T0328431

The Green and the Brown

This study provides the first comprehensive discussion of conservation in Nazi Germany. Looking at Germany in an international context, it analyzes the roots of conservation in the late nineteenth century, the gradual adaptation of racist and nationalist language among conservationists in the 1920s, and the inner distance to the republic of Weimar. It describes how the German conservation movement came to cooperate with the Nazi regime and discusses the ideological and institutional lines between the conservation movement and the Nazis. Uekoetter further examines how the conservation movement struggled to do away with a troublesome past after World War II, making the environmentalists one of the last groups in German society to face up to its Nazi burden. It is a story of ideological convergence, of tactical alliances, of careerism, of implication in crimes against humanity, and of deceit and denial after 1945. It is also a story that offers valuable lessons for today's environmental movement.

Frank Uekoetter is a researcher in the History Department at Bielefeld University, Germany. He is the author of two monographs and editor, alone or in part, of four collections. He is also author of articles published in *Business History Review*, *Environment and History*, and *Historical Social Research*.

Studies in Environment and History

Editors
Donald Worster, University of Kansas
J. R. McNeill, Georgetown University

The Green and the Brown

A History of Conservation in Nazi Germany

FRANK UEKOETTER

Bielefeld University

CAMBRIDGE UNIVERSITY PRESS
Cambridge, New York, Melbourne, Madrid, Cape Town,
Singapore, São Paulo, Delhi, Mexico City

Cambridge University Press
32 Avenue of the Americas, New York, NY 10013-2473, USA

www.cambridge.org
Information on this title: www.cambridge.org/9780521612777

First published 2006
Reprinted 2013

A catalog record for this publication is available from the British Library.

Library of Congress Cataloging in Publication Data

Uekoetter, Frank, 1970–
The green and the brown : a history of conservation in Nazi Germany /
Frank Uekoetter.
  p. cm. – (Studies in environment and history)
Includes bibliographical references and index.
ISBN-13: 978-0-521-84819-0 (hardback)
ISBN-10: 0-521-84819-9 (hardback)
ISBN-13: 978-0-521-61277-7 (pbk.)
ISBN-10: 0-521-61277-2 (pbk.)
  1. Nature conservation – Germany – History – 20th century.   2. National socialism and
science.   I. Title.   II. Series.
QH77.G3U35 2006
333.70943´0904 – dc22   2006001011

ISBN 978-0-521-84819-0 Hardback
ISBN 978-0-521-61277-7 Paperback

Für Werner

Contents

Acknowledgments

This book is the product of an intellectual journey that had far more resemblance to a roller-coaster ride than I, or anyone, could have imagined when I came to the topic in 2001. At that time, the German minister for the environment, Jürgen Trittin, pushed aggressively for a conference on the topic, a remarkable move given the fact that public interest in the Nazi past of conservation was almost nonexistent. The task of organizing this conference fell to Joachim Radkau, historian at Bielefeld University, who turned for help to a doctoral student who had just finished his dissertation – in other words, to me. The result was a symposium on "Conservation in Nazi Germany," which took place in Berlin in July 2002. The first conference of its kind, it attracted a surprisingly large number of participants, along with intensive coverage by the media, demonstrating that the issue was clearly more than an academic topic. I am greatly indebted to the speakers at the Berlin conference who helped to make the symposium such a rousing success. At the same time, the conference volume provided a great opportunity to reflect on the state of research and the general approach to the topic. While this book differs from the conference volume in many respects, and seeks to break new ground in some, it clearly could not have been written in this form without the work of seventeen formidable academics.

In writing this book, I enjoyed encouragement and support from more people than I can mention here. Donald Worster inspired this book and guided it, together with John McNeill, as series editors, toward its completion. Their comments were a great help in revising the manuscript, as were the remarks of an anonymous third reviewer. It was a pleasure to work with Frank Smith and Eric Crahan at the Americas branch of

Cambridge University Press. For their assistance in the use of archival material, I thank the staff of the German Bundesarchiv in Berlin, Koblenz, and Freiburg; the Geheimes Staatsarchiv in Berlin; the Deutsches Literaturarchiv in Marbach; the state archives in Darmstadt, Dresden, Düsseldorf, Freiburg, Karlsruhe, Nürnberg, Schleswig, Stuttgart, and Würzburg; the Westfälisches Archivamt in Münster; the county archives in Warendorf and Altena; and the city archives in Bielefeld, Leipzig, Reutlingen, and Telgte. I was on many occasions a guest at the library of the Bundesamt für Naturschutz in Bonn-Bad Godesberg; the interlibrary loan office of Bielefeld University supplied me with books and articles in a timely manner. Joachim Radkau accompanied this project with his unique blend of encouragement and critique. His seminar at Bielefeld University, cosponsored by Werner Abelshauser, provided a valuable proving ground for my ideas at different stages. Sandra Chaney, Ute Hasenöhrl, and Heinrich Spanier read the manuscript fully or in part and provided valuable comments; Jotham Parsons did a terrific job proofreading the manuscript. During the preparation of the first draft, my wife, Simona, took a new job in Munich, resulting in the irony that this book, first conceived in the city of Prague, is now being finalized within walking distance of the Nazi Party's former headquarters. The twisted road toward this book probably deserves no other conclusion.

Frank Uekoetter
Munich, September, 2005

Abbreviations

BArch	Bundesarchiv
DLA	Deutsches Literaturarchiv Marbach am Neckar
GDR	German Democratic Republic
GLAK	Badisches Generallandesarchiv Karlsruhe
GStA	Geheimes Staatsarchiv Berlin
HStAD	Hauptstaatsarchiv Düsseldorf
HStADd	Hauptstaatsarchiv Dresden
HStAS	Hauptstaatsarchiv Stuttgart
KAW	Kreisarchiv Warendorf
KMK	Kreisarchiv des Märkischen Kreises, Altena
LASH	Landesarchiv Schleswig-Holstein
NSDAP	Nationalsozialistische Deutsche Arbeiterpartei (Nazi Party)
RVH	Reichsbund Volkstum und Heimat
SS	Schutzstaffel (Protective Detachment)
StAB	Stadtarchiv Bielefeld
StAD	Staatsarchiv Darmstadt
StAF	Staatsarchiv Freiburg
StAL	Stadtarchiv Leipzig
StAN	Staatsarchiv Nürnberg
StAR	Stadtarchiv Reutlingen
StAT	Stadtarchiv Telgte
StAW	Staatsarchiv Würzburg
WAA	Westfälisches Archivamt Münster

A Note on Vocabulary

Writing a book in a language that is not one's native language is never easy. But writing a book on the Nazi era in the English language presents a challenge all of its own. No one who has never tried it can truly understand the trouble and pain that one encounters in translating the vocabulary of the Nazi era. The trouble starts with words like *Heimat* that encompass an entire cosmos of meanings that no word in the English language can really capture – and it ends with phrases like *Reichskommissariat für die Festigung des deutschen Volkstums*, a true monster in terminological and other respects. Trying to bring out all implications of this terminology in another language is bound to produce frustration – or, alternatively, gigantic footnotes whenever one of the ominous words pops up.

Therefore, it seems that a few notes on my choice of words are called for. Whenever I encountered a word that has no direct equivalent in the English language, I have chosen the word that, in my opinion, comes as close as possible to the German original. When the word or expression appears for the first time, I have added the German word in brackets, clarifying the terminology for the Germanophone reader and reminding all others that the word's connotations in the English language may be deceiving. This approach may be prone to misunderstandings, and it inevitably suggests to English readers that they may miss a few fine points of the story, but it is the best one that I am aware of. Also, I have used the German expression for some organizations and institutions without offering a translation. In all these cases, the role of these institutions becomes clear from the context, whereas the precise meaning of the German words is of no relevance for an understanding of the story. The poem on page 164 has intentionally been printed in both languages, and I will make no attempt to claim that the translation is anything but inadequate.

In addition to these general remarks, it seems advisable to say a little more about a few specific words. I have used *conservation* and *nature protection* as synonyms in this study, and I made no distinction between conservation and preservation: all of these words are the English equivalents of *Naturschutz*. Thus, any allusion to American concepts of resource management ("wise use") would be misleading. As the narrative shows, even the use of nature as a tourist attraction was met with scornful disregard in the German conservation community. The word *Naturdenkmal* (natural monument) means an object of relatively small scale – e.g., a tree or a rock – that conservationists deemed worthy of preservation; no German bureaucrat would have thought of an object the size of the Grand Canyon as a natural or national monument. The first German conservation office, the *Staatliche Stelle für Naturdenkmalpflege*, thus signaled its penchant for conservation *en miniature* already in its title. I have not translated *völkisch*; the word is translated as "folkish" in the American edition of Hitler's *Mein Kampf*, but that word clearly sounds far too harmless for a mixture of chauvinist, racist, and xenophobic ideas. I occasionally speak of a German *Volksgemeinschaft*, a word that literally translates into "community of nationals" or "community of the folk," but such a translation would mute the dual implications of the word: it was egalitarian in that the term transcended barriers of class and tradition but also racist in that it admitted only those of Aryan origin into the "national community." The same holds true for the corresponding term *Volksgenosse* (National Comrade), which designates a member of the *Volksgemeinschaft*.

In some cases, the search for an English equivalent was simply hopeless. According to the dictionary, *Führer* translates into either leader or head, but both words give a terribly inadequate impression of Hitler's pivotal role in Nazi politics. The organization *Kraft durch Freude* is mentioned with the addition "tourist association" to describe its work, but the concept that the name implied is impossible to convey in a similarly brief form; briefly, *Kraft durch Freude* linked the promise of pleasant experiences during one of the tourist trips that the Nazis offered many Germans for the first time with a reminder that these trips were ultimately intended as an uplift of the individual's work ethic in the service of the nation, thus connecting individual relaxation with national strength. The concept of *Lebensraum* in Eastern Europe that was so central to Hitler's thinking means more than "living space," the literal translation, because the Nazi notion of *Lebensraum* was based on the racist concept of a hierarchy of races, where the Aryan race was destined to subjugate the inferior Slavic people. *Heimat* was already a complex word before the terrorist attacks of September 11, 2001, soon after which the German media began to translate the United States Department of Homeland Security as *Ministerium für Heimatschutz*. *Heimat* alludes to a place of indeterminate size where one feels at home; often (but not necessarily), *Heimat* alludes to a home *region*, and the *Heimat* protection movement was always a strong defender of regionalism. At the same time, *Heimat* is filled with romantic associations, and the word evokes associations of coziness.

Gleichschaltung was a process during the first months of Nazi rule that sought to "streamline" those parts of German society that implied, like trade unions or states' rights, a threat to Hitler's dictatorial powers. However, the process soon led to the reorganization of countless civic organizations, with the goal of creating one national organization in the place of the previous pluralism. *Dauerwald* is a silviocultural doctrine that allows trees of different ages to stand next to each other; I refrained from a translation in part because Aldo Leopold used the German term in his essay on "Deer and *Dauerwald* in Germany." The word *Weltanschauung* describes a holistic worldview based on a certain set of key principles, with the Nazis, of course, opting for racist principles; *Weltanschauung* is one of the words that entered the English vocabulary because of the Nazi experience. Finally, I chose not to translate *Gauleiter* because the position was more complex than a simple term could capture. *Gauleiters* were leaders of the NSDAP in one of its forty-two German districts, but in addition to party chairmanship, *Gauleiters* often took up further tasks, acting as ministers, prime ministers, or Reich Commissioners (*Reichsstatthalter*) for a certain state. The extent of the *Gauleiters'* powers was significant, but they depended strongly on the specifics of each individual case.

The Nazis and the Environment: A Relevant Topic?

In February 1938, five years after Adolf Hitler and the Nazi Party came to power, the German conservationist Wilhelm Lienenkämper published an essay on "the protection of nature from a Nazi perspective."[1] Three years earlier, the Nazi government had passed a national conservation law with great fanfare, and now, Lienenkämper thought, the time was ripe for a preliminary summary of the results. He was full of praise for the law itself and celebrated it as an achievement for the ages. For him, the conservation law was not an accidental by-product of Nazi rule but a direct expression of the "new *Weltanschauung*." Whereas the protection of nature had formerly been something "that one can choose to do or not," National Socialism now bestowed on it a new sense of urgency. As Lienenkämper enthusiastically proclaimed:

The new ideology, and with it the national conservation law, imposes a new postulate for totality. They refuse all kinds of compromise and demand strict, literal fulfillment.... Time and again, we are nowadays talking about sacrifice as a key idea of our society. Those refusing the call for sacrifice are under attack, and rightly so. But when conservationists are likewise asking for sacrifice in the interest of their movement and on the basis of the law, people come up with a thousand 'ifs' and 'buts', with economic interests and special concerns; we are not always proceeding with the firmness and rigidity that we are used to in other fields. The idea of National Socialism demands totality and sacrifice. And we have to bring

---

[1] The term *conservation* is used here as a synonym for nature protection. Any allusion to American concepts of resource use or a juxtaposition of conservation against preservation would be misleading. The "Note on Vocabulary" at the beginning of this book provides a more comprehensive discussion of the author's choice of words.

that message time and again to those people who for some reason see the nature protection movement as a marginal and subordinate one.[2]

The protection of nature as an expression of National Socialist *Weltanschauung*, totality and sacrifice in the interest of the common good, Nazi rule as a showcase of firmness and rigidity – one does not need to know about the horrible toll of Nazi rule to think that such a quotation is shocking indeed. Thus, it should come as no surprise that quotations of this kind have created quite a stir in recent years. Some historians have published long compilations of similarly appalling quotations, suggesting that National Socialism permeated conservation thinking to the core.[3] On first glance, Lienenkämper's article seems to nourish this kind of reading. But does it?

It is interesting to note that the longer one reflects on Lienenkämper's article, the more ambiguous it appears. The trouble starts with the question of whether he was serious about his core argument: did he really think that the protection of nature was a key goal of Nazi rule? After all, there were laws and programs installed after the conservation law of 1935 that the Nazi leadership obviously took much more seriously: the Nuremberg Racial Laws of the same year that placed German Jews in a lower citizenship category, for example, or the Four Year Plan of 1936 to make the German economy ready for war. Did Lienenkämper really think that conservation could stand on a par with racial purity and rearmament on the Nazis' agenda? And what were the motives behind this article: did Lienenkämper correlate conservation and National Socialism for ideological or for tactical reasons? Given the deplorable state of conservation work that he mentioned, one could imagine that he simply tried to strengthen the conservationists' case by plundering the Nazis' ideological arsenal for anything that might be useful. Was that his true intention? And if so, how would this change our interpretation of the text?

The ambiguities become stronger when one looks at the article in a broader context. The conservationists' cause enjoyed some support among some Nazi leaders, as this book will show, but the Nazis never made the protection of nature a truly urgent part of their policy. So could one not read Lienenkämper's article as a document of desperation – the

---

[2] Wilhelm Lienenkämper, "Der Naturschutz vom Nationalsozialismus her gesehen," *Sauerländischer Gebirgsbote* 46 (1938): 26. All translations from German by the author.
[3] The best-known examples are the publications of Joachim Wolschke-Bulmahn and Gert Gröning. The Appendix provides a more comprehensive discussion of the development and state of research.

outcry of a dedicated conservationist who saw his concern sidelined by the government? In this case, the article would not demonstrate the proximity of conservation and the Nazi state but rather the opposite: the deep *gap* separating them. Also, basing an indictment on ugly quotations inevitably brings up the question of how to deal with those people who, as far as we know, never adopted Nazi rhetoric to the extent that Lienenkämper did. This problem is by no means a marginal one: the lion's share of conservationist publications between 1933 and 1945 could be printed again today without raising eyebrows. So how do we deal with the large number of publications devoid of Nazi rhetoric? Was Lienenkämper simply one of those "Nazi hotheads" that a popular postwar myth blamed for the Nazis' atrocities?

The situation becomes even more complex if one adds a moral perspective to the general picture. The shock that many readers experience over quotations from the conservation literature of the Nazi era is certainly genuine. But what is the reason for it? The novelist Ephraim Kishon, an Israeli author with a wide readership in Germany, once expressed his displeasure over certain trends of modern art, and when others pointed him to similar trends in Nazi Germany, epitomized in the infamous exposition on "degenerate art" of 1937, he replied laconically, "I will not start smoking because Adolf Hitler hated cigarettes."[4] Would it be possible to deal with the conservationists' Nazi past in a similar vein? Nobody would consider a ban on German shepherds because a member of this species, Blondi, was Hitler's most cherished partner during the last years of his life (until he had Blondi killed by poison as a trial run for his own suicide).[5] So if the Nazis embraced conservation – and vice versa – does that constitute more than a curious but ultimately meaningless footnote of history? If one thinks of conservation as "good" and the Nazis as "bad," and any connection between both as "strange," does one not fall into a crude and naïve essentialization of "eternal good" and "universal evil"?

Publications on conservation in Nazi Germany usually ignore questions of this kind and simply take the relevance of the topic as given. But it is easy to see that such a stance is unsatisfactory in both analytical and moral terms: it implies, after all, a moral condemnation before one has clarified the terms by which to make a decision. Rushing to a verdict and

[4] See Joachim Radkau, "Naturschutz und Nationalsozialismus – wo ist das Problem?," in Joachim Radkau and Frank Uekötter (eds.), *Naturschutz und Nationalsozialismus* (Frankfurt and New York, 2003), 41.
[5] Ian Kershaw, *Hitler 1936–1945: Nemesis* (London, 2000), 825.

condemning every link between the conservationists and the Nazi regime may look like good political judgment on first glance, but it quickly leads to a dead end. The ambiguities of Lienenkämper's stance provide a fitting case in point: was he a true believer in the gospel of Nazi conservation or rather an opportunist trying to drape his own concerns in Nazi language? Did he represent a staunch alliance between the conservation movement and the Nazi regime or rather argue for an alliance that never materialized? Obviously, even a blunt statement like Lienenkämper's is open to a wide range of interpretations and with that a wide range of moral judgments. It would be unwise, to say the least, to blame Lienenkämper before knowing what to blame him for.

Therefore, inquiring deeper into the story's relevance does by no means undermine the general importance of the topic. Quite the contrary, it demonstrates that dealing with the topic is indeed rewarding, if not crucial, for environmentalists even more than 60 years after the Nazis' demise. In fact, it seems that the ensuing story has relevance also beyond the realms of environmental history. After all, the history of the conservation movement in Nazi Germany is part of the general history of the relationship between intellectuals and the Nazi regime. Since its birth in the late nineteenth century, intellectuals had played a pivotal role in the German conservation movement, and the dominance of university-educated people among the conservationists of the 1930s is unmistakable. On this background, this book opens a new avenue toward the history of intellectuals in Nazi Germany: it demonstrates the stunning ability of the Nazi regime to befriend intellectuals even when they were not in league with the Nazis' overarching ideology. The history of the conservation movement in Nazi Germany provides a sobering reminder of the extent to which intellectuals can be seduced.

To place the story in such a broad context, a book of this kind is well advised to start with a discussion of the general context of conservation in Nazi Germany. After all, conservation was neither an invention of the Nazis nor a German peculiarity. Like most of its European counterparts, the German conservation movement emerged in the late nineteenth century, when industrialization and urbanization led to a massive transformation of the natural environment, and conservation had become a fixture in most European countries long before the Nazis' rise to power. Conservationists were anything but immune to the nationalist sentiments permeating all European societies in the late nineteenth and early twentieth centuries, and that left a marked imprint on the political philosophy of conservation, as this book will show for the German case. But this did not preclude contacts and a candid exchange of ideas: it is noteworthy that these contacts, though by no means as intensive as in the current environmental movement, never actually ceased to exist and, in some cases, even ran directly counter to public sentiment. It is irritating, to mention just one example, to see a German conservationist pointing to the much-despised Polish government as a model during the Nazi era.[6] Therefore, it is important to see the German conservation movement in the international context of the interwar years: did the German movement differ from that in other countries and, if so, in what ways?

A comparison between Germany and England shows some similarity in the original motives but marked differences regarding institutional structures. In Germany, the state quickly assumed a central role in conservation policy; in England, it played a rather marginal, supportive role for decades. Founded in 1894, England's National Trust for Places of Historic Interest or Natural Beauty became the dominant institution in the field, acquiring or purchasing nature reserves along with gardens and historical monuments. The British parliament gave support to its work with the passage of the National Trust Act of 1907, which made the Trust's acquisitions "inalienable," thus giving public legitimacy to its role as a trustee "for the benefit of the nation." A more active role of the British state was under discussion in the 1930s but did not materialize until the National Parks and Access to the Countryside Act of 1949. The success of conservation in Nazi Germany thus contrasts strongly with the stalemate in the British Isles.[7] The French case likewise reveals more differences than similarities: although German conservationists were highly critical of touristic exploitation of nature from the outset, the Touring Club of France and the Alpine Club of France were among the most important early conservation organizations on the other side of the Rhine.[8] The

---

[6] WAA LWL Best. 702 No. 191, Provinzmittel für den Naturschutz. Memorandum of the Sauerländischer Gebirgsverein, ca. 1934. Similarly, Walther Schoenichen, *Urdeutschland. Deutschlands Naturschutzgebiete in Wort und Bild*, vol. 2 (Neudamm, 1937), 11. On the development of international conservation efforts, see Hanno Henke, "Grundzüge der geschichtlichen Entwicklung des internationalen Naturschutzes," *Natur und Landschaft* 65 (1990): 106–12; and Anna-Katharina Wöbse, "Der Schutz der Natur im Völkerbund – Anfänge einer Weltumweltpolitik," *Archiv für Sozialgeschichte* 43 (2003): 177–90.

[7] This account of English conservation is based on Karl Ditt, "Die Anfänge der Naturschutzgesetzgebung in Deutschland und England 1935/49," in Radkau and Uekötter, *Naturschutz und Nationalsozialismus*, 107–43; and David Evans, *A History of Nature Conservation in Britain*, 2nd edition (London and New York, 1997).

[8] Michael Bess, *The Light-Green Society: Ecology and Technological Modernity in France, 1960–2000* (Chicago and London, 2003), 68. See also E. Cardot, *Manuel de l'Arbre* (Paris, 1907), 74; Danny Trom, "Natur und nationale Identität. Der Streit um den Schutz der

contrast with the United States is even more striking: almost a century elapsed between the designation of Yellowstone as a national park in 1872 and the creation of the first national park in Germany in 1969.[9] Moreover, there was no equivalent in Germany to the monumentalism that was the driving force behind the protection of Yellowstone and Yosemite Valley or the cult of wilderness that became so central to both American environmentalism and American nationalism.[10] To be sure, German conservationists maintained a certain fascination for American conservation, and the Nazi era in fact saw a frustrated attempt to create a number of national parks. But when Walther Schoenichen noted in his book *Urdeutschland* ("Primeval Germany") that Yellowstone National Park was thirty-four times larger than the Lüneburg Heath, one of the largest German nature reserves, and that the total acreage of all 600 German nature reserves combined did not even add up to one-third of Yellowstone, the differences between German and American conservation become plainly apparent.[11] Even a patriotic German conservationist could not help but concede that "compared with the wonders of Africa and America, we are miserably poor (*bettelarm*) in natural treasures."[12]

With Germany and Italy emerging as allies during the 1930s, the comparison between these two countries deserves special attention. The similarities and differences between Hitler's Germany and Mussolini's Italy have attracted much interest among historians, not least because of their relevance on the background of more general theories of Nazi rule.[13] Was there a distinct fascist style of conservation? Some Italian conservation

---

'Natur' um die Jahrhundertwende in Deutschland und Frankreich," in Etienne François, Hannes Siegrist, and Jakob Vogel (eds.), *Nation und Emotion. Deutschland und Frankreich im Vergleich* (Göttingen, 1995), 147–67.

[9] See Hans-Dietmar Koeppel and Walter Mrass, "Natur- und Nationalparke," in Gerhard Olschowy (ed.), *Natur- und Umweltschutz in der Bundesrepublik Deutschland* (Hamburg and Berlin, 1978), 810.

[10] See Alfred Runte, *National Parks. The American Experience*, 3rd edition (Lincoln, Nebr., 1997); and Roderick Nash, *Wilderness and the American Mind*, 4th edition (New Haven, Conn., and London, 2001).

[11] Walther Schoenichen, *Urdeutschland. Deutschlands Naturschutzgebiete in Wort und Bild*, vol. 1 (Neudamm, 1935), 5n. For a more extensive comparison among Germany, England, and the United States, see Karl Ditt, "Naturschutz zwischen Zivilisationskritik, Tourismusförderung und Umweltschutz. USA, England und Deutschland 1860–1970," Matthias Frese and Michael Prinz (eds.), *Politische Zäsuren und gesellschaftlicher Wandel im 20. Jahrhundert. Regionale und vergleichende Perspektiven* (Paderborn, 1996), 499–533.

[12] Hans Stadler, "Landschaftsschutz in Franken," *Blätter für Naturschutz und Naturpflege* 18 (1935): 45.

[13] The classic study in this regard is Ernst Nolte, *Three Faces of Fascism: Action Française, Italian Fascism, National Socialism* (London, 1965). For a stimulating recent comparison

efforts look strikingly similar to German approaches on first glance. Mussolini supported the planting of forests to make the climate cooler and embolden the Italian warrior spirit, thus adhering to the same parallelism between landscapes and national characters that characterized much of the German conservation literature.[14] During the famed draining of the Pontine Marshes in the 1930s, Mussolini set aside some 8,000 acres for a nature reserve over the objections of his minister of agriculture, thus creating Circeo National Park, Italy's third, in 1934. However, on second glance, the differences between Germany and Italy appear more significant than the similarities. Hitler never engaged in conservation efforts as prominently as Mussolini, leaving the topic mostly to subordinates such as Hermann Göring, Fritz Todt, and Heinrich Himmler. More significantly, the general impression of conservation in fascist Italy is one of gradual decline, whereas the German conservation movement clearly thrived during the Nazi era.[15] In fact, even Circeo National Park does not provide a good example of fascist Italy's commitment to the environment if one takes a closer look: in his environmental history of Italy, Antonio Cederna speaks of a nature reserve "born dead."[16] And with doubts persisting generally about the similarities between Italian fascism and Nazism, it seems that the potential of this line of inquiry is rather limited.[17]

While the fascist school of Nazi interpretation has declined in recent years, the theory of totalitarianism experienced a boom, in large measure because of the collapse of the socialist regimes in Eastern Europe. However, a comparison between Nazi Germany and Stalinist Russia quickly demonstrates the limits of such approach in this context. German conservation worked in public, and with few exceptions, conservationists did not experience prosecution, or even fear it to a significant extent, whereas in the Soviet Union, conservationists laid low in the 1930s so as not to

between Germany and Italy, see Sven Reichardt, *Faschistische Kampfbünde. Gewalt und Gemeinschaft im italienischen Squadrismus und in der deutschen SA* (Cologne, 2002).

[14] John R. McNeill, *Something New under the Sun: An Environmental History of the Twentieth Century* (London, 2001), 329.

[15] See James Sievert, *The Origins of Nature Conservation in Italy* (Bern, 2000), esp. pp. 199–214.

[16] Antonio Cederna, *La Distruzione della Natura in Italia* (Torino, 1975), 196. Conditions in the park were so bad that the International Union for the Conservation of Nature considered deleting it from its list of national parks (*ibid.*, 200).

[17] See Renzo de Felice, *Die Deutungen des Faschismus* (Göttingen and Zürich, 1980), esp. p. 255; and Karl Dietrich Bracher, *Zeitgeschichtliche Kontroversen. Um Faschismus, Totalitarismus, Demokratie* (Munich and Zürich, 1984), 13–33. Even the recent synthesis by Michael Mann cannot help but acknowledge a number of important differences between Italian fascism and German Nazism: Michael Mann, *Fascists* (Cambridge, 2004), 360–2.

appear as an autonomous, and hence potentially dangerous, group. Aesthetic and cultural motives played a strong role in German conservation from the outset, whereas Russian conservation had been closely aligned with science since tsarist times. In Germany, conservation enjoyed, at least temporarily, the favor of some of the most powerful Nazis, whereas in the Soviet Union, the conservationists generally sought to escape Stalin's attention and actually succeeded in doing so until 1951, when a decree dissolved two-thirds of the country's nature reserves and reduced the total acreage under protection by almost 90 percent.[18] As David Blackbourn quipped in his contribution to the 2002 Berlin conference, "A conference on conservation and Stalinism would certainly be much shorter than this one."[19] It is too early to make a final assessment of the contrast between Germany and the Soviet Union; after all, the environmental history of socialism is only starting to be written.[20] But with the current state of research, it seems that a typical pattern of conservation work in totalitarian states is nowhere in sight.

For several decades, the school of totalitarianism has had a powerful rival in German historiography in the polycentric school of Nazi interpretation. Whereas the totalitarian model assumes the dictator's dominance in decision-making, the polycentric model stresses the multitude of institutions and interest groups competing with each other. In its earliest formulation, this line of reasoning goes back to Franz Neumann's study of the Nazi state written during World War II. "The ruling class of National Socialist Germany is far from homogeneous. There are as many interests as there are groups," Neumann wrote.[21] Rather than seeing the Nazi regime as a monolithic bloc with strict top-down processes, where the Führer's will was diligently carried out by myriads of underlings, the polycentric approach stresses the administrative chaos in Nazi Germany and the rivalry among different institutions. An extensive

---

[18] This description of Soviet conservation is based on Douglas R. Weiner, *A Little Corner of Freedom: Russian Nature Protection from Stalin to Gorbachëv* (Berkeley and Los Angeles, 1999); and Douglas R. Weiner, *Models of Nature: Ecology, Conservation and Cultural Revolution in Soviet Russia* (Pittsburgh, 2000).

[19] David Blackbourn, "'Die Natur als historisch zu etablieren.' Natur, Heimat und Landschaft in der modernen deutschen Geschichte," in Radkau and Ueköter, *Naturschutz und Nationalsozialismus*, 71.

[20] For some of the most recent contributions, see Klaus Gestwa, "Ökologischer Notstand und sozialer Protest. Der umwelthistorische Blick auf die Reformunfähigkeit und den Zerfall der Sowjetunion," *Archiv für Sozialgeschichte* 43 (2003): 349–83; and Alla Bolotova, "Colonization of Nature in the Soviet Union. State Ideology, Public Discourse, and the Experience of Geologists," *Historical Social Research* 29, 3 (2004): 104–23.

[21] Franz Neumann, *Behemoth: The Structure and Practice of National Socialism 1933–1944* (New York, 1963 [first edition 1942]), 396.

literature has shown that there was an enormous amount of infighting among Nazi leaders, with Hitler routinely suspending these disputes instead of resolving them, and that coordination between bureaucracies was notoriously weak, ultimately culminating in what Hans Mommsen has called "an unparalleled institutional anarchy."[22] From this background, Hitler emerges not as an omnipotent dictator but rather as a supreme authority that often evaded clear decisions and even refrained from issuing general guidelines. Hitler could decide what he wanted to decide, but he left much room for initiatives from the second tier of Nazi leaders, provided that these could somehow claim to adhere to the spirit of the Third Reich.

The history of conservation in Nazi Germany provides a showcase of this institutional anarchy, for the inconsistency of the Nazis' environmental policy is plainly apparent. Countless books and articles explained how Germany's strength hinged on its rootedness in the land, all while the intensification of agricultural production and the hasty buildup of industry in preparation for war were changing the face of the beloved *Heimat*. The Nazis passed the national conservation law of 1935, one of the best laws of its time, and then watched while many agencies and institutions ignored its provisions. Fritz Todt, the head of Autobahn construction and supreme engineer of Nazi Germany, hired a number of "Landscape Advocates" (*Landschaftsanwälte*) to assure that the construction of the Autobahn went on in accordance with the demands of the German landscape, but his planners routinely ignored the Advocates' advice. In fact, the conservation movement itself became more and more fragmented, and rivalries among conservationists flourished to such an extent that fights between fellow conservationists sometimes seemed to be more important than the fight for the protection of nature. At the same time, Nazi leaders showed little inclination to advance a more consistent policy. Hermann Göring, the semiofficial "second man" in the Nazi state, was instrumental in the passage of the 1935 national conservation law, but his work

---

[22] Hans Mommsen, "Nationalsozialismus," *Sowjetsystem und demokratische Gesellschaft. Eine vergleichende Enzyklopädie*, vol. 4 (Freiburg, 1971), col. 702. For some of the studies that have shaped this picture, see Martin Broszat, *Der Staat Hitlers. Grundlegung und Entwicklung seiner inneren Verfassung* (Munich, 1969); Peter Hüttenberger, "Nationalsozialistische Polykratie," *Geschichte und Gesellschaft* 2 (1976): 417–42; and Dieter Rebentisch, *Führerstaat und Verwaltung im Zweiten Weltkrieg. Verfassungsentwicklung und Verwaltungspolitik 1939–1945* (Stuttgart, 1989). See also Gerhard Hirschfeld and Lothar Kettenacker (eds.), *The "Führer State": Myth and Reality. Studies on the Structure and Politics of the Third Reich* (Stuttgart, 1981), for a pointed discussion on the character of Nazi rule.

as Germany's supreme forester and as chief of the Four Year Plan ran strongly against conservation interests. Hitler showed even less interest in conservation issues, and his sporadic initiatives bordered on the comical. A brochure of 1941, entitled "The Führer Wants Our Hedgerows Protected," demonstrated the conservationists' gratitude for what was, in all likelihood, an offhand remark that some paladins had transformed into an official decree, but it also showed something else: it inadvertently revealed Hitler's lack of support for other, more important, conservation goals.[23]

It would be wrong to conceive of the totalitarian and the polycentric approaches as fundamentally at odds with each other. It is impossible to understand some aspects of the following story without referral to the totalitarian character of Nazi rule. The Nazi regime reacted allergically to anything that resembled public protest or even a systematic campaign for a certain natural treasure, and it cared little about the general spirit of the protest. Even Ludwig Finckh, one of the most aggressive right-wing ideologists within the entire conservation community, was monitored by the Gestapo during his campaign to save the scenic Hohenstoffeln Mountain from mining interests. The conservation movement also lost several of its members, especially those who were Jewish or deemed Jewish according to the Nazis' race-based definition, and the social democratic *Naturfreunde* tourist association. But other than that, the totalitarian character of Nazi rule was of little importance for the conservation community, and debates among the conservationists were characterized by a surprisingly large degree of freedom of expression. The reason is simple: it was difficult, if not impossible, to deduce an authoritative conservation ethic from the key pillars of Nazi ideology. If we see anti-Semitism and the quest for *Lebensraum* in Eastern Europe as the two fundamentals of Hitler's political ethos, as Eberhard Jäckel has argued in a seminal monograph, it is easy to see that deducing clear "dos" and "don'ts" for the conservation community was next to impossible.[24] Since its inception in the late nineteenth century, the German conservation movement had blamed industrialization and urbanization for the destruction of nature, and there was no way to shift the blame to a small band of Jewish conspirators. To be sure, this

[23] GLAK Abt. 235 no. 47680, Der Führer hält seine schützende Hand über unsere Hecken. Hans Schwenkel, Reichsbund für Vogelschutz. For the original decree of the German Peasant Leader (*Reichsbauernführer*) of January 23, 1940, see WAA LWL Best. 702 no. 191, Dienstnachrichten des Reichsnährstandes no. 7 of February 10, 1940, edition B.

[24] See Eberhard Jäckel, *Hitlers Weltanschauung: A Blueprint for Power* (Middletown, Conn., 1972).

did not prevent some conservationists from trying to bridge this gap, and the ensuing quotations define a historic low in conservation rhetoric. But these quotations never evolved into a full-fledged conservation ethic, let alone specific guidelines for conservation policy. Conservationists often touted the convergence of conservation and National Socialism as a meeting of like-minded spirits, but as Chapter 2 will show, the closer one looks at the ideological bridge between the two camps, the more fragile it appears.

In his biography of Hitler, Ian Kershaw proposed a synthesis of these divergent approaches. Using an expression from a speech of Werner Willikens, State Secretary in the Prussian ministry of agriculture, in February 1934, he argued that "working towards the Führer" was the key principle of policy in the Nazi state. Willikens argued that "everyone with opportunity to observe it knows that the Führer can only with great difficulty order from above everything that he intends to carry out sooner or later. On the contrary, until now everyone has best worked in his place in the new Germany if, so to speak, he works towards the Führer." Some may fail in their anticipation of the Führer's will, but others will "have the finest reward of one day suddenly attaining the legal confirmation of his work."[25] Kershaw argued that this speech shed an instructive spotlight on the general character of the Nazi regime: "Through 'working towards the Führer', initiatives were taken, pressures created, legislation instigated – all in ways which fell into line with what were taken to be Hitler's aims, and without the dictator necessarily having to dictate."[26] The great advantage of this perspective is that it provides an explanation why the institutional anarchy did not lead to chaos and inefficiency in the Nazi state, at least not sufficiently as to prevent the Nazis from realizing their racist fantasies to a stunning extent. For Kershaw, the cumulative result of so many people "working towards the Führer" was a polycentric dynamism that remained alive during the entire life span of the Nazi regime; during the war, the "cumulative radicalization" of Nazi rule opened the door for the Nazis' well-known crimes against humanity. This general dynamism is also evident in the conservation community. Within a few months after the Nazis' seizure of power, the conservationists were lobbying for several new pieces of legislation: a nature protection law, a *Heimat* protection law,

---

[25] Ian Kershaw, *Hitler 1889–1936: Hubris* (London, 1998), 529. Kershaw first presented this argument in "'Working Towards the Führer.' Reflections on the Nature of the Hitler Dictatorship," *Contemporary European History* 2 (1993): 103–18.
[26] Kershaw, *Hitler 1889–1936*, 530.

a law for the protection of birds, and a law curtailing outdoor advertising. Only one of these laws eventually materialized, but that was enough to win the allegiance of the conservation movement for the Nazis.

It is important to see this general situation through the lenses of the contemporary conservation movement. Contacts between the conservationists and the Nazis were rare before 1933, not so much out of mutual disagreements but as a result of traditional sentiments in the nature protection community. The conservation movement was not apolitical in a strict sense, but it was certainly uninterested in party politics and in any alliance with other political movements. However, this attitude was no longer viable during the Nazi era. If one wanted to make some inroads under the new regime – and conservationists quickly stressed that they had high hopes in this regard – an apolitical stance was the surest recipe for failure. It is no coincidence that Walther Schoenichen, the head of the Prussian Agency for the Protection of Natural Movements, joined the Nazi party two months after the seizure of power and quickly wrote a monograph on "conservation in the Third Reich" as a gesture of deference.[27] The order of the day was now to depict conservation as a quintessential concern of the Nazi regime, to use personal and institutional connections in one's favor, to lobby for attention – in short, to work toward the Führer. With that, the conservation movement was standing on a slippery slope, and it is disheartening to see that conservationists observed few taboos in their rapprochement to the Nazis. The shameful attempt to use Heinrich Himmler's authority in a conservation conflict during the war demonstrates an appalling lack of political morality, and it attests to the dynamism of "working toward the Führer" that some of the key figures involved were not even members of the Nazi party.

The emerging alliance between the conservation movement and the Nazis is the subject of three chapters that look at the relationship from different perspectives. Chapter 3 describes the different groups that played a role during the Nazi era and the legal and institutional fundamentals of conservation work. Chapter 4 offers four case studies of local

---

[27] NSDAP Membership no. 1510121, from March 1, 1933; Walther Schoenichen, *Naturschutz im Dritten Reich. Einführung in Wesen und Grundlagen zeitgemäßer Naturschutz-Arbeit* (Berlin-Lichterfelde, 1934). Schoenichen later declared in a membership application that he became a member in December 1932, thus moving his date of entry before Hitler's seizure of power. (BArch Berlin Document Center RSK I B 201, p. 444.) Unfortunately, some researchers also mention this wrong date of entry: see Gert Gröning and Joachim Wolschke-Bulmahn, *Liebe zur Landschaft. Teil 1: Natur in Bewegung. Zur Bedeutung natur- und freiraumorientierter Bewegungen in der ersten Hälfte des 20. Jahrhunderts für die Entwicklung der Freiraumplanung* (Münster, 1995), 149.

conservation conflicts in different parts of Germany: the fight over the Hohenstoffeln Mountain in southwest Germany, which was threatened by a quarry; the Schorfheide nature reserve near Berlin, where Hermann Göring, who was Nazi Germany's supreme conservationist, forester, and hunter at the same time, acted out his penchant for hunting; the regulation of the Ems River in northern Germany, where conservation issues were marginalized in favor of increased agricultural production; and finally, the conflict over the Wutach Gorge during World War II, where conservationists managed to stall a hydroelectric project for more than a year in spite of the exigencies of the war economy. Of course, these case studies cover only a fraction of the numerous conservation conflicts between 1933 and 1945, but they do provide an impression of the different types of conflicts during the Nazi era. Chapter 5 completes the picture with a look at the everyday business of conservation, which was characterized not so much by spectacular conflicts as by countless small-scale issues and a huge amount of paperwork. At the same time, Chapter 5 discusses developments after 1939, for conservation work by no means ended with the onset of World War II. Far into the war, conservationists managed to maintain at least a semblance of "business as usual," but this work looks even more ambivalent than the other efforts of the Nazi era in retrospect: during the war, some members of the conservation community became accomplices to genocide.

Environmental history is not only the history of people seeking to protect nature but also the history of the environment itself, and Chapter 6 pays tribute to that.[28] How did the 12 years of Nazi rule change the countryside? Did the alliance of conservation and National Socialism really pay off in ways that would have been difficult to achieve under other circumstances? And how does the impact of the Nazi era differ from that of previous and later times? In the interest of clarity, it should be stressed from the outset that the response will necessarily remain sketchy in this chapter because of the lack of prior research on this subject. Most Germans now acknowledge the importance of remembering the Nazi era, but few have thought of the Nazis' impact on the German *landscape* so far, and uncertainty reigns on how to deal with this impact. The stir over a luxury resort on the Obersalzberg in Bavaria in 2005, the site of Hitler's mountain retreat, exemplifies this void in Germany's collective memory.

---

[28] See David Blackbourn, *A Sense of Place: New Directions in German History. The 1998 Annual Lecture of the German Historical Institute London* (London, 1999).

Proximity to the Nazi regime turned into a burden after 1945, and Chapter 7 discusses the impact of the Nazi experience after the German defeat. Most conservationists would have liked to ignore this past, but that turned out to be difficult: history kept coming back to haunt them. However, instead of trying to face up to its own responsibility, the conservation movement developed a set of ideas and attitudes that, though highly dubious from a historical standpoint, managed to quell the nascent discussion within a matter of years. Briefly, the argument was that conservation was not a political issue and that the national conservation law of 1935 had only coincidentally been passed under the Nazi regime – thus, there was no further need for reflection or soul-searching. Interestingly, this attitude survived the generation of wartime conservationists and even persists to the present: it is no coincidence that the German environmental movement has taken longer than many other groups to recognize its own Nazi past.

"A relevant topic?" The seemingly naïve question turns out to be important, and in fact indispensable, for it forces us to think more thoroughly about the concepts guiding our thinking. At the same time, the question makes clear that this book, and in fact any treatise on the environment and the Nazis, is more than a purely academic enterprise. Inevitably, the issue at stake in any such discussion is also the perspective that it opens on the current environmental movement: how does modern environmentalism look against this historic background – and what are the lessons that today's environmentalists should learn from this part of their history? Some proposals have already been made in this regard, but they often came across as rather simplistic. For example, some researchers have argued that the current criticism of nonnative species is following up on Nazi clichés in a fateful way. However, it is easy to show that this interpretation is based on a selective reading of the sources: there was never a uniform opinion on nonnative species among German conservationists of the interwar years, let alone the rigor and fanaticism that one would expect in an ideologically charged field. Other researchers have taken an even bolder approach, using the issue as an excuse for a fundamental attack on conservationism per se. But that line of reasoning is even easier to dismiss. There is no way – at least no logically consistent way – to tarnish environmentalism in general through a reference to the Nazi era: in fact, such an argument constitutes an *abuse of history*. If you came upon this book hoping to be told that today's environmentalists are actually Nazis in disguise, then I hope you paid for it before reaching this sentence.

In the quest for lessons from this story, it is generally unwise to give primary attention to the ideological side of the issue. To be sure, the ideological baggage of German conservationism was anything but unproblematic long before 1933, and if the history of conservation in Nazi-era Germany came to be seen as an object lesson in the importance of keeping a close eye on the moral underpinnings of conservation, it could not be criticized from either a political or a historical point of view. But at the same time, a narrow focus on ideology easily produces a deceptive and ultimately misleading picture. It is important to realize that, in 1933, the German conservation community was not a group of ideological bloodhounds who were just waiting for a chance to act out their racist and anti-Semitic ambitions. Quite the contrary, it was a set of ardent nature lovers who generally cared mostly about the outdoors and little, if at all, about politics. To be sure, this perspective does not in any way excuse the ugly excursions into racist and anti-Semitic clichés that dot the literature of the Nazi era. In fact, environmentalists are well advised not even to try to excuse remarks of this kind. But such a perspective does make the conservationists of the Nazi era more similar to today's environmentalists. And that opens the path to what I see as the key lesson of this story.

It is instructive to imagine the situation of German conservationists on the verge of World War II: if they compared the contemporary situation with that of a decade ago, it was easy to become optimistic, if not enthusiastic. The national conservation law had revived nature protection in all parts of Germany, and a rapid succession of orders from the Reich Conservation Agency mirrored the busy atmosphere in conservation circles; with the law of 1935, the conservationists' cause had received the blessing of the second man in the country, and even Hitler himself would side with the cause a bit later, if only on the issue of hedgerows. A large number of new nature reserves had been designated within a brief period of time, thanks to provisions in the law that sped up the previously lengthy negotiations with property owners. Of course, it is easy to counter this positive overall balance in retrospect: the Nazi leaders' interest in conservation was actually rather flimsy, the general dynamism was in many cases little more than paperwork, and the improvements were more than counterbalanced by losses caused by the cultivation of previously unused land, the regulation of rivers, and a rapid industrialization in preparation for war, all likewise results of Nazi policies. However, the conservationists of the Nazi era rarely took stock in such a sober way, and they gave even less thought to the general principles that conservation policy was based on. As we will see, the improvements for the conservation community were in no small part caused by a lack of consideration for the civil rights of those who happened to own a natural treasure. But this fact never became a significant issue in conservation circles, not even after the Nazis were gone.

It is not difficult to imagine how conservationists of the Nazi era would have responded to a more balanced view: it made no sense to stand up against certain Nazi policies, especially in the field of agriculture; you had to take what you could get, and you had to leap at opportunities. It is on *this* attitude that the rapprochement of the conservation movement to the Nazi regime was based, and it is *this* attitude that needs to be challenged retrospectively. Without much thought to universal principles such as democracy and human rights, the German conservation movement acted on the basis of an exceedingly simple political philosophy: any legal provision, and any alliance with the Nazi regime, is fine as long as it helps our cause. Rarely does one get the impression, going through the records and books of the Nazi era, that there was something that the conservationists would *not* do to push their own agenda; and what that was leading to became clear in its crassest form during the war, when conservationists were honestly trying to mobilize Heinrich Himmler for their cause at a time when he was not only the head of the German police and the infamous SS but also the chief organizer of the Holocaust. In retrospect, one may legitimately call this a politically naïve attitude; in fact, one probably *should* call it that. But it is a naïveté that probably did not end with the demise of the Nazi regime.

The title of this book is *The Green and the Brown*. Of course, this title is misleading in a way: the "green" and the "brown" were not two camps at a distance, like Stendhal's *The Red and the Black*, but two groups that shared many convictions and came to work together to a stunning extent. The green *were* brown to some extent – all too many of them. The story that emerges is a complicated one, with many facets that defy a simple narrative or a clear-cut explanation. It is a story of ideological convergence, of tactical alliances, of simple careerism, of implication in crimes against humanity, and of deceit and denial after 1945. It is a story that many environmentalists will find disturbing. That is what makes it important.

2

Ideas: Diverse Roots and a Common Cause

What are the intellectual roots of German conservation? For Schoenichen, the former head of the Prussian Agency for the Protection of National Monuments, the answer was simple: "The idea of conservation is essentially an outgrowth of romanticism," he wrote in his overview of German conservation published in 1954.[1] Today's historians will need to provide a more complex answer. Schoenichen was right in his emphasis that the idea of conservation was indeed much older than the organized conservation movement that arose around 1900, but romanticism was only one of multiple strands that defined thinking on conservation issues in Germany. In fact, it is a matter of debate whether there was actually a clearly defined philosophy of nature protection in Germany at any time, and especially during the first decades of conservation history. During the nineteenth century, conservation was a sentiment rather than a social movement, and its key proponents were often freelance authors who showed little interest in molding their ideas into a clear political agenda, let alone formal organizations. The best-known example was Wilhelm Heinrich Riehl, whose 1854 book *Naturgeschichte des Volkes* ("Natural History of the German People") celebrated rural life, the German forests, and a natural "right to wilderness."[2] However, the book, based mostly on Riehl's personal experiences while traveling through Germany's regions, was much more than a treatise on conservation: it put forward a harmonious ideal of

---

[1] Walther Schoenichen, *Naturschutz, Heimatschutz. Ihre Begründung durch Ernst Rudorff, Hugo Conwentz und ihre Vorläufer* (Stuttgart, 1954), 1.

[2] Wilhelm Heinrich Riehl, *Land und Leute. Die Naturgeschichte des Volkes als Grundlage einer deutschen Social-Politik*, vol. 1 (Stuttgart and Tübingen, 1854).

social relations, with nature being a harbinger of peace, and key concepts, such as modesty and honor, revealed Riehl's longing for an idealized premodern society.[3] Another nineteenth-century protagonist of conservation with a more regional influence was Hermann Landois, a native of Münster who was a Catholic priest, the founder of Münster's zoological garden and natural history museum, a popularizer of biology, and proponent of the protection of birds. One of his students was Hermann Löns, whose passion for the Lüneburg Heath became one of the fixtures of German nature protection.[4] In both cases, conservation was not a separate issue but part of a wide spectrum of societal and scientific ideas. It is illustrative that the most important organizations on conservation issues in the late nineteenth century were beautification societies, where the protection of nature was part of a broader program of regional aesthetic uplift.[5]

The cheerful mixture of conservation and other ideas in the nineteenth century may look sympathetic in retrospect, but it was not conducive to the formation of a social movement. Riehl's writings made for great reading and remained popular long after his death, but deducing from them a clear political agenda and a plan of action was next to impossible: social movements need a clear set of goals to gain momentum.[6] Therefore, it was perhaps inevitable that the ideological richness of early conservation began to dwindle when conservation became a political cause. Toward the end of the nineteenth century, a new type of regional association emerged that favored active reclamation, thus moving beyond the more constrained agenda of the beautification societies. The Siebengebirge in the upper Rhine valley provides a case in point: a beautification society founded in 1869 (*Verschönerungsverein für das Siebengebirge*) focused

---

[3] See Peter Steinbach, "Wilhelm Heinrich Riehl," in Hans-Ulrich Wehler (ed). *Deutsche Historiker*, vol. 6 (Göttingen, 1980), 43. See also Konrad Ott, "Geistesgeschichtliche Ursprünge des deutschen Naturschutzes zwischen 1850 und 1914," in Werner Konold, Reinhard Böcker, and Ulrich Hampicke (eds.), *Handbuch Naturschutz und Landschaftspflege* (Landsberg, 2004), 3–5; Konrad Ott, Thomas Potthast, Martin Gorke, and Patricia Nevers, "Über die Anfänge des Naturschutzgedankens in Deutschland und den USA im 19. Jahrhundert," *Jahrbuch für europäische Verwaltungsgeschichte* 11 (1999): 1–55.

[4] Barbara Rommé (ed.), *Professor Landois. Mit Witz und Wissenschaft* (Münster, 2004); Walter Werland, *Münsters Professor Landois. Begebenheiten und Merkwürdigkeiten um den Zoogründer* (Münster, 1977).

[5] See Alon Confino, *The Nation as a Local Metaphor. Württemberg, Imperial Germany, and National Memory, 1871–1918* (Chapel Hill, N. C., 1997), 108–11; and Celia Applegate, *A Nation of Provincials. The German Idea of Heimat* (Berkeley and Los Angeles, 1990), 63–65.

[6] See Joachim Raschke, *Soziale Bewegungen. Ein historisch-systematischer Grundriß* (Frankfurt and New York, 1988), 165.

on the designation of hiking trails and the purchase of terrain to secure the area's attractiveness and accessibility for tourists. But when a number of quarries threatened the familiar landscape, the beautification society felt unable to conduct an aggressive political campaign, leading to the formation of a separate "Society for the Rescue of the Siebengebirge" (*Verein zur Rettung des Siebengebirges*) in 1886.[7] The next step in the development of an organized conservation movement came around 1900, when a number of national associations evolved that continue to play an important role in environmental policy to the present day. Nonetheless, the spectrum of ideas remained impressive: it ranged from the Federation for Heimat Protection (*Bund Heimatschutz*), which linked conservation with regional cultural policy to the Bird Protection League (*Bund für Vogelschutz*), which relied on a rather lowbrow concept of compassion for "our feathered friends."[8] Even within the *Heimat* protection movement, the range of approaches went, as Friedemann Schmoll wrote, "from pragmatic conservation work to quasireligious worship of nature."[9] The German conservation movement was always a pluralistic one and never developed a universally binding canon of conservation ideas.

The multitude of approaches found its reflection in a multitude of organizations. In fact, the agenda was so much in flux within some organizations that they kept changing their names on a regular basis: an association in Westphalia operated under six different names within four decades. Starting with a title that included the breeding of canary birds as part of its agenda, it came to focus on the protection of birds, then included nature protection in its title and finally, in 1934, became known as Westphalian Nature Protection Association (*Westfälischer Naturschutzverein*); three years later, it changed its name again to Westphalian Natural History Association (*Westfälischer Naturwissenschaftlicher Verein*).[10] On a European scale, the fragmentation of the German conservation movement was something of an exception – in many other countries, a single association

---

[7] Friedemann Schmoll, *Erinnerung an die Natur. Die Geschichte des Naturschutzes im deutschen Kaiserreich* (Frankfurt and New York, 2004), 199.

[8] See Andreas Knaut, *Zurück zur Natur! Die Wurzeln der Ökologiebewegung* (Supplement 1 [1993] of *Jahrbuch für Naturschutz und Landschaftspflege*, Greven, 1993); Anna-Katharina Wöbse, "Lina Hähnle und der Reichsbund für Vogelschutz. Soziale Bewegung im Gleichschritt," in Radkau and Uekötter, *Naturschutz und Nationalsozialismus*, esp. pp. 312–14; Reinhard Johler, "Vogelmord und Vogelliebe. Zur Ethnographie konträrer Leidenschaften," *Historische Anthropologie* 5 (1997): 1–35.

[9] Schmoll, *Erinnerung*, 456.

[10] See WAA Best. 717 Zug. 23/1999 Naturschutzverein, Satzungen des Westfälischen Naturschutzvereins e.V. von 1934, p. 4; and WAA LWL Best. 702 no. 186.

came to dominate the field – and some members regretted the duplication of work and parallel efforts. "It is sad to see how jealousy and dispute rules among the associations, wasting a lot of money and work at the expense of the common cause," Konrad Guenther, a natural scientist at Freiburg University, complained in 1910.[11] However, the plurality of organizations was also to some extent a mirror of the strong regional orientation of many efforts. One needs to keep in mind that there was no German nation-state until 1871, and regionalist sentiments remained strong even decades after the foundation of the Emperor's Reich. In the field of conservation, regionalism was also a result of the geographic diversity of Germany: the protection of nature looked very different in the north German lowlands, the mountain regions like the Sauerland or the Black Forest, or the Bavarian Alps. The nationwide Federation for Heimat Protection, which was a loose umbrella organization for numerous regional associations with distinct agendas, provided perhaps as much unity as the regionalist sentiments could bear.[12] It was no coincidence that the conservation movement was one of the few social movements that the Nazis never managed to merge into a uniform national organization.

The plurality of organizations inevitably led to numerous conflicts and rivalries that consumed a significant part of the movement's energies; the idea that a multitude of approaches to conservation could be an asset rather than a problem was never popular among German conservationists.[13] But in spite of a considerable amount of infighting, the movement managed to preserve some degree of coherence and never split into fully independent factions. There were, after all, a few points on which most conservationists did agree. One of these was the notion of *Heimat*, the love of the regional homeland. But part of the attractiveness of *Heimat* was that it made for an inherently diffuse concept, uniting nature and culture, landscapes and people, and thus left much room for individual preferences.[14] A second popular notion saw conservation as an inherently

[11] Konrad Guenther, *Der Naturschutz* (Freiburg, 1910), 262.

[12] Thomas Lekan, *Imagining the Nation in Nature: Landscape Preservation and German Identity, 1885–1945* (Cambridge, Mass., 2003), 61.

[13] See Frank Uekoetter, "The Old Conservation History – and the New. An Argument for Fresh Perspectives on an Established Topic," *Historical Social Research* 29, 3 (2004): 181.

[14] As mentioned in the "note on vocabulary," the concept of *Heimat* is a German peculiarity and ultimately impossible to translate into English. According to Alon Confino, "its singularity in European culture was the merging of local, regional, and national identities in one common representation of the nation.... Only in Germany,... an iconography of landscape and cityscape as a representation of the nation became a common

idealistic enterprise. A rallying cry against the destructive powers of materialism was always sure to get applause in conservation circles – though not everyone would phrase it as aggressively as Wilhelm Lienenkämper, one of the more flamboyant conservationists, who referred to the "merciless extermination of the utilitarian perspective" as the "First Commandment" of conservation during the Nazi era.[15] In contrast to the American definition of the word, conservation did not have implications of use in Germany. Another point of agreement was the strong orientation toward enlisting the help of state authorities; the proximity of many organizations to the state, which offered information, money, and other kinds of support, was stronger in Germany than in most other European countries.[16] But, ultimately, it was not a certain canon of ideas that united the conservation community but a common identity: "you are worthless as a conservationist if you do not partake with your heart, if you do not act out of love and a deeply felt belief in the beauty, in the eternal powers and miracles of our *Heimat* nature," a conservation pamphlet from the Nazi era declared.[17] Conservationists felt that they were part of a small group of idealists who had truly understood the peril nature was in and tried to do something about it, and this passion for nature left much room for individual preferences. More than other social movements, the conservation movement was a haven for individualists: it is no coincidence that hiking was a key activity among German conservationists, and it was understood that hiking was a solitary enterprise; excursions with large groups, where communication would dilute the experience of nature, were

symbolic capital." (Confino, *Nation*, 212n.) John Alexander Williams notes that "*Heimat* was an extraordinarily slippery and unstable idea with an overabundance of conflicting meanings." (John Alexander Williams, "'The Chords of the German Soul are Tuned to Nature': The Movement to Preserve the Natural Heimat from the Kaiserreich to the Third Reich," *Central European History* 29 [1996]: 358.) For the author's attempt to define *Heimat* nonetheless, see Frank Uekoetter, "Heimat, Heimat ohne alles? Warum die Vilmer Thesen zu kurz greifen," *Heimat Thüringen* 11, 4 (2004): 8–11.

15 HStAD NW 60 no. 1603 p. 300. For further information on Lienenkämper, see Kuno Müller, "Zur Geschichte der ehemaligen Kreisstelle für Naturschutz Altena-Lüdenscheid bis zum Jahre 1936," *Der Märker* 31 (1982): 147–54, Walter Hostert, *Geschichte des Sauerländischen Gebirgsvereins. Idee und Tat. Gestern – Heute – Morgen* (Hagen, 1966), 129n; and Herbert Schulte, "Vorkämpfer für den Naturschutz," in Heimatbund Märkischer Kreis (ed.), *Herscheid. Beiträge zur Heimat- und Landeskunde* (Altena, 1998), 121–2.

16 See Frank Uekötter, "Naturschutz und Demokratie. Plädoyer für eine reflexive Naturschutzbewegung," *Natur und Landschaft* 80 (2005): 137–40.

17 KAW Landratsamt Warendorf C 303, Der Westfälische Naturschutz braucht auch Dich! (Ein Mahnruf des Bundes "Natur und Heimat) (ca. 1936). The phrasing carried biblical allusions and resembled the choice of words in I Corinthians, 13.

generally abhorred. During the Nazi era, conservationists derided the mass tourism sponsored by the *Kraft durch Freude* tourist association as "horde hiking."[18]

With a view to the Nazi experience, the political stance of the conservation movement deserves special attention. In spite of the strong regionalism within the rank and file, the German conservation movement has always been, as most bourgeois movements of its time, a nationalist one. "The love of nature is the root for the love of the fatherland," Konrad Guenther wrote in his seminal monograph on conservation in 1910.[19] In 1913, when the centennial of the German victory over Napoleon and the twenty-fifth anniversary of the reign of the German Emperor Wilhelm II were approaching, the head of the Prussian Agency for the Protection of Natural Monuments, Hugo Conwentz, suggested a conservation drive to celebrate the occasion. Citing a number of precedents, like the foundation of the Friedrichshain city park in Berlin in 1840, Conwentz wrote that "some communities could express their support for the patriotic cause by putting some scenic part of their surroundings under protection."[20] But this kind of nationalism was far removed from the chauvinism in other parts of contemporary German society, and the conservation movement represented, as nationalisms go, a rather cool-headed variant. It is interesting to note that, although German nationalism overheated during World War I, culminating in the formation of the protofascist German Fatherland Party (*Deutsche Vaterlandspartei*), in 1917, the German conservationists remained rather moderate, though they were by no means immune to the general radicalization of political rhetoric.[21] As late as 1917, a conservation journal published an eulogy of British conservation, whereas a *Heimatschutz* journal in Brandenburg appeared with an encomium on the region's nature that, though nationalist at times, culminated in the sentence, "Modest in our demands, we are staying in our home country" – not the worst slogan in times of war and a stance that differed markedly from the expansionist fantasies that the German government was still hoping to realize at that time.[22] The nation was

---

[18] Susanne Falk, *Der Sauerländische Gebirgsverein. "Vielleicht sind wir die Modernen von übermorgen"* (Bonn, 1990), 113. See also Roland Siekmann, *Eigenartige Senne. Zur Kulturgeschichte der Wahrnehmung einer peripheren Landschaft* (Lemgo, 2004), 340n.

[19] Guenther, *Naturschutz*, iv.

[20] LASH Abt. 301 no. 1193, Anregung für 1913. Attachment to a letter of Hugo Conwentz, September 9, 1912.

[21] See Lekan, *Imagining*, 74.

[22] H. Salomon, "Der Naturschutz bei unseren Feinden," *Blätter für Naturschutz und Heimatpflege* 3 (1917): 5; Paul Förster, "Die Entdeckung der Heimat," *Heimatschutz*

FIGURE 2.1. The so-called Green Gate in Danzig, the first seat of Hugo Conwentz's Prussian Agency for the Protection of Natural Monuments. Photo from Hans Klose, *Fünfzig Jahre Staatlicher Naturschutz* (Giessen, 1957).

important for the conservationists, but it did not rank higher than the fate of nature. When Germany had to cede a part of its North to Denmark in 1920, Conwentz diligently supplied the Danish conservationists with a list of nature reserves.[23]

The ideas that went along with nationalist sentiments look more ambivalent in retrospect. The rhetoric of the early German conservation movement displayed, as Konrad Ott remarked, "all the themes of conservative cultural criticism," thus making conservation part of a climate of cultural despair that was strong among German academics around 1900.[24] Some early publications on the history of nature protection have

in Brandenburg 8 (1917): 41–5. The classic treatise on wartime planning within the German government is Fritz Fischer, *Griff nach der Weltmacht. Die Kriegszielpolitik des kaiserlichen Deutschlands 1914/18* (Düsseldorf, 1961).

[23] LASH Abt. 301 no. 4066, Staatliche Stelle für Naturdenkmalpflege in Preussen to the Oberpräsident in Kiel, February 24, 1921.

[24] Ott, "Geistesgeschichtliche Ursprünge," 2.

pointed to these tendencies to suggest that they set the conservation movement on a direct course toward National Socialism,[25] but the more recent
literature is unanimous in its rejection of such a line of reasoning.[26] Mock-
ing the evidence presented in earlier publications as little more than "a
diligent collection of xenophobic keywords," Friedemann Schmoll has
argued for a more balanced approach that looks not only at the rather
small number of anti-Semitic statements from conservationists but also at
the general context; and on that background, the German conservation
movement did not stand out as a particularly anti-Semitic part of society.[27]
When the *Pfälzerwald Verein* was founded in the West German Palatinate region in 1902, its founders included "a Catholic priest, a Protestant
clerk, and a Jewish businessman."[28] The early conservation movement
comprised people such as Hermann Löns, who, in 1913, claimed that
conservation was also "a fight for the power of the nation and the flour-
ishing of the race."[29] But again, it is just as important to note the limited
resonance that statements of this kind achieved. "Regional conservationists' vision of landscape planning remained overwhelmingly aesthetic and
provincial rather than racist and nationalist," Thomas Lekan wrote.[30] The
conservation movement was not free from the uglier expressions of right-
wing political philosophy before 1914, but voices of this kind remained
a minority. As Celia Applegate wrote, nature continued to represent "an
inclusive and tolerant impulse. Nature was to be neutral, above party and
confessional strife."[31]

[25] See Ulrich Linse, *Ökopax und Anarchie. Eine Geschichte der ökologischen Bewegungen in Deutschland* (Munich, 1986), esp. p. 35; Werner Hartung, *Konservative Zivilisationskritik und regionale Identität. Am Beispiel der niedersächsischen Heimatbewegung
1895 bis 1919* (Hannover, 1991), esp. p. 305n; and Gert Gröning and Joachim Wolschke-
Bulmahn, "Landschafts- und Naturschutz," in Diethart Kerbs and Jürgen Reulecke (eds.),
Handbuch der deutschen Reformbewegungen 1880–1933 (Wuppertal, 1998), 30n.

[26] Schmoll, *Erinnerung*, 467; Thomas Rohkrämer, *Eine andere Moderne? Zivilisationskritik, Natur und Technik in Deutschland 1880–1933* (Paderborn, 1999), 138n; Lekan,
Imagining, 111n; Confino, *Nation*, 212.

[27] Friedemann Schmoll, "Die Verteidigung organischer Ordnungen. Naturschutz und Antisemitismus zwischen Kaiserreich und Nationalsozialismus," in Radkau and Uekötter,
Naturschutz und Nationalsozialismus, 169. See also Friedemann Schmoll, "Bewahrung
und Vernichtung. Über Beziehungen zwischen Naturschutz und Antisemitismus in
Deutschland," in Freddy Raphaël (ed.), "*... das Flüstern eines leisen Wehens...*" *Beiträge
zu Kultur und Lebenswelt europäischer Juden* (Constance, 2001), 345–67.

[28] Applegate, *Nation*, 67.

[29] Hermann Löns, "Naturschutz und Rassenschutz," *Blätter für Naturschutz* 4 (1913): 1.

[30] Thomas Lekan, "'It Shall Be the Whole Landscape!' The Reich Nature Protection Law
and Regional Planning in the Third Reich," in Franz-Josef Brüggemeier, Mark Cioc, and
Thomas Zeller (eds.), *How Green Were the Nazis? Nature, Environment, and Nation in
the Third Reich* (Athens, 2005), 90.

[31] Applegate, *Nation*, 77.

Things were looking less harmless after World War I, however, which generally was a catalyst for extreme voices in German politics. Racist, völkisch, and anti-Semitic voices became significantly more pronounced, moving from a fringe phenomenon to a prominent part of the still quite diverse choir of conservationists.[32] For example, Konrad Guenther enlisted conservation in the task of resurrecting the German race: "if we did not find the German *Heimat*, then all efforts to mould the Germans into one nation would be futile."[33] A few years later, Guenther warned that failure in the protection of nature would mean a "betrayal of Germandom (*Deutschtum*)" and evoked the memory of the battles between the Roman Empire and the Germanic tribes in antiquity, where "throngs and throngs of blond heroes" streamed out of the German forests to fend off the Roman invasion, thus demonstrating that "the source of Germanic national character was inexhaustible... because it lay in the darkness of the forests, where it was beyond the reach of enemy hands."[34] In 1923, during the French occupation of the Ruhr region, the industrial heartland of Germany, the Federation for Heimat Protection played a prominent role in anti-Allied agitation.[35] In 1929, a treatise on the "*Heimat* sentiment" bemoaned the "deluge of Western European and American ideas," fearing that these might "erode the soil that we are standing on, unless the Germans regain their senses" – a thinly veiled critique of Western democracy.[36] Countless articles described intrinsic linkages between the natural environment and national character that, though not antidemocratic by themselves, nourished thinking in terms of faceless collectives rather than individual rights.[37] Even the beauty of nature was not immune to a nationalist twist: in 1921, a resolution of the League of German Mountain and Hiking Associations (*Verband Deutscher Gebirgs- und Wandervereine*) on the Hohenstoffeln Mountain stressed the importance of preserving the beauty of the German *Heimat* soil "after the

---

[32] See Lekan, *Imagining*, 13; William H. Rollins, *A Greener Vision of Home. Cultural Politics and Environmental Reform in the German Heimatschutz Movement, 1904–1918* (Ann Arbor, 1997), 262; Williams, "Chords"; and Willi Oberkrome, "*Deutsche Heimat.*" *Nationale Konzeption und regionale Praxis von Naturschutz, Landschaftsgestaltung und Kulturpolitik in Westfalen-Lippe und Thüringen (1900–1960)* (Paderborn, 2004), 514.

[33] Konrad Guenther, *Heimatlehre als Quelle neuer deutscher Zukunft* (Freiburg, 1922), 5. See also Williams, "Chords," 339.

[34] Konrad Guenther, "Naturschutz als Wissenschaft und Lehrfach," *Blätter für Naturschutz und Naturpflege* 14 (1931): 16.

[35] Oberkrome, *Deutsche Heimat*, 24.

[36] Max Kästner, "Vom Heimatgefühl," in Landesverein Sächsischer Heimatschutz (ed.), *Naturschutz in Sachsen* (Dresden, 1929): 9.

[37] See Lekan, *Imagining*; and Martin Greiffenhagen, *Das Dilemma des Konservatismus in Deutschland* (Frankfurt, 1986).

German nation has lost so many values."[38] In some cases, conservation organizations even came under the influence of eugenic ideas.[39] It was significant that Schoenichen succeeded Conwentz as head of the Prussian Agency for the Protection of Natural Monuments after his death in 1922: while Conwentz had been a rather sober natural scientist with little interest in the broader cultural implications of conservation, Schoenichen was more prone to reactionary sentiments and racist ideas, having depicted the Jews as a race, characterized by an "aquiline nose," as early as 1910.[40]

With this shift in conservation thinking, it is clear that the door was more open for Nazi ideology after 1918 than before the war. Still, it is important to refrain from simple teleological interpretations in this regard. For all the rightist rhetoric gathering in the 1920s, it is striking that this generally did not lead to an aggressive stance against the Weimar Republic. To be sure, there were some exceptions: Hans Wilhelm Stein, the founding chairman of the Thuringian *Bund der Thüringer Berg-, Burg- und Waldgemeinden*, gave refuge to the murderers of Walther Rathenau, the German secretary of state, in 1922.[41] But Stein had to resign after his implication in one of the most shocking acts of right-wing terror became clear, and the involvement of conservation associations in antidemocratic action remained an isolated and temporary phenomenon; the general atmosphere in the conservation community was very different from the aggressive, hate-filled atmosphere within many rightist splinter groups during the Weimar years. The *Heimat* movement as a whole never denounced democracy in public, not least to avoid jeopardizing financial support from the state. In some cases, the *Heimat* community even moved to the left in response to a leftist state government.[42] In short, it showed a pragmatic and unenthusiastic option for democracy, at least for the time being.[43] From the conservationists' point of view, the main

---

[38] GLAK Abt. 237 no. 36121, Verband Deutscher Gebirgs- und Wandervereine to the Badisches Staatsministerium, November 7, 1921.

[39] Oberkrome, *Deutsche Heimat*, 87.

[40] Walther Schoenichen, *Einführung in die Biologie. Ein Hilfsbuch für höhere Lehranstalten und für den Selbstunterricht* (Leipzig, 1910), 136. For a biographical sketch of Conwentz, see Knaut, *Zurück*, 40–50.

[41] Rüdiger Haufe, "Geistige Heimatpflege. Der 'Bund der Thüringer Berg-, Burg- und Waldgemeinden' in Vergangenheit und Gegenwart," in Radkau and Ueköttet, *Naturschutz und Nationalsozialismus*, 440.

[42] Oberkrome, *Deutsche Heimat*, 33n, 59.

[43] See Heinrich August Winkler, *Der lange Weg nach Westen vol. 1. Deutsche Geschichte vom Ende des Alten Reiches bis zum Untergang der Weimarer Republik* (Munich, 2000), 468.

problem about the Weimar Republic was not so much its democratic character as the sharp contrast between the harsh clashes in everyday political
life and the movement's harmonious ideals; as Celia Applegate remarked,
the *Heimat* movement was on "a search for security in a society ridden
by crisis."[44] However, the movement's distaste for the hustle and bustle
of party politics did not preclude broad support on conservation issues
across the political spectrum. In 1931, for example, the new conservation law for the state of Hesse passed by a wide majority, with only the
Communists voting against it.[45]

In retrospect, the prominence of racist and völkisch ideas even before
the Nazis' rise to power may appear shocking; but it is important to see
them against the background of contemporary politics. Compared with
other, more aggressive groups, the rightist tendencies within the conservation movement were weak: given the strength of antidemocratic sentiments during the Weimar years, it would have been more surprising if
the conservationists had stayed immune to these tendencies.[46] In fact, the
presence of these ideas was probably less dangerous than the reaction of
the movement's rank and file, which simply accepted them without much
ado. The conservation community never developed an intellectual climate
that encouraged an open discussion of the change of conservation rhetoric
after 1918. Therefore, reactionary and racist ideas floated freely through
the contemporary literature: not everyone embraced them, but nobody
took issue with them. Even the Social Democratic *Naturfreunde* tourist
organization showed little interest in a debate on the relationship between
conservation and democracy or human rights.[47] As a result, rightist ideas
won a place in conservation thinking without being challenged significantly. Even Siegfried Lichtenstaedter, who spoke about "conservation
and Jewishness" at a meeting of the Bavarian Conservation League, did
not use this occasion to criticize right-wing tendencies but rather laid
out why "one can recommend the promotion of nature protection to

[44] Applegate, *Nation*, 151. Similarly, Williams, "Chords," 344.

[45] Ludwig Spilger, "Das neue Naturschutzgesetz," *Volk und Scholle* 10, 2 (1932): 43.

[46] See the classic work of Kurt Sontheimer, *Antidemokratisches Denken in der Weimarer
Republik. Die politischen Ideen des deutschen Nationalismus zwischen 1918 und 1933*
(Munich, 1962).

[47] See Augustin Upmann and Uwe Rennspieß, "Organisationsgeschichte der deutschen
Naturfreundebewegung bis 1933," in Jochen Zimmer (ed.), *Mit uns zieht die neue Zeit.
Die Naturfreunde. Zur Geschichte eines alternativen Verbandes in der Arbeiterkulturbe-
wegung* (Cologne, 1984), esp. p. 96n; and Gunnar Wendt, "Proletarischer Naturschutz
in der Weimarer Republik – Der Touristenverein 'Die Naturfreunde' im Rheinland,"
Geschichte im Westen 19 (2004): 42–65.

religious Jews."[48] The general opinion was that if someone adopted racist or anti-Semitic ideas, that was his or her personal affair and one could live with it.

With this lack of discussion and a harmonious ideal of politics, the conservation movement was certainly not in a position to leap to the defense of German democracy when it came under acute pressure in the early 1930s. After 1929, the parliamentary system went into a downward spiral that led, in Karl Dietrich Bracher's famous phrase, to "the dissolution of the republic of Weimar."[49] Within the conservation community, the prevalent reaction was apathy and lack of interest. Of course, it was clear to most conservationists that their issues could play only a marginal role at a time of worldwide economic depression – the Great Depression hit Germany especially hard since the late 1920s – but the problem went deeper than that: the power struggle at work and the street violence so prevalent in the final years of the republic was anathema to the longings of the conservationists. When political controversies threatened to dominate discussions at the general assembly of a *Heimat* association in the Palatinate region in 1931, a passionate pledge for harmony and consolation ended the strife: "We do not want controversies, we want peace. We are not a party but nonpartisan mediators. . . . The party seeks division, but we long for reconciliation. . . . Parties are saying: Marx, Lenin, Hitler. We are saying: Pestalozzi, Goethe, Mozart."[50] While extremists

---

[48] *Blätter für Naturschutz und Naturpflege* 14 (1931): 171. Gert Gröning has argued that Lichtenstaedter's booklet of the same title included a pledge for democracy, but such an interpretation is grossly misleading. It ignores not only the main thrust of the argument, but it also blanks out that Lichtenstaedter saw anti-Semitism as a mere nuisance, rather than a threat that one had to fight tooth and nail: referring to anti-Semitic sentiments in contemporary society, he urged Jews to exert "a certain moderation" in conservation work so as not to make conservation appear as a quintessential Jewish concern – the complete opposite of a determined fight! Even more, Lichtenstaedter wrote that anti-Semitism was stronger in the "broader masses" than in "smaller, morally higher circles," a strong indication that he saw anti-Semitism among the conservationists themselves as a marginal problem. (Compare Gert Gröning, "Siegfried Lichtenstaedter. 'Naturschutz und Judentum, ein vernachlässigtes Kapitel jüdischer Sittenlehre' – ein Kommentar," in Gert Gröning and Joachim Wolschke-Bulmahn [eds.], *Arbeitsmaterialien zum Workshop "Naturschutz und Demokratie!?"* [Hannover, 2004], 41–4; and Siegfried Lichtenstaedter, *Naturschutz und Judentum. Ein vernachlässigtes Kapitel jüdischer Sittenlehre* [Frankfurt, 1932]. Quotations p. 39.)

[49] Karl Dietrich Bracher, *Die Auflösung der Weimarer Republik. Eine Studie zum Problem des Machtverfalls in der Demokratie* (Stuttgart, 1955).

[50] *Pfälzisches Museum – pfälzische Heimatkunde* 49 (1932): 84. Johann Heinrich Pestalozzi was a Swiss educator and social reformer who lived from 1746 to 1827. He was a pioneer of modern elementary education.

from the right and the left were undermining the last remnants of democracy, conservationists behaved as if all this was of no concern to them. Almost, that is: when Germany was bracing for the federal elections of July 1932, in which the Nazi party would win a 37.4 percent share of the vote that essentially deadlocked the German parliament, the Federation for Heimat Protection petitioned the German government because it feared an election campaign with advertisements in the open landscape "devoid of respect for the face of the *Heimat*" and therefore called on the government "to take decisive measures for the protection of scenic beauty in town and countryside."[51] Opposition to billboards and other kinds of outdoor advertising had a long tradition within the conservation community, and yet one cannot help but find the Federation's petition a fitting closure to the history of conservation in the Weimar Republic. In the midst of a violent and exceedingly bitter election campaign that would decide on the future of Germany's democracy, the conservationists were worrying about ugly billboards.

All in all, it was a highly ambivalent position that the German conservation movement occupied on the eve of the Nazis' seizure of power. Rightist ideas had a place in the German conservation movement long before 1933, but it seems unlikely that they were close to a majority opinion.[52] The Nationalsozialistische Deutsche Arbeiterpartei (NSDAP) was certainly not most conservationists' party of choice, and not only because the conservationists were generally averse to party politics. The situation was similar from the Nazis' point of view: for them, the conservation movement did not stand out as an oppositional or even dangerous group, but neither did it win instant sympathies. Paul Schultze-Naumburg, one of the cofounders of the Federation for Heimat Protection in the early 1900s, was in touch with Hitler and Joseph Goebbels during the 1920s and became a leading figure in the Nazis' Fighting League for German Culture (*Kampfbund für deutsche Kultur*) from 1929. Other than that, contacts between the conservationists and the Nazi movement were almost nonexistent.[53] Of eighteen prominent conservationists whom historian

[51] GLAK Abt. 235 no. 48254, Der Reichsminister des Innern to the Landesregierungen, July 2, 1932. The result of the Nazi Party was matched by a 14.5 percent share of the vote by the communists, meaning two parties that explicitly sought to abolish democracy held an absolute majority of the seats. With that, any kind of parliamentary government became impossible. (Heinrich August Winkler, *Weimar 1918–1933. Die Geschichte der ersten deutschen Demokratie* [Munich, 1998], 505–7.)

[52] See Lekan, *Imagining*, 101, 148.

[53] On Schultze-Naumburg, see Knaut, *Zurück*, 54–60, and Norbert Borrmann, *Paul Schultze-Naumburg 1869–1949. Maler, Publizist, Architekt. Vom Kulturreformer der*

Raymond Dominick screened for membership in the NSDAP, only one had joined before 1933. Nine more conservationists entered the party during the first 5 years of the Nazis' reign, and membership was refused in a tenth case, but the opportunism of these members was already familiar to contemporary observers and a frequent cause for mockery among the party's old guard.[54] Within 4 months of Hitler's rise to power, the NSDAP grew from 850,000 to some 2.5 million members, resulting in a temporary ban on new memberships on May 1, 1933.[55]

Against the background of the conservationists' turn to the right, it would appear that the conservation movement had little trouble presenting itself in a Nazi light. However, the ideological merger of conservation and National Socialism turned out to be much more difficult than one would expect. The themes of Hitler's writings and speeches were not only far removed from the conservationists' issues, but they also revealed to the careful reader a number of statements with severe antienvironmental implications. The most notorious was Hitler's call for an intensification of agriculture in his quest for autarky. Years later, conservationists were still shuddering when they recalled Hitler's wish that "no square meter of German soil shall remain uncultivated," for such a vision was nothing short of a horror scenario from the conservationists' point of view.[56] In his 1941 brochure on Hitler's intervention for the protection of hedgerows, Hans Schwenkel complained of the "overzealous people" who took this quote as a blank check to "cleanse" the landscape of all woodland, noting that Hitler's statement had been "widely misunderstood" in Germany – a rare case of a public renunciation of a Hitler quote.[57] According to Jeffrey Herf, Hitler thought "that the Germans must succeed in the

Jahrhundertwende zum Kulturpolitiker im Dritten Reich (Essen, 1989). On the Kampfbund, see Jürgen Gimmel, *Die politische Organisation kulturellen Ressentiments. Der "Kampfbund für deutsche Kultur" und das bildungsbürgerliche Unbehagen an der Moderne* (Münster, 2001). Willi Oberkrome gives the rather anecdotal example of Manfred Fuhrmann, who founded the *Lippische Naturschutzvereinigung* in 1925 as an alternative to the mainstream *Heimat* leagues but quickly isolated himself because of his radical rhetoric and ended up as a regional NSDAP leader. (Oberkrome, *Deutsche Heimat*, 73–5. See also Siekmann, *Eigenartige Senne*, 343–5.)

54 Raymond H. Dominick III, *The Environmental Movement in Germany. Prophets and Pioneers 1871–1971* (Bloomington and Indianapolis, 1992), 112n.

55 Broszat, *Staat Hitlers*, 253.

56 See WAA Best. 717 file "Reichsstelle (Bundesstelle) für Naturschutz (und Landschaftspflege)," Der Direktor der Reichsstelle für Naturschutz, Denkblätter der Reichsstelle für Naturschutz über die künftige Wahrnehmung von Naturschutz und Landschaftspflege, June 26, 1945, p. 2. See also Radkau, "Naturschutz," 45.

57 GLAK Abt. 235 no. 47680, Der Führer hält seine schützende Hand über unsere Hecken. Hans Schwenkel, Reichsbund für Vogelschutz, p. 2.

FIGURE 2.2. Adolf Hitler playing with a German shepherd in his mountain retreat on the Obersalzberg. Photo from Ullstein Bild.

battle against nature in order to win in the battle among nations and races."[58] To be sure, Hitler made repeated references to Nature (with a capital N) in his *Mein Kampf*, depicting it as an agent of history, but this Nature was completely different from the one that the conservationists were seeking to protect. "Nature knows no political boundaries. First, she puts living creatures on this globe and watches the free play of forces. She then confers the master's right on her favorite child, the strongest in courage and industry."[59] Obviously, Hitler's Nature did not require protection!

It would certainly overstate the point to deduce a clear antienvironmental ethic from Hitler's statements, not least because it would imply a misperception of the role of ideology in the Nazi state. Nazi ideology was never a rigid set of ideas and principles that called for exegetical studies but rather an amorphous conglomerate of concepts, notions, and resentments, where even key concepts like *Volk* and race, community and

---

[58] Jeffrey Herf, *Reactionary Modernism. Technology, Culture, and Politics in Weimar and the Third Reich* (Cambridge, 1984), 194. Similarly, Oberkrome, *Deutsche Heimat*, 142.

[59] Adolf Hitler, *Mein Kampf*, trans. Ralph Manheim (Boston and New York, 1999), 134.

Führer, were open to divergent readings.[60] In fact, even Hitler's call for the cultivation of every square meter of arable land stood in contrast to his argument in *Mein Kampf*, where he had denounced internal colonization because it would weaken the Aryan urge to seek new *Lebensraum* beyond German borders.[61] However, Hitler's political decisions reveal little in the way of environmental thinking. When a petitioner claimed that Hitler had promised to save a beech forest near Stettin from being harmed by Autobahn construction, an aide's inquiry with the dictator produced a negative result: according to an internal memorandum of May 31, 1934, Hitler "was of the opinion that while beech forests obviously should be preserved as far as possible during the construction of the Autobahn, they would have to yield to the demands of such a great technological project in case of conflict."[62] Even Hitler's mountain retreat on the Obersalzberg near Berchtesgaden, one of the most scenic parts of Bavaria, did not imply an emotional attachment to nature. For Hitler, the Alpine scenery was little more than a backdrop to show himself against and a refuge from the ministerial bureaucracy in Berlin. "He had no eye for the beauty of nature," Ernst Hanfstaengl, a close associate of Hitler in the 1920s, wrote in his memoirs, describing Hitler as "a city person who only felt at home on cobblestones."[63] While Göring, one of only three senior Nazis allowed to own a house on the Obersalzberg, went on hiking and climbing excursions in the nearby Watzmann mountain range, Hitler never sought to explore the Obersalzberg on foot.[64] Because he abhorred physical stress, Hitler's walks on the Obersalzberg always led gently downhill to a special tea house, where a car was waiting to carry him back up again.[65] In *Mein Kampf*, Hitler was full of praise for the merits of physical training, but he obviously made an exception for himself.[66]

---

[60] Lutz Raphael, "Radikales Ordnungsdenken und die Organisation totalitärer Herrschaft. Weltanschauungseliten und Humanwissenschaftler im NS-Regime," *Geschichte und Gesellschaft* 27 (2001): 28n. It is no coincidence that Alfred Rosenberg, who produced the only systematic attempt at a philosophy of National Socialism with his *Myth of the Twentieth Century*, had a precarious standing as the Nazis' chief ideologist. (Reinhard Bollmus, *Das Amt Rosenberg und seine Gegner. Studien zum Machtkampf im national-sozialistischen Herrschaftssystem* [Stuttgart, 1970].)

[61] Hitler, *Mein Kampf*, 135.

[62] BArch R 43 II/227 p. 41n.

[63] Ernst Hanfstaengl, *Zwischen Weißem und Braunem Haus. Memoiren eines politischen Außenseiters* (Munich, 1970), 80.

[64] Horst Höfler and Heinz Zembsch (eds.), *Watzmann. Mythos und wilder Berg* (Zürich, 2001), 98.

[65] Kershaw, *Hitler 1889–1936*, 534. Similarly, Ulrich Chaussy, *Nachbar Hitler. Führerkult und Heimatzerstörung am Obersalzberg* (Berlin, 2001), 131n.

[66] Hitler, *Mein Kampf*, 408–10.

Interest in environmental issues was somewhat stronger among the second tier of Nazi leaders, most prominently Hermann Göring and Fritz Todt. Göring was a passionate hunter from childhood and usurped responsibility for conservation as Germany's supreme forester in 1935.[67] But Göring was a Nazi leader with a multitude of offices and functions, and conservation quickly found itself near the bottom of his priorities. It is revealing that Erich Gritzbach's biography, a quasiofficial account of Göring's life – the book's revenues went to Göring, not to the author![68] – devoted only four pages to his conservation work, two of which dealt with his beloved Schorfheide nature reserve.[69] Fritz Todt was a trained engineer who was responsible for the construction of the Autobahn as the Inspector General for the German Roadways (*Generalinspekteur für das deutsche Straßenwesen*) and "Leader of German Technology" (*Führer der deutschen Technik*). He argued for a reconciliation of technology and culture, with technological artifacts being harmoniously embedded into the landscape; the best-known result was the employment of Landscape Advocates as general advisors on landscaping issues in the construction of the Autobahn.[70] With respect to conservation ideology, it is important to note that Göring and Todt both came to conservation from a more practical side. The situation was different with Heinrich Himmler, the leader (*Reichsführer*) of the SS, the backbone of the Nazi police state and embodiment of its racial ideology, who delved deep into racist fantasies and imagined himself as a reincarnation of the early medieval King Henry I. Himmler's perception of landscapes was intrinsically linked with notions of national character, inspiring the infamous plans to "Germanize" the Eastern European landscape during the war, but his excursions into conservation issues in the German heartland remained sporadic.[71]

However, limited interest among Nazi leaders did not prevent many conservationists from attempting to redefine conservation as a quintessential goal of the new regime. Walther Schoenichen pointed the way in

---

[67] Leonard Mosley, *The Reich Marshal. A Biography of Hermann Goering* (London, 1974), 179. On his usurpation of authority over conservation, see p. 68n.

[68] Volker Knopf and Stefan Martens, *Görings Reich. Selbstinszenierungen in Carinhall* (Berlin, 1999), 47.

[69] Erich Gritzbach, *Hermann Göring. Werk und Mensch* (Munich, 1938), 94–8. The Schorfheide nature reserve is discussed extensively in Chapter 4, Section 2.

[70] See Herf, *Reactionary Modernism*, 199–207; Thomas Zeller, *Straße, Bahn, Panorama. Verkehrswege und Landschaftsveränderung in Deutschland von 1930 bis 1990* (Frankfurt and New York, 2002); and Karl-Heinz Ludwig, "Technik," in Wolfgang Benz, Hermann Graml, and Hermann Weiß (eds.), *Enzyklopädie des Nationalsozialismus* (Munich, 1997), 262–4.

[71] See Josef Ackermann, *Heinrich Himmler als Ideologie* (Göttingen, 1970), esp. p. 226n.

1933 with an article in the *Völkischer Beobachter*, the Nazis' widely read newspaper, several articles in his own conservation journal, and a book, *Conservation in the Third Reich*, in 1934.[72] Some historians have taken these pledges of allegiance at face value, but the tactical nature of these publications becomes clear when one compares these publications, for the depiction of the relationship between Nazi ideology and the ethos of conservation differed markedly from one to another. Schoenichen's publications, along with numerous similar ones of that time, were clearly written out of a strategic desire to appease the powers-that-be, and his book actually included little in the way of new agendas but rather argued for a thinly veiled continuation of Weimar conservation policy. Nonetheless, it is rewarding to take a closer look at these publications, for their frequently convoluted logic and distortions of facts provide a measure of the difficulties that conservationists encountered in their ideological rapproachement to the Nazis.[73] To be sure, the leaps of logic never became an issue during the Nazi era, and the publications managed to provide the conservation movement with an aura of inconspicuousness, making for an almost total absence of censorship: during the Nazi era, conservationists could run into trouble with the police state if they were stirring public unrest or were adherents of anthroposophy but never because their stances on conservation issues were deemed ideologically inappropriate. Still, the frequent adaptation to Nazi rhetoric must not conceal the fact that a truly consistent blend of conservation and Nazi ideology was nowhere in sight.

It is one of the more remarkable features of the history of conservation in the Nazi era that there was never a rivalry between the conservation community and a group of ideologists who proposed a different kind of conservation in a true Nazi spirit. There was no equivalent in conservation to the concept of "German physics" that sought to counter mainstream physics with a nationalist phantasm, or of Walter Frank's *Reichsinstitut für Geschichte des neuen Deutschlands*, which

---

[72] Walther Schoenichen, "Der Naturschutz im nationalen Deutschland," *Völkischer Beobachter, Norddeutsche Ausgabe* 46, 84 (March 23, 1933): 6; Walther Schoenichen, "'Das deutsche Volk muß gereinigt werden'. – Und die deutsche Landschaft?," *Naturschutz* 14 (1933): 205–9; Walther Schoenichen, "Der Naturschutz – ein Menetekel für die Zivilisation!" *Naturschutz* 15 (1933/1934): 1–3; Schoenichen, *Naturschutz im Dritten Reich*.

[73] For a masterful exploration of this theme, see Ludwig Fischer, "Die 'Urlandschaft' und ihr Schutz," in Radkau and Uekötter, *Naturschutz und Nationalsozialismus*, 183–205.

sought to rewrite German history in a Nazi vein.[74] Even the landscape planners' work within the Reich Commissariat for the Strengthening of German Nationality (*Reichskommissariat für die Festigung des deutschen Volkstums*), whose involvement in the genocide in Eastern Europe represents perhaps the darkest chapter of this story, was not an ideological challenge to the conservationists' mainstream. Quite the contrary, the Reich Commissariat made a point of recruiting mainstream experts.[75] The reason is simple: from a worldview that saw human history essentially as a struggle between different races, it was impossible to deduce directions for the protection of nature. Not that the conservationists did not try to develop a race-based approach to conservation. In his publications on the German wilderness (*Urwaldwildnis*), Schoenichen stressed the heroic character of the struggle in nature and suggested a link to certain völkisch traits of the German character – but no one could seriously believe that these natural processes were a German peculiarity.[76] At a conference in 1939, Hans Schwenkel elaborated on how the German folk character was rooted in the land and how this strengthened the case for landscape protection – and yet he had to concede, at least with one sentence, that "all these things of course depend on the blood-based origin (*blutsmäßige Herkunft*)," thus acknowledging the gap between his own concern for the environment and the Nazis' obsession with racial purity.[77] Even Hans Stadler, a Franconian conservationist who sought to work on a party ticket and presented himself as the favorite of the regional *Gauleiter*, did not make an attempt to develop a distinct Nazi style of conservation. When asked whether party membership was mandatory to join his network of conservation representatives, he vigorously denied any preference for party members: "There has not been any talk about party membership in Franconian conservation, for a tree or a quarry cannot stand right or

---

[74] See Steffen Richter, "Die 'deutsche Physik,'" in Herbert Mehrtens and Steffen Richter (eds.), *Naturwissenschaft, Technik und NS-Ideologie. Beiträge zur Wissenschaftsgeschichte des Dritten Reiches* (Frankfurt, 1980), 116–41; and Helmut Heiber, *Walter Frank und sein Reichsinstitut für Geschichte des neuen Deutschlands* (Stuttgart, 1966).

[75] See Klaus Fehn, "'Lebensgemeinschaft von Volk und Raum.' Zur nationalsozialistischen Raum- und Landschaftsplanung in den eroberten Ostgebieten," in Radkau and Uekötter, *Naturschutz und Nationalsozialismus*, 207–24; and Michael A. Hartenstein, *Neue Dorflandschaften. Nationalsozialistische Siedlungsplanung in den "eingegliederten Ostgebieten" 1939 bis 1944*. Wissenschaftliche Schriftenreihe Geschichte 6 (Berlin, 1998).

[76] See Fischer, "Urlandschaft", 187–90.

[77] StAD G 15 Friedberg B 101, Niederschrift über die Arbeitsbesprechung und Bereisung am 19. und 20. Juni in Frankfurt a.M. und Umgebung, p. 13.

left politically, but will always remain neutral." In fact, Stadler reasoned that nonmembers might be preferable, for they would not be burdened with party work and would probably have more time.[78]

On a general level, the conservationists' emphasis on the strong connection between the people and the land went along well with Nazi concepts of Germanness and "blood and soil." With keywords such as "old-Germanic animal life" or praise for "the holy ground of our ancestors," an otherwise harmless presentation quickly sounded like exemplary Nazi talk.[79] But a closer look quickly reveals the enduring fragility of the intellectual bridge between the two camps. There were, after all, a few stumbling blocks that inevitably stood in the way of a seamless merger. One of them was the issue of Darwinism. To this day, evolution and conservation are uneasy bedfellows, as Thomas Potthast has shown in his monograph on the topic.[80] However, the relationship was far more explosive during the Third Reich because of the importance of social Darwinism for Nazi ideology. To some extent, Darwinism and conservation went together in that they nourished anxieties of degeneration; but beyond that point, the divergence between the two lines of thought was impossible to ignore.[81] When Schoenichen described nature as "a pluralism of single organisms, closely dependent on each other functionally," the split was a rather tacit one.[82] But when the Bavarian conservationist Hans Kobler celebrated "the wonderful harmony" of nature, his strong ideological bias – he sought to enlist conservation in "the defense against the Bolshevist spirit" – could not conceal that this perspective was incompatible with the Darwinian concept, so dear to the Nazis, of survival of the fittest.[83] In the field of

---

[78] StAW Landratsamt Ebern no. 1336, Der Regierungs-Beauftragte der NSDAP für Naturschutz in Unterfranken to Hauptlehrer Hoch in Ebern, March 11, 1935. Stadler's attempt to develop a network of conservation representatives within the NSDAP is discussed more extensively in Chapter 3.

[79] WAA LWL Best. 702 no. 184b vol. 2, Gemeinsame Arbeitstagung der westfälischen Naturschutzbeauftragten und der Fachstelle Naturkunde und Naturschutz im Westfälischen Heimatbund on February 12–13, 1938, p. 4.

[80] See Thomas Potthast, *Die Evolution und der Naturschutz. Zum Verhältnis von Evolutionsbiologie, Ökologie und Naturethik* (Frankfurt and New York, 1999).

[81] It is no coincidence that Paul Brohmer's blueprint for biology instruction in a Nazi spirit is far removed from any thought about the protection of nature, and in fact runs counter to conservation ideas with its marginalization of rare species and peculiarities of nature. (Paul Brohmer, *Biologieunterricht unter Berücksichtigung von Rassenkunde und Erbpflege*, 3rd edition [Osterwieck and Berlin, 1936, 12n.])

[82] Walther Schoenichen, *Biologie der Landschaft*, Landschaftsschutz und Landschaftspflege 3 (Neudamm and Berlin, 1939), 12.

[83] StAW Landratsamt Bad Kissingen No. 1237, Hans Kobler, Vortrag, gehalten bei der Bezirksversammlung der Gendarmerie in Garmisch-Partenkirchen on November 7, 1938, p. 4n.

forestry, Wilhelm Bode has stressed that the *Dauerwald* concept, which is discussed more extensively below, matched the Nazis' social Darwinism, but that turned out to be a mainly theoretical link.[84] During the Nazi era, Arnold Freiherr von Vietinghoff-Riesch, a key proponent of the *Dauerwald* concept, stressed that "malformations, symptoms of disease and weaker stands of plants are of great importance for the preservation of nature as a whole, for plants and animals are living in them and through them."[85] With views like that, it was hard to argue for something like a eugenics of conservation.

The tension between Darwinism and conservation never led to a major dispute during the Nazi era.[86] Some of the bolder members of the conservation community even used Darwinist quotations and claimed them as support for the conservationists' cause.[87] A second stumbling block turned out to be more difficult, if not impossible to ignore: the issue of *Heimat*. The regionalist orientation of the vast number of conservationists ran directly counter to the centralism of the Nazi state, and no reasoning could more than camouflage this enduring tension.[88] The Nazis' uncertainty in this regard is plainly apparent. In 1933, they turned the annual "Day of Westphalia" (*Westfalentag*) into a mass event in the provincial capital, where 150,000 people celebrated the supposed merger of *Heimat* sentiment and National Socialism. However, the Nazi leaders refrained from a repetition the following year despite their well-known penchant

---

[84] Wilhelm Bode, Martin von Hohnhorst, *Waldwende. Vom Försterwald zum Naturwald*, 4th edition (Munich, 2000), 95. The limits of the forests' propagandistic merits became clear in the movie *Ewiger Wald* ("Eternal Forest"), which achieved a disappointing result; Hitler did not like the movie either. (Ulrich Linse, "Der Film 'Ewiger Wald' – oder: Die Überwindung der Zeit durch den Raum. Eine filmische Übersetzung von Rosenbergs 'Mythus des 20. Jahrhunderts,'" *Zeitschrift für Pädagogik* 31 [1993]: 72n.) For more on the *Dauerwald* concept, see pp. 69–71.

[85] Arnold Freiherr von Vietinghoff-Riesch, *Naturschutz. Eine nationalpolitische Kulturaufgabe* (Neudamm, 1936), 135. Similarly, Walther Schoenichen, *Urdeutschland* vol. 2, 181.

[86] Günter Zwanzig drew attention to the fact that there was no preamble to the animal protection law of November 1933, presumably because of the difficulties in consolating social Darwinism and animal ethics. (Günter W. Zwanzig, "Vom Naturrecht zum Schöpfungsrecht. Wertewandel in der Geschichte des Naturschutzrechts," *Berichte der Bayerischen Akademie für Naturschutz und Landschaftspflege* 18 [1994]: 23.)

[87] See WAA LWL Best. 702 no. 184, Wilhelm Lienenkämper, Der Deutsche und seine Landschaft. Vom gegenwärtigen Stand der Naturschutzbewegung. Easter edition of the conservation supplement of the Lüdenscheider Generalanzeiger, March 31, 1934; and Künkele, "Naturschutz und Wirtschaft," *Blätter für Naturschutz und Naturpflege* 19 (1936): 25.

[88] See Karl Ditt, "'Mit Westfalengruß und Heil Hitler.' Die westfälische Heimatbewegung 1918–1945," in Edeltraud Klueting (ed.), *Antimodernismus und Reform. Beiträge zur Geschichte der deutschen Heimatbewegung* (Darmstadt, 1991), 202; and Winfried Speitkamp, "Denkmalpflege und Heimatschutz in Deutschland zwischen Kulturkritik und Nationalsozialismus," *Archiv für Kulturgeschichte* 70 (1988): 166.

for spectacular festivities, though the "Day of Westphalia" continued on a smaller scale during the Third Reich.[89] Increasingly stripped of its regionalist emphasis, "*Heimat* ceased to mean much of anything," Celia Applegate wrote in her study on "the German idea of *Heimat*": "although *Heimat* cultivation did persist in the Third Reich, its meaning – politicized, paganized, and nationalized – became ultimately abstract."[90] The notion of *Heimat* was revived in Nazi propaganda during the war, and *Heimat* leagues received detailed instructions from the Reich Propaganda Office in 1942 on how a recollection of past exigencies in their respective regions should strengthen the people's endurance in the face of wartime hardships, but that was little more than the enlistment of the last ideological reserves.[91]

Conservationists also had a hard time incorporating anti-Semitism into their rhetoric. At this point, the gap between the two camps was probably the most pronounced: although the Nazis blamed the Jews for almost everything from economic woes to World War II, there was essentially no way for the conservationists to present the environmental toll of industrialization and urbanization as the work of a small band of Jews. At the most, the Jews could be blamed for some minor problems, and even these attempts quickly bordered on the absurd. In a letter of 1937, Hans Stadler claimed that "*Holzjuden*" – presumably Jewish merchants specializing in the timber trade – had bought and processed "the last of the strong oaks and the last of the beautiful walnut trees" in the region and were now seeking to exterminate the pear trees.[92] Lashing out once more against the excesses of outdoor advertising in 1939, Schoenichen remarked "that it would be a worthwhile cause for inquiry in how far this social-psychic disease [i.e., outdoor advertising] is the result of an infection with Jewish poison."[93] In a treatise "on the essence of German conservation" one year earlier, Hans Schwenkel declared that "pursuant to the First Book of Moses, the Jew does not know nature protection.... Only cultivated

---

[89] Karl Ditt, *Raum und Volkstum. Die Kulturpolitik des Provinzialverbandes Westfalen 1923–1945* (Münster, 1988), 208n.

[90] Applegate, *Nation*, 18, 212. See also Heinz Gollwitzer, "Die Heimatbewegung. Ihr kulturgeschichtlicher Ort gestern und heute," *Nordfriesland* 10 (1976): 12; Ditt, *Raum*, 387; and Oberkrome, *Deutsche Heimat*, 167.

[91] StAB HA 506, Westfälischer Heimatbund, Heimatgebiet Minden-Ravensberg, Arbeitstagung in Bielefeld on May 4, 1942.

[92] StAW Landratsamt Ebern no. 1336, Der Regierungsbeauftragte für Naturschutz in Unterfranken to the Bezirksbeauftragten für Naturschutz in Mainfranken, March 12, 1937.

[93] Schoenichen, *Biologie*, 76. Nonetheless, one employee of the Reich Conservation Agency, Kurt Hueck, had a Jewish wife. (BArch B 245/255 p. 433.)

man, and almost exclusively the Nordic man, develops a completely new relationship towards nature, namely one of reverence, which is also the foundation of conservation."[94] There can be no doubt that quotations of this kind were both ugly and unnecessary, but they could not conceal that the link between conservation and anti-Semitism had an air of artificiality.[95]

Finally, the conservation movement was also at odds with the Nazis' concept of *Volksgemeinschaft*, which saw all Germans of Aryan origin as "national comrades" (*Volksgenossen*). To be sure, the *Volksgemeinschaft* concept remained a somewhat diffuse one, and it is a matter of enduring dispute among historians whether the Nazis actually maintained an active social policy.[96] However, as Hans-Ulrich Wehler argued, although the propaganda cliché of the equality of all national comrades remained unimplemented, the Nazis did manage to spread a "'sentiment of social equality' that seemed to transcend traditional class and status boundaries."[97] Inevitably, this social ethos remained a significant stumbling block for a movement that had always had its main constituency in a small segment of the general population, namely the educated classes. Even the Bavarian Conservation League (*Bund Naturschutz in Bayern*), one of the largest and most popular conservation associations of the interwar years, remained ambivalent in its outreach to society: in 1920, an advertising leaflet explicitly called on all classes of people to enlist but simultaneously urged "civil servants, clerics, and teachers" to "join completely."[98] The conservation literature is full of emphatic pledges to make conservation popular in all of German society, but when the conservationists spoke among themselves, they often struck a rather different tone: "We are still lacking true and honest fighters for the protection of nature in

[94] Hans Schwenkel, "Vom Wesen des deutschen Naturschutzes," *Blätter für Naturschutz* 21 (1938): 74. See also Hans Kobler, "Naturschutz und Bolschewismus," *Blätter für Naturschutz* 22 (1939): 67n; and Williams, "Chords," 381.

[95] The conservationists' hesitancy to embrace anti-Semitic rhetoric is all the more remarkable if seen against the strong anti-Jewish stance of alpine associations: see Rainer Amstädter, *Der Alpinismus. Kultur – Organisation – Politik* (Wien, 1996); and Helmuth Zebhauser, *Alpinismus im Hitlerstaat. Gedanken, Erinnerungen, Dokumente* (Munich, 1998).

[96] See Ian Kershaw, *The Nazi Dictatorship. Problems and Perspectives of Interpretation*, 4th edition (London, 2000), 161–82.

[97] Hans Ulrich Wehler, *Deutsche Gesellschaftsgeschichte vol. 4. Vom Beginn des Ersten Weltkriegs bis zur Gründung der beiden deutschen Staaten 1914–1949* (Munich, 2003), 771.

[98] StAW Landratsamt Kitzingen no. 879, advertising leaflet of the Bund Naturschutz in Bayern, November 12, 1920.

Germany, and at the same time, we have an excessive number of so-called nature-lovers," Wilhelm Lienenkämper noted in a 1936 speech to a group of conservation advisors, juxtaposing them as "combat troops" for the cause of conservation against the lukewarm interest in the rest of society.[99] The trend toward a more exclusive self-definition remained strong among the conservationists of the Nazi era, even though it went not only against the more inclusive ideals of the Nazi regime but also against the conservationists' own interests. Few conservationists were as honest as Schoenichen in a book published in 1942, in which he regretfully noted that conservation "had behaved too exclusively" in earlier times.[100]

Significant as these divergences were, their impact on the conservationists' daily business was clearly limited. None of these points of disagreement ever led to more general doubts about Nazi rule among conservationists, and as a result, there was no path from the conservation community to the opposition. Furthermore, it seems that the Nazi regime never saw these divergences as major problems and never seemed to consider an ideological purge of the conservation community. For the Nazis, the gains of such a move in terms of ideological coherence were far less important than the costs in terms of political unrest that this would have brought in an otherwise harmless camp. Still, it is important to realize the enduring gap between conservation and Nazi ideology, for it offers an explanation of why rightist ideology never permeated all aspects of conservation work during the Nazi era. To the contrary, ideologically charged statements remained surprisingly rare in the conservation literature, and they never pushed other ways of reasoning to the margins.[101] In fact, resorting to Nazi rhetoric was frequently a sign of weakness and ideological restraint a sign of strength. Thomas Zeller has argued that the growing use of Nazi language among Fritz Todt's Landscape Advocates during the 1930s was mostly a result of their widespread lack of influence.[102] In a desperate fight against his demotion as head of Münster's natural history

99 WAA LWL Best. 702 no. 195, Wesen und Aufbau der Naturschutzarbeit im Regierungsbezirk Arnsberg. Vortrag vom Bezirksbeauftragten Lienenkämper auf der Finnentroper Naturschutztagung on January 13, 1936, p. 12n.

100 Walther Schoenichen, *Naturschutz als völkische und internationale Kulturaufgabe* (Jena, 1942), 75.

101 Even Lienenkämper's "alphabet of conservation" was largely devoid of Nazi ideology. (WAA LWL Best. 702 no. 184b vol. 2, Wilhelm Lienenkämper, Das Naturschutz-ABC.)

102 Zeller, *Straße, Bahn, Panorama*, 204.

museum, Hermann Reichling wrote a plea "for the restoration of the inner connection between folk and nature" that smacked of Nazi rhetoric.[103]

Therefore, it was consequential that the Hitler quotations that conservationists, like many other groups, used to sustain their cause focused on rather innocuous themes. The most frequent quotation called for the preservation of the German landscape as a contribution to German potency: "It is imperative to preserve the German landscape, for it is, and always was, the ultimate foundation of the power and strength of the German people."[104] A second, less frequent quotation struck a similar vein: "We will not only create a Germany of power, but also a Germany of beauty" – as Hitler quotations go, certainly one of the more harmless ones.[105] In both cases, the link between conservation and Nazi goals was a rather indirect one, and as contributors to a mythical German strength, the conservationists were on a par with countless other groups. Even more important, the emphasis in these quotations was on aesthetic, rather than racist or anti-Semitic, categories. Finally, the quotations were convenient for the conservation community in that they simply legitimized the work that they had been doing for decades and did not call for adjustments in the light of the Nazis' priorities. Besides, it is doubtful that the quotations received much attention beyond conservation circles. Those who had read *Mein Kampf*, or had listened to his speeches, knew full well that for Hitler, the essence of the race lay in the blood and not in the land.

The agreement between conservation and Nazi ideology was always strongest when it came to ways and means. Both were adamant in their

[103] WAA LWL Best. 702 no. 184b vol. 1, Aufruf by Hermann Reichling, Kommissar für Naturdenkmalpflege der Provinz Westfalen, of October 1933. See also Rollins, *Greener Vision*, 263.

[104] See Vietinghoff-Riesch, *Naturschutz*, 58; Ditt, *Raum*, 330; O. Kraus, "Naturschutz und Ödlandaufforstung," *Blätter für Naturschutz* 23 (1940): 4; WAA LWL Best. 702 no. 195, Wesen und Aufbau der Naturschutzarbeit im Regierungsbezirk Arnsberg. Vortrag vom Bezirksbeauftragten Lienenkämper auf der Finnentroper Naturschutztagung on January 13, 1936, p. 16; WAA LWL Best. 702 no. 184b vol. 2, Wilhelm Lienenkämper, Das Naturschutz-ABC, p. 16; LASH Abt. 320 Eiderstedt no. 1806, advertising leaflet of the Verein Jordsand, sent to the Kreisverwaltung des Kreises Eiderstedt on October 29, 1936; LASH Abt. 320 Eiderstedt no. 1846, Lamprecht and Wolf, Aufgaben des Natur- und Heimatschutzes im Kreise Husum (n.d.), p. 1; HStAD NW 60 no. 1603 pp. 204r, 299r; StAR Nachlass Ludwig Finckh II a folder 15, letter paper of Ludwig Finckh; and Barch B 245/3 p. 260.

[105] See Hans Schwenkel, *Taschenbuch des Naturschutzes* (Salach/Württemberg, 1941), 37; Hans Schwenkel, "Aufgaben der Landschaftsgestaltung und der Landschaftspflege," *Der Biologe* 10 (1941): 133; and WAA LWL Best. 702 no. 184b vol. 2, Wilhelm Lienenkämper, Das Naturschutz-ABC, p. 10.

critique of liberalism, seeing it as "negating life."[106] Closely aligned with
the rejection of free-wheeling liberalism was a disdain for materialism:
both movements saw themselves as idealistic enterprises, though for different causes. "It is really necessary to confront the master bookkeepers
of the present *material republic* by faith in an *ideal* Reich," Adolf Hitler
wrote in *Mein Kampf*.[107] Not to be forgotten, either, is the fact that the
marginal role of women in public life during the Nazi era meshed well
with sentiments within the conservation movement. In one of his usual cri-
tiques of materialism and liberalism, Schoenichen also lashed out against
female emancipation: "Nothing is more revealing of the lunacy of the liberalist *Weltanschauung* than what it has done with the women. It opened
all kinds of male professions for them, allowing them to become lawyers,
teachers, and ministry officials while robbing them of the one thing that
nature wants to play a role in a woman's life: motherhood."[108] The only
woman of some prominence within the conservation community was Lina
Hähnle, the longtime leader of the Bird Protection League, who ran her
association like a patriarch almost to her death in 1941.[109] Finally, both
movements counted on the state for support in the realization of their
goals. While some conservationists were hesitant to probe the depths of
Nazi rhetoric, there was never any doubt about the vital importance of
close cooperation with state authorities. However, in defining themes and
goals, the conservationists continued to enjoy a large degree of freedom.
The German conservation community was probably not "a little corner
of freedom," as Douglas Weiner described the status of conservation in
the Soviet Union; the contacts with Nazi authorities were far too intense
to justify such a description.[110] But it was a realm where the Nazi regime
allowed, as totalitarian governments go, a considerable degree of independent thinking.

In 1939, the Third Reich Garden Exhibit (*Reichsgartenschau*) took
place in Stuttgart. With the Nazi regime reaching its apogee of popularity,

---

[106] StAN Rep. 212/19[VII] no. 2535, letter of the Bürgermeister der Stadt Weissenburg, May 5,
    1936. Similarly, Oberkrome, *Deutsche Heimat*, 143.
[107] Hitler, *Mein Kampf*, 437. Emphasis original.
[108] Schoenichen, "Der Naturschutz – ein Menetekel," 1.
[109] See Wöbse, "Lina Hähnle." In Germany, women generally played a marginal role in
    environmental conflicts during the first half of the twentieth century, unlike the United
    States, where women constituted a significant force in the drive against urban air pol-
    lution. (Cf. Frank Uekötter, *Von der Rauchplage zur ökologischen Revolution. Eine
    Geschichte der Luftverschmutzung in Deutschland und den USA 1880–1970* [Essen,
    2003], 52–6.)
[110] See Weiner, *Little Corner*.

and with Heinrich Wiepking-Jürgensmann and two other landscape architects close to the Nazi regime among the jury, one would expect an exposition with a distinct ideological flavor.[111] Surprisingly, the opposite was true. The prize committee chose Hermann Mattern for the design of the park, even though Mattern was not a member of the Nazi Party and had worked for Jewish clients, thus making him "politically unreliable" in the eyes of the Nazis.[112] Built on the site of a former quarry, the park won praise for its smooth transitions between different types of uses: although sharp demarcations had been the rule previously, Mattern and his colleagues selected from a wide range of species to make for a new, harmonious landscape experience. The park lacked any trace of Nazi monumentalism and was in fact never seen as an outgrowth of Nazi ideology, even after 1945. Nonetheless, Alwin Seifert was enthusiastic about the result, extolling "the elated ease and relaxation of the entire area, which allows for strolls in a completely peaceful state of mind."[113] Clearly, the rapprochement between Nazism and conservation ideology remained incomplete, even in the heyday of the Nazi regime.

[111] See Gert Gröning and Joachim Wolschke-Bulmahn, *Grüne Biographien. Biographisches Handbuch zur Landschaftsarchitektur des 20. Jahrhunderts in Deutschland* (Berlin and Hannover, 1997), 14–15, 415–19.

[112] See *ibid.*, 244–51.

[113] Günter Mader, *Gartenkunst des 20. Jahrhunderts. Garten- und Landschaftsarchitektur in Deutschland* (Stuttgart, 1999), 104, 106, 108.

3

Institutions: Working Toward the Führer

If anything can be said in summary about the relationship between conservation ideas and Nazi ideology, it is that taken by itself, that relationship cannot explain the general dynamism in the cooperation between the green and the brown.[1] It was, after all, a much too complicated mix of ideas: at some points, ideas overlapped, whereas others were more or less at odds, and the fundamental pillars of Nazi ideology were so distant from the ethos of nature protection that a distinct Nazi brand of conservation never came into being. Accordingly, one would expect an equally diverse set of contacts between the conservation community and the Nazi regime: a wide spectrum from sympathy to opposition, with indifference probably being the most frequent attitude.

However, the actual picture differs markedly from such a scenario. The distance between the conservation community and the Nazis was much smaller in practice than one would expect from the background of the divergent philosophies: cooperation was far too intensive, and far too cordial, to be explained by a partial coincidence of goals. Thus, an analysis of the ideological relationship needs to be supplemented by a discussion of institutional ties. For the conservation movement, the Nazi regime offered a number of unprecedented opportunities, which conservationists tried to seize to the greatest extent possible. It was institutional links that created the atmosphere of sustained sympathy, if not unbridled enthusiasm, that permeated the conservation literature of the Nazi era. But it was also these links that, in retrospect, put the conservation movement on a downward slope.

[1] In this regard, this monograph is fundamentally at odds with Manfred Klein, *Naturschutz im Dritten Reich* (Ph.D. dissertation, Mainz University, 2000).

44

Of course, conservation ideology is not irrelevant in the light of the institutional rapprochement.[2] But countless episodes in the Nazi history of conservation cannot be explained by ideas alone, and some even ran directly counter to ideological divisions. Once again, Wilhelm Lienenkämper provides a case in point: a convinced Nazi and party member since 1933, the closest ally in his conservation drive in the Sauerland region was Wilhelm Münker, an independent spirit with the air of political unreliability whom the Nazis had forced to resign as the longtime leader of the German Youth Hostel Federation.[3] And why did Alwin Seifert, perhaps the most influential anthroposophist in Nazi Germany, side with Fritz Todt, Germany's supreme engineer, and clash with Richard Walther Darré, the Reich Peasant Leader (*Reichsbauernführer*) who entertained a certain interest in organic farming?[4] The change at the top of the Reich Conservation Agency (*Reichsstelle für Naturschutz*) in 1938 was revealing: whereas Walther Schoenichen had paid tribute to the Nazis' cause in his publications, his successor Hans Klose kept a low profile in ideological terms and was not even a member of the Nazi Party. By one account, Klose was also a "Quarter-Jew" (*Vierteljude*) by Nazi definitions, a person with one Jewish grandparent.[5]

In 1933, the conservationists in charge were already the second generation of German conservation. The first generation, with key figures like Hugo Conwentz, Ernst Rudorff, and Wilhelm Wetekamp, had mostly left the scene by the mid-1920s, bequeathing an institutional network that

[2] In this context, the definition of institutions is inspired by Douglass North, who saw institutions as "a set of rules, compliance procedures, and moral and ethical behavioral norms designed to constrain the behavior of individuals in the interest of maximizing the wealth or utility of principals." (Douglass C. North, *Structure and Change in Economic History* [New York and London, 1981], 201n.) The definition thus moves beyond the formal institutions that this chapter concentrates on and includes the modes of behavior discussed in Chapters 4 and 5.

[3] See NSDAP Membership no. 3283027; and Hartmut Müller, "'Machtergreifung' im Deutschen Jugendherbergswerk," Deutsches Jugendherbergswerk (ed.), *Weg-Weiser und Wanderer. Wilhelm Münker. Ein Leben für Heimat, Umwelt und Jugend* (Detmold, 1989), 60–77. For the close cooperation between Lienenkämper and Münker, see WAA LWL Best. 702 no. 184b vol. 2 and no. 191.

[4] See Joachim Radkau, *Natur und Macht. Eine Weltgeschichte der Umwelt* (Munich, 2000), 297; and Thomas Zeller, "Molding the Landscape of Nazi Environmentalism. Alwin Seifert and the Third Reich," in Brüggemeier, Cioc, and Zeller, *How Green*, 156. On Darré's interest in organic farming, see Gesine Gerhard, "Richard Walther Darré – Naturschützer oder 'Rassenzüchter'?," in Radkau and Uekötter, *Naturschutz und Nationalsozialismus*, 257–71.

[5] Heinrich Rubner, *Deutsche Forstgeschichte 1933–1945. Forstwirtschaft, Jagd und Umwelt im NS-Staat* (St. Katharinen, 1985), 83.

easily bore comparison with other countries. The history of dedicated conservation agencies started in Bavaria in 1905 with the foundation of the State Commission for the Care of Nature (*Landesausschuß für Naturpflege*).[6] Prussia followed suit in 1906 with Hugo Conwentz's Prussian Agency for the Protection of Natural Monuments (*Staatliche Stelle für Naturdenkmalpflege in Preußen*).[7] The agency's resources were limited during its first years, and Conwentz, director of the West Prussian Provincial Museum in Danzig, since 1880, had to work on a part-time basis until 1910.[8] But with Prussia comprising some two-thirds of the German population, the Agency for the Protection of Natural Monuments was by far the most influential institution of its kind. Other German states usually took the Prussian agency as a model, and even observers in other countries were full of praise. At the first International Conference for the Protection of the Countryside (*Congrès international pour la protection des paysages*) in Paris in 1909, participants took note that Prussia was the first country with a state organization for the protection of natural monuments.[9] In 1922, a Russian conservationist even addressed Conwentz as "the apostle of the humane nature protection movement."[10]

During the Weimar Republic, this institutional network developed in a rather uneven way. Several states took steps to strengthen their legal frameworks and the institutions enforcing them, in spite of the rapid succession of crises during the Weimar years. The state of Lippe was first with a *Heimat* protection law in 1920, followed by the state of Anhalt, which, undeterred by the hyperinflation crisis, passed a conservation law in June 1923.[11] In 1927, the minister of education in the state of Baden took the initiative to create a network of conservation advisors similar to the

[6] Richard Hölzl, *Naturschutz in Bayern von 1905–1933 zwischen privater und staatlicher Initiative. Der Landesausschuß für Naturpflege und der Bund Naturschutz* (M.A. thesis, University of Regensburg, 2003), 46.

[7] For an account of its early work, see Hugo Conwentz (ed.), *Beiträge zur Naturdenkmalpflege* vol. 1 (Berlin, 1910).

[8] Knaut, *Zurück*, 40.

[9] GLAK Abt. 233 no. 3029, Kaiserlich Deutsche Botschaft in Frankreich to the Reichskanzler, November 11, 1909, p. 2.

[10] BArch B 245/214 p. 50.

[11] Siekmann, *Eigenartige Senne*, 343; Walther Schoenichen and Werner Weber, *Das Reichsnaturschutzgesetz vom 26. Juni 1935 und die Verordnung zur Durchführung des Reichsnaturschutzgesetzes vom 31. Oktober 1935 nebst ergänzenden Bestimmungen und ausführlichen Erläuterungen* (Berlin-Lichterfelde, 1936), 125.

Prussian model, with a state conservation agency (*Landes-Naturschutz-stelle*) tied to the natural history museum in Karlsruhe.[12] In 1922, the Bavarian ministry of the interior even merged the state's own network of conservation advisors with that of the Bavarian Conservation League, thus giving official status to a dedicated group of activists.[13] To be sure, the advisors did not have the right to take decisions: as in the rest of Germany, the conservation advisors assumed the role of independent consultants, whereas the authority to decide remained within the general administration.[14] However, the blend between official and civic conservation authorities clearly indicated that the administration would have an open ear for their demands. Other states refrained from copying the Bavarian model, but close cooperation between civic leagues and the state was generally the rule. For example, the Westphalian Nature Protection Association received 40,600 Reichsmarks from the provincial administration for its conservation work between 1921 and 1934, supplemented by 16,250 Reichsmarks from the city of Münster.[15] Between 1925 and 1931, the conservationists held four National Conservation Conferences (*Naturschutztage*), providing a much-needed forum for an exchange of ideas and a chance to demonstrate the importance of the issue to the general public.[16] In 1931, the state assembly in Hesse passed a state-of-the-art conservation law that drew on a conservation exposition held in the state capital 3 years earlier.[17]

Much of this work remained focused on the small-scale improvements that had been the mainstay of prewar conservation. Natural monuments,

---

[12] GLAK Abt. 235 no. 6548, Minister des Kultus und Unterrichts to the Bezirksämter, April 4, 1928.

[13] StAN Rep. 212/19[VII] no. 2536, Staatsministerium des Innern to the Bezirksämter, July 14, 1922.

[14] See Michael Wettengel, "Staat und Naturschutz 1906–1945. Zur Geschichte der Staatlichen Stelle für Naturdenkmalpflege in Preußen und der Reichsstelle für Naturschutz," *Historische Zeitschrift* 257 (1993): 388.

[15] WAA LWL Best. 717 no. 104, Nachweisung der an den Westfälischen Naturschutzverein gezahlten Beihilfen.

[16] Hans Klose, "Der Weg des deutschen Naturschutzes," in Hans Klose and Herbert Ecke (eds.), *Verhandlungen deutscher Landes- und Bezirksbeauftragter für Naturschutz und Landschaftspflege. Zweite Arbeitstagung 24.–26. Oktober 1948 Bad Schwalbach und Schlangenbad* (Egestorf, 1949), 37; Adelheid Stipproweit, "Naturschutzbewegung und staatlicher Naturschutz in Deutschland – ein historischer Abriß," in Jörg Calließ and Reinhold E. Lob (eds.), *Handbuch Praxis der Umwelt- und Friedenserziehung. Band 1: Grundlagen* (Düsseldorf, 1987), 34.

[17] See StAD G 21 A no. 8/21 and G 33 A no. 16/6.

like rock formations or scenic trees, received the lion's share of attention, not large nature reserves or even national parks. In 1925, the largest
nature reserve in the state of Hesse comprised only six acres.[18] However, the later Weimar years saw a growing trend toward a more inclusive
approach to conservation: increasingly, the issue at stake was the landscape as a whole. For example, Schoenichen proposed a special administrative body for the area along the Rhine in 1929 to assure a coordinated
approach to the protection of the scenic landscape.[19] In 1931, the Fourth
National Conservation Conference in Berlin called on the state adminis-
trations to consult with conservation representatives on all matters of city
and landscape planning, followed by a similar resolution of the German
Federation for Heimat Protection the next year.[20] "It does not suffice to
preserve isolated natural monuments, which are easily seen as curiosi-
ties," the government's comment to the Hessian conservation law of 1931
declared.[21] However, the law's stipulations on landscape protection were
notably vague, and other state governments were even more hesitant in
their responses to the conservationists' shifting agenda. A decree of the
ministry of trade and industry of 1931 calling for more attention to the
landscape in the projection of power lines was actually one of the more
forceful gestures.[22]

Thus, the conservation efforts of the Weimar era looked rather modest,
especially when compared with the achievements of the prewar years. In
some respects, the conservationists even lost ground. Before the war, Conwentz had created a comprehensive network of provincial conservation
committees (*Provinzialkomitees für Naturdenkmalpflege*).[23] However,

[18] StAD G 33 A no. 16/6 p. 29.
[19] HStAD Landratsamt Siegkreis no. 586, Der Direktor der Staatlichen Stelle für Natur-
     denkmalpflege in Preußen to the Minister für Wissenschaft, Kunst und Volksbildung,
     October 16, 1929, p. 3. See also Thomas Lekan, "Regionalism and the Politics of Land-
     scape Preservation in the Third Reich," *Environmental History* 4 (1999): 392; and Her-
     mann Josef Roth, "Naturschutz und Landschaftspflege im Westerwald und südlichen
     Bergischen Land," in Josef Ruland (ed.), *Erhalten und Gestalten. 75 Jahre Rheinischer
     Verein für Denkmalpflege und Landschaftsschutz* (Neuss, 1981), 412.
[20] *Nachrichtenblatt für Naturdenkmalpflege* 8, 3 (June 1931): 17; Oberkrome, *Deutsche
     Heimat*, 132.
[21] StAD G 21 A no. 8/21, Der Hessische Finanzminister to the Justizminister, January 29,
     1930, Begründung zum Naturschutzgesetz, p. 1.
[22] StAB HA 506, Der Minister für Handel und Gewerbe to the Regierungspräsidenten,
     January 26, 1931. On the conservationists' critique of power lines, see Hans Schwenkel,
     "Die Verdrahtung unserer Landschaft," *Schwäbisches Heimatbuch* 1927: 87–111; and
     Lekan, *Imagining*, 108.
[23] *Beiträge zur Naturdenkmalpflege* 2 (1912): 169–74.

wartime and postwar exigencies had left significant gaps in this network, and the Prussian government never made a systematic attempt to restore it in its entirety. Therefore, the fate of conservation often depended on local initiatives. In 1921, the regional administration in Cologne announced the formation of a new conservation committee, followed by the administration of the Rhine Province in 1926.[24] In 1927, complaints over the state of conservation work at a meeting of county commissioners in the Aachen area led to a surge of activity during the following years.[25] Even in Westphalia, where an active Provincial Committee had created fifty-six nature reserves by 1932, conservation had a precarious standing because it relied on only two institutions.[26] The state of conservation work remained highly uneven during the Weimar years, leaving much room for bold initiatives but also a rather chaotic administrative structure. It was telling that a ministerial decree of 1934 spoke of a "widespread lack of clarity" about the proper organization of conservation work.[27]

Perhaps the greatest disappointment for the conservation community was the failure of a Prussian conservation law. The Weimar Constitution had defined the care of natural monuments as one of the duties of government, and as early as 1920 the Prussian parliament had urged the government to produce a draft for a new nature protection law in a timely fashion. However, no such draft emerged in the next 12 years.[28] Some historians have blamed this failure on the difficult issue of compensation claims.[29] This issue was indeed subject to prolonged internal

[24] HStAD Landratsamt Siegkreis no. 606, Der Regierungspräsident Köln to the Landräte und Oberbürgermeister des Bezirks, September 21, 1921, and Der Oberpräsident der Rheinprovinz to the Regierungspräsidenten der Provinz, June 17, 1926.

[25] HStAD BR 1011 no. 44 p. 4.

[26] Ditt, *Raum*, 142; WAA LWL Best. 702 no. 195, Wesen und Aufbau der Naturschutzarbeit im Regierungsbezirk Arnsberg. Vortrag vom Bezirksbeauftragten Lienenkämper auf der Finnentroper Naturschutztagung on January 13, 1936, p. 13n.

[27] WAA LWL Best. 702 no. 184b vol. 1, Der Preußische Minister für Wissenschaft, Kunst und Volksbildung to the Oberpräsidenten and Regierungspräsidenten, June 30, 1934, p. 1.

[28] See article 150 of the Weimar constitution; GStA HA I Rep. 90 A no. 1798 p. 211; and *Sitzungsberichte der verfassunggebenden Preußischen Landesversammlung, Tagung 1919/21*, vol. 9 (Berlin, 1921), col. 11782n. For an overview on legislation before the national conservation law, see Gustav Mitzschke, *Das Reichsnaturschutzgesetz vom 26. Juni 1935 nebst Durchführungsverordnung vom 31. Oktober 1935 und Naturschutzverordnung vom 18. März 1936 sowie ergänzenden Bestimmungen* (Berlin, 1936).

[29] See Wettengel, "Staat und Naturschutz," 378; and Charles Closmann, "Legalizing a *Volksgemeinschaft*. Nazi Germany's Reich Nature Protection Law of 1935," in Brüggemeier, Cioc, and Zeller, *How Green*, 28.

discussions; but the smooth passage of conservation laws in other states shows that these problems were by no means insurmountable.[30] Examining the internal files, it seems that the failure of the Prussian conservation law was first and foremost a classic case of bureaucratic mismanagement: no administrative body pushed aggressively for the law, resulting in lackluster discussions among the lower ranks of the ministerial bureaucracy. In August 1921, more than a year after the parliament's resolution, the minister of education sent out letters to learn about the laws in force in other German states.[31] By 1923, the administration had developed a first draft, which it sent out to selected recipients for comment.[32] However, the draft did not advance further because the minister of education had different priorities. Responding to criticism in parliament in 1926, a ministry official declared that work on the conservation law would not resume until the passage of the pending law for the protection of historical monuments.[33] In March 1927, the ministry of education finally invited to an interdepartmental conference on a first draft, followed by two more meetings in April and May.[34] But after that, it took until January 1928 for the ministry of education to produce a second draft of the law.[35] This draft left out the tricky issue of compensation, and the ministry of justice had just given its consent to this approach when the ministry of the interior called for a halt because the law was in conflict with its plans for a general administrative reform.[36] With that, the conservation law finally disappeared from the government's agenda, to the great frustration of the conservation community, which had been expecting the passage of such a law for a number of years.[37] Disappointment grew even greater when the Prussian government issued a deregulation directive in March 1932 that

[30] See StAD G 21 A no. 8/21; and Schoenichen and Weber, *Reichsnaturschutzgesetz*, 125n.

[31] GStA HA I Rep. 90 A no. 1798 p. 219.

[32] LASH Abt. 301 no. 4066, Der Preußische Minister für Wissenschaft, Kunst und Volksbildung to the Oberpräsidenten, the Regierungspräsidenten in Liegnitz, Lüneburg and Düsseldorf and the Verbandspräsident des Siedlungsverbandes Ruhrkohlenbezirk, September 3, 1923.

[33] *Sitzungsberichte des Preußischen Landtags, 2. Wahlperiode 1. Tagung*, vol. 8 (Berlin, 1926), col. 11621.

[34] GStA HA I Rep. 90 A no. 1798, pp. 268–9, 276–82.

[35] *Ibid.*, pp. 287–91.

[36] *Ibid.*, pp. 296–7, 305–6, 308, 317.

[37] See Carl Schulz, "Botanische und zoologische Naturdenkmäler," in Walther Schoenichen (ed.), *Der biologische Lehrausflug. Ein Handbuch für Studierende und Lehrer aller Schulgattungen* (Jena, 1922), 197; StAD G 21 A no. 8/21, Der Direktor der Staatlichen Stelle für Naturdenkmalpflege in Preußen to the Ministerium der Justiz, June 27, 1927; and *Blätter für Naturschutz und Naturpflege* 13 (1930): 51.

urged officials to cut back on government decrees and to create nature reserves "only for the protection of very important or unique areas."[38]

Thus, it should come as no surprise that in 1933 few conservationists felt that the Weimar Republic had been a favorable experience. But as pervasive as discontent was, it is important to realize that this sentiment did not necessarily translate into sympathy for the Nazis, even less so because, in a number of cases, the first result of the Nazi seizure of power was the loss of fellow conservationists who were Jewish or deemed Jewish according to Nazi definitions. Protest against the removal of Jews was just as rare within the conservation network as it was in the rest of German society, and yet one should not underestimate the impact that such measures had for a movement with a strong corporate identity. When the county commissioner of Freiburg in southern Germany learned that he had to discharge Robert Lais as the county's conservation advisor because he was "interrelated with Jews" (*jüdisch versippt*), he did not withhold his true feelings: "I could only comment on the dismissal of Professor Lais with the greatest sense of regret."[39] He even initially refused to accept the candidate whom the NSDAP proposed as a replacement, noting on the party candidate "that I am not sure whether he will fulfill his office with the same dedication and love as Professor Lais."[40] Shortly after coming to power, the Nazis disbanded the *Naturfreunde* tourist association because of its affiliation with the Social Democratic Party, though some of its activities continued within other organizations.[41] Ludwig Lesser had to resign as president of the German Horticultural Society (*Deutsche Gartenbau-Gesellschaft*) in 1933 because of his Jewish origin and later emigrated to Sweden; the landscape gardener Georg Bela Pniower, a member of the Social Democratic Party and "Half-Jew" (*Halbjude*) according to Nazi definitions, was banned from his profession.[42] The Prussian Agency for

---

[38] LASH Abt. 301 no. 4065, Der Preußische Minister für Wissenschaft, Kunst und Volksbildung to the Regierungspräsidenten, March 21, 1932.

[39] GLAK Abt. 235 no. 6550, Der Landrat als Vorsitzender der Bezirksnaturschutzstelle Freiburg-Land to the Minister des Kultus und Unterrichts, July 3, 1936.

[40] *Ibid.*, Der Landrat als Vorsitzender der Bezirksnaturschutzstelle Freiburg-Land to the Minister des Kultus und Unterrichts, October 7, 1936.

[41] See Christiane Dulk and Jochen Zimmer, "Die Auflösung des Touristenvereins 'Die Naturfreunde' nach dem März 1933," in Zimmer, *Mit uns zieht*, 112–17; Oberkrome, *Deutsche Heimat*, 201; Lekan, *Imagining*, 188; and Oliver Kersten, "Zwischen Widerstand und Anpassung – Berliner Naturfreunde während der Zeit des Nationalsozialismus," *Grüner Weg 31a* 10 (January, 1996): 16–23.

[42] Joachim Wolschke-Bulmahn, "Von Anpassung bis Zustimmung. Zum Verhältnis von Landschaftsarchitektur und Nationalsozialismus," *Stadt und Grün* 46 (1997): 386n.

the Protection of Natural Monuments lost Benno Wolf, a baptized Protestant with Jewish ancestors, who resigned from the agency in 1933. He died in the Theresienstadt concentration camp in 1943.[43]

The losses within the conservation community were significant, though nowhere as dramatic as the losses in the fields of science and culture, where a broad band of eminent authorities, from Albert Einstein to Thomas Mann, left their native country. For most conservationists, the more pressing concern was the uncertainty as to what the Nazis would mean to their community. Disorientation, more than sympathy or antipathy, was the dominant state of mind. To be sure, many conservation organizations cheerfully welcomed the new regime, but close attention to their choice of words was often revealing. In many cases, they were quick to add that they had already been working in Hitler's spirit for quite a while and that as a result there was no need for change.[44] Interestingly, there were almost no comments in the conservation literature on the "Hitler-Oaks" and "Hitler-Lindens" that ardent Hitlerites were planting in hundreds of towns and villages.[45] Later on, conservationists would celebrate the planting of trees on special days as "concordant with the spirit of the Führer," but in the midst of the reverberations surrounding the Nazis' ascension to power, the conservationists were just too disoriented to come up with such a rationale.[46]

Of course, the conservationists never feared prosecution similar to the Social Democrats or even the Jews and had no reason to do so. However, the new regime's plan for agriculture certainly gave cause for concern. Even before his cheerful article welcoming Hitler's regime, Schoenichen published an article on the perils of land reclamation schemes that the new regime promised to pursue on a grand scale with an intensification of Labor Service projects (*Arbeitsdienst*).[47] Entitled "An Appeal of the

---

43 *Natur und Landschaft* 78 (2003): 437; R. G. Spöcker, "Ahasver Spelaeus. Erinnerungen an Dr. Benno Wolf," *Mitteilungen des Verbands deutscher Höhlen- und Karstforscher* 32, 1 (1986): 4–8. Since 1996, the Association of German Speleologists (*Verband deutscher Höhlen- und Karstforscher*) has awarded a Dr.-Benno-Wolf-Preis to honor his memory.

44 See Susanne Falk, "'Eine Notwendigkeit, uns innerlich umzustellen, liege nicht vor.' Kontinuität und Diskontinuität in der Auseinandersetzung des Sauerländischen Gebirgsvereins mit Heimat und Moderne 1918–1960," in Frese and Prinz, *Politische Zäsuren*, 401–17; Ditt, *Raum*, 207n; and Oberkrome, *Deutsche Heimat*, 141n.

45 Ian Kershaw, *The "Hitler Myth." Image and Reality in the Third Reich* (Oxford, 1987), 55.

46 WAA LWL Best. 702 no. 184b vol. 2, Wilhelm Lienenkämper, Das Naturschutz-ABC, p. 9. See also Schoenichen, *Naturschutz im Dritten Reich*, 89.

47 Walther Schoenichen, "Appell der deutschen Landschaft an den Arbeitsdienst," *Naturschutz* 14 (1933): 145–9. A Labor Service had been in existence in Germany since

German Landscape to the Labor Service," the article went back to the annual conference of conservation representatives in December 1932, where discussions on the potential impact of the Labor Service projects had been prominent.[48] The conference revealed the participants' worries as much as the lack of a clear plan for action. "It is imperative to get the authorities in charge to take the justified demands of nature and *Heimat* protection into account in the design of Labor Service projects," the conservationists decided, but they were unable to cite a law or decree that gave some kind of legitimacy to their concern, let alone a force that would match that of a labor project in the middle of an economic depression.[49] Even Schoenichen's article could not help but strike a pessimistic note at times: "The German landscape will need to make its own sacrifices when the treasures and powers lying within it are put to use for the grand healing project."[50] In a statement on a land reclamation project in the Donauried Moor in Baden, the state's conservation advisor laconically declared, "Since the experts obviously think that they will gain precious soil through cultivation, it seems that the concerns of conservation, as always, will have to yield."[51]

In his "appeal to the Labor Service," Schoenichen called for "approaches that derive from empathic immersion into the myth of the *Heimat* soil."[52] But as so often, the actual response had less to do with myth and ideology than with administrative logic and the art of the possible. Schoenichen asked the Prussian conservation advisors to prepare special maps on an ad hoc basis showing all areas that were sensitive from a conservation standpoint.[53] To save time, the advisors were urged

---

1931, but the Nazi regime greatly expanded it and made it mandatory in 1935. Whereas 177,000 people worked in the Labor Service in January 1933, membership was at 797,000 a year later. (Kiran Klaus Patel, *"Soldaten der Arbeit." Arbeitsdienste in Deutschland und den USA 1933–1945* [Göttingen, 2003], 55, 149.)

[48] HStAD BR 1011 no. 43, letter of the Direktor der Staatlichen Stelle für Naturdenkmalpflege in Preußen, May 8, 1933. An earlier critique is Max Kästner, "Die Gefahr der Naturschändung durch den Freiwilligen Arbeitsdienst," *Mitteilungen des Landesvereins Sächsischer Heimatschutz* 21 (1932): 254–63.

[49] WAA LWL Best. 702 no. 185, Jahresbericht der Bezirksstelle für Naturdenkmalpflege im Gebiete des Ruhrsiedlungsverbandes in Essen, May 5, 1933, p. 5. Similarly, *Blätter für Naturschutz und Naturpflege* 16 (1933): 80.

[50] Schoenichen, "Appell," 145.

[51] GLAK Abt. 235 no. 48254, Landesnaturschutzstelle to the Ministerium des Kultus, Unterrichts und der Justiz, August 1, 1933. Similarly, BArch B 245/23 p. 6.

[52] Schoenichen, "Appell," 147.

[53] In 1936, the approach was extended to all of Germany. (StAN Rep. 212/19[VII] no. 2539, decree of the Reichsstelle für Naturschutz, May 13, 1936).

to refrain from special inquiries: "it will suffice if those familiar with the
region get together and define those areas that they see as significant."
Schoenichen urged his fellow conservationists to take a bold approach
and to note down all areas of any relevance but highlight those areas
of special importance: "it will be necessary to surrender in some cases
later on." After completion, the maps were forwarded to the authorities
in charge of reclamation projects with a request to save these areas from
destruction as far as possible. In a display of humanist education, the conservation administration chose a Latin name for the project and spoke of
"noli-tangere areas" and "noli-tangere maps." Presumably, the urge to
give some kind of authority to these maps also played a role in this choice
of words: *noli tangere* is the Latin expression for "do not touch."[54]

It was the conservationists' first systematic attempt at landscape planning, and they went to work quickly. As early as May 1933, the regional
conservation advisor for the Ruhr region reported the completion of three
county maps with the help of the county conservation advisors.[55] But
speed could not resolve the fundamental problem of this approach: even
if the planning authorities knew the sensitive areas, they were in no way
obliged to respect this information in their work. The noli-tangere maps
were nothing but a conservationists' wish list that others saw as simply
noncommittal advice. Therefore, the preparation of these plans was often
an irritating experience for the conservation community: after registering
the natural treasures in their area systematically, they could then do nothing but wait and see how one after the other was going to be destroyed.
In fact, a reclamation official from the northern town of Neumünster
made it clear from the outset what he thought of this intrusion into his
own affairs: "Of course, we cannot always show consideration for the
noli-tangere areas. That would mean to refrain from a number of recla-
mations of special value for agriculture. Refraining from large projects,
which are of extreme importance with a view to job creation nowadays,
would mean sabotaging the current projects, created upon instigation of
the Führer."[56] After that, it was indeed hard to be optimistic about the
prospects of conservation in the environs of Neumünster.[57]

---

[54] StAN Rep. 212/19[VII] no. 2539, Der Direktor der Staatlichen Stelle für Naturdenkmalpflege in Preußen to the Kommissare für Naturdenkmalpflege, January 2, 1934.

[55] WAA LWL Best. 702 no. 185, Jahresbericht der Bezirksstelle für Naturdenkmalpflege im
Gebiete des Ruhrsiedlungsverbandes in Essen, May 5, 1933, p. 15.

[56] LASH Abt. 734.4 no. 3348, Der Kulturbaubeamte in Neumünster to the Landrat in
Pinneberg, December 8, 1933.

[57] Some noli-tangere maps won praise later on as preparations for the landscape reserves
created under the National Conservation Law of 1935. (StAW Landratsamt Bad Kissingen

For some time, the animal protection laws of 1933 provided a ray of hope for the conservation community. Between April and November 1933, the regime passed three laws that significantly tightened the rules governing the treatment of animals. A 1999 publication even speaks admiringly of "quite progressive" laws.[58] The key motivation had little to do with environmental considerations, however. Since the late nineteenth century, protests against vivisection were closely aligned with anti-Semitism because of the Jewish custom of kosher butchering.[59] However, the laws did not simply ban the killing of animals according to Jewish rites but rather made it illegal "to torment animals unnecessarily or to mistreat them brutally."[60] The authors of the laws even offered a nonanthropocentric line of reasoning: "We no longer punish animal torture because it hurts human feelings due to man's compassion for the creation but because the animal as such needs protection against abusive behavior."[61] However, enforcement lagged far behind these noble goals.[62] Only one month after the passage of the animal protection law in November 1933, a decree from the minister of the interior Wilhelm Frick used the forced reorganization of the animal protection organizations (*Gleichschaltung*) to exclude them from work in the universities' animal protection commissions.[63]

It gradually dawned on the Nazis that vivisection was important to research, including research instrumental to the overarching goal of

no. 1234, Staatsministerium des Innern to the Regierungspräsidenten, August 8, 1940, p. 4; BArch B 245/19 p. 168.) However, only rarely did this transform the noli-tangere maps into a rewarding experience. Tellingly, the topic was almost absent from the conservation literature.

[58] Johannes Caspar, *Tierschutz im Recht der modernen Industriegesellschaft. Eine rechtliche Neukonstruktion auf philosophischer und historischer Grundlage* (Baden-Baden, 1999), 272. Similarly, Klaus J. Ennulat and Gerhard Zoebe, *Das Tier im neuen Recht. Mit Kommentar zum Tierschutzgesetz* (Stuttgart, 1972), 22. For an intensive discussion of these laws, see Edeltraud Klueting, "Die gesetzlichen Regelungen der nationalsozialistischen Reichsregierung für den Tierschutz, den Naturschutz und den Umweltschutz," in Radkau and Uekötter, *Naturschutz und Nationalsozialismus*, 78–88.

[59] Miriam Zerbel, "Tierschutz und Antivivisektion," in Kerbs and Reulecke, *Handbuch der deutschen Reformbewegungen*, 41–3.

[60] Klueting, "Regelungen," 85.

[61] Clemens Giese and Waldemar Kahler, *Das deutsche Tierschutzrecht. Bestimmungen zum Schutze der Tiere* (Berlin, 1939), 20. See also Heinz Meyer, "19./20. Jahrhundert," in Peter Dinzelbacher (ed.), *Mensch und Tier in der Geschichte Europas* (Stuttgart, 2000), 560. According to Luc Ferry, this was the first reasoning of this kind in an animal protection law worldwide: Luc Ferry, *Le nouvel ordre écologique. L'arbre, l'animal et l'homme* (Paris, 1992), 194.

[62] Cf. Boria Sax, *Animals in the Third Reich. Pets, Scape goats, and the Holocaust* (New York and London, 2000), 117n. See also StAN Rep. 212/19[VII] no. 2924.

[63] Daniel Jütte, "Tierschutz und Nationalsozialismus – eine unheilvolle Verbindung," *Frankfurter Allgemeine Zeitung* no. 289 (December 12, 2001): N 3.

FIGURE 3.1. The animals salute Göring: a cartoon in the *Kladderadatsch*, a humorous journal, published at a time when the Nazis were producing one animal protection law after another. Printed with permission from Heidelberg University.

rearmament. As a result, the laws' original intentions were quickly abandoned, and regulations were successively watered down. A decree imposing a total ban on vivisection, enacted on August 16, 1933, by Hermann Göring as prime minister of Prussia, survived for only 3 weeks, being revised by a decree of September 5 with more lenient provisions. In the end, the ministry of the interior handed out blank permits to university institutes to conduct experiments with animals and refrained from any closer supervision of experimental practice. The law continued to impose some limits to laboratory work, and researchers were keen to keep their more delicate experiments under wraps: researchers at the University of Freiburg once conducted a frantic search for a cat with electrode implants in its brain that had escaped during a nighttime experiment.[64] But in general, the law's impact remained limited. In 1936, the Chamber of Veterinarians (*Tierärztekammer*) of Darmstadt filed a formal complaint against the lax enforcement of the law on people who had conducted illegal castrations, fearing that the practice "may completely paralyze the effect of the law."[65] Nazi leaders took pride in presenting themselves as friends of animals, and this sentiment even found its way into Heinrich Himmler's speech at the SS leaders' conference (*SS-Gruppenführertagung*) in Posen on October 4, 1943, one of the most infamous justifications of Nazi terror, where Himmler took pride in the assertion that the Germans were "the only nation of the world with a decent attitude towards animals."[66] When discussions arose within the administration in 1940 to prohibit useless pets to save precious foodstuffs for human consumption, a personal intervention from Hitler stopped the plan.[67] In the end, the administration did publish a decree against pets, but it pertained only to animals in the possession of non-Aryan citizens, an act that many Jews found humiliating.[68]

Hope persisted within the conservation community that the animal protection law would be only the first of a number of laws in its favor. Rumors spread during the early Nazi years of a whole host of allegedly pending laws: on nature protection, on *Heimat* protection, on the protection of birds, and on the protection of the countryside from ugly billboards.[69] However, none of these laws materialized during the first

---

[64] Daniel Jütte, "'Von Mäusen und Menschen.' Die Auswirkungen des nationalsozialistischen Reichstierschutzgesetzes von 1933 auf die medizinische Forschung an den Universitäten Tübingen, Heidelberg, Freiburg im Breisgau 1933–1945. Beitrag zum Schülerwettbewerb Deutsche Geschichte" (manuscript, Stuttgart, 2001), 9–11, 27, 55.

[65] StAD G 24 no. 1504, letter of the Hessische Tierärztekammer Darmstadt, Geschäftsstelle Büdingen, March 22, 1936.

[66] Internationaler Militär-Gerichtshof Nürnberg (ed.), *Der Prozess gegen die Hauptkriegsverbrecher vor dem Internationalen Militärgerichtshof*, vol. 29 (Nuremberg, 1948), 123.

[67] Götz Aly, *Hitlers Volksstaat. Raub, Rassenkrieg und nationaler Sozialismus* (Frankfurt, 2005), 351.

[68] Victor Klemperer, *LTI. Notizbuch eines Philologen* (Leipzig, 2001), 132.

[69] See BArch R 22/2117 pp. 6r, 74; GStA HA I Rep. 90 A no. 1798 pp. 352–3; StAW Landratsamt Obernburg no. 209, Staatsministerium des Innern to the Staatskanzlei, May 28, 1934; GLAK Abt. 237 no. 36122, Begehung des Steinbruchs Hohenstoffeln, memorandum of May 1934; WAA LWL Best. 702 no. 191, Provinzmittel für den Naturschutz. Undated memorandum of the Sauerländischer Gebirgsverein; Thomas Scheck, *Denkmalpflege und Diktatur. Eine Untersuchung über die Erhaltung von Bau- und Kulturdenkmälern im Deutschen Reich zur Zeit des Nationalsozialismus unter besonderer Berücksichtigung der preußischen Provinz Schleswig-Holstein* (Ph.D. dissertation, Kiel University, 1993),

two years of Nazi rule: the Heimat protection laws enacted in the states of Saxony and Braunschweig in 1934 brought "no satisfactory solution" in the eyes of contemporary observers and received only scant attention.[70] Quite the contrary, the conservationists faced a fundamental challenge to their organizational structure during the first 2 years when the Nazis sought to force the diverse associations into line in accordance with the idea of Gleichschaltung. For the conservationists, this experience was certainly more disturbing than the limited accomplishments that the movement had made until early 1935. After all, limited success was something that the conservation movement had been used to for decades, and the impression that the general trends of modern society were at odds with the demands of conservation had always been a common denominator of the nature protection community. But a threat to the conservation movement's institutional integrity was something altogether different.

The original intention behind the Gleichschaltung campaign was to neutralize the states as political actors and to extinguish political opposition. But the campaign soon evolved into a general streamlining of all societal actors into a corporatist system of organizations, and careerism abounded in the process. The Reich League for National Character and Heimat (Reichsbund Volkstum und Heimat or RVH), set up to unite all associations in the fields of conservation, regional culture, and the preservation of historic monuments, provides a case in point. Incorporated formally on July 27, 1933, the RVH comprised some five million members by the end of the year.[71] But formal membership was something very different from actual support, and the conservation community by no means ceded authority willingly to the League, as Gert Gröning and Joachim Wolschke-Bulmahn have suggested.[72] Quite the opposite, it was a move that deeply disturbed a conservative membership base that overwhelmingly adhered to the traditional organizational structures. Much criticism centered on the RVH's organizational leader, Werner Haverbeck, who

236–46, 312–16; Blätter für Naturschutz und Naturpflege 18 (1935): 72; Heimat und Landschaft 7 (1933): 11; and Werner Lindner, Außenreklame. Ein Wegweiser in Beispiel und Gegenbeispiel (Berlin, 1936), 110.

[70] Mitzschke, Das Reichsnaturschutzgesetz, xiv. See also Hans Jungmann, Gesetz zum Schutze von Kunst-, Kultur- und Naturdenkmalen (Heimatschutzgesetz) (Radebeul-Dresden, 1934), 54n, 79–82; Walther Fischer, "Heimatschutz und Steinbruchindustrie," in Landesverein Sächsischer Heimatschutz (ed.), Denkmalpflege, Heimatschutz, Naturschutz. Erfolge, Berichte, Wünsche (Dresden, 1936), 70; and HStADd Best. 10702 no. 1425.

[71] Scheck, Denkmalpflege, 89, 230.

[72] Gröning and Wolschke-Bulmahn, "Landschafts- und Naturschutz," 30.

had been a top officer in the Hitler Youth and the National Socialist's student body: Haverbeck was 23 years old when he became secretary of the League.[73] Also, it became increasingly clear that there was a wide gap between Haverbeck's goals and those of the conservation community. Whereas Haverbeck sought a centralist and activist organization directed especially toward the youth and the working class, the rank and file stood by its tradition, favoring a regionalist approach with the middle classes as the primary audience.[74] Finally, the League became caught up in the rivalry between Alfred Rosenberg and Joseph Goebbels over authority in the field of cultural policy. The conflict was resolved temporarily at the end of 1933 when the RVH was incorporated into Goebbels' Reich Chamber of Culture (*Reichskulturkammer*).[75]

The *Heimat* community was an overwhelmingly peaceful group, but Haverbeck's plan soon brought them into a rebellious mood. Of course, their opposition never took the form of an open revolt because of the totalitarian character of Nazi rule. Instead, the associations conducted a silent battle of attrition and tried to use their connections to fend off all intrusions into their internal affairs. The Bavarian Conservation League was perhaps the most fortunate in that regard because the president of the RVH, Karl Alexander von Müller, a historian at Munich University, was among its members. The Bavarian Conservation League quickly approached Müller and won the assurance that there would be "no change in the association's internal business." To forestall any unwanted intrusions on the local level, the League's chairman informed all branch offices and regional representatives of Müller's statement and asked them to bring contraventions immediately to the attention of the executive committee.[76] At the same time, Werner Haverbeck was driving through the German regions in a big Mercedes bought with RVH funds to seize the associations' assets.[77]

---

[73] See Scheck, *Denkmalpflege*, 88–90.

[74] Ditt, *Raum*, 214.

[75] Scheck, *Denkmalpflege*, 229n.

[76] StAW Landratsamt Bad Kissingen no. 1237, Bund Naturschutz in Bayern to the Gruppenvorstände and Vertrauensmänner, October 10, 1933. See also Josef Ruland, "Kleine Chronik des Rheinischen Vereins für Denkmalpflege und Landschaftsschutz," in Ruland, *Erhalten und Gestalten*, 28; Karl Peter Wiemer, *Ein Verein im Wandel der Zeit. Der Rheinische Verein für Denkmalpflege und Heimatschutz von 1906 bis 1970*. Beiträge zur Heimatpflege im Rheinland 5 (Cologne, 2000), 108–12; and Karl Zuhorn, "50 Jahre Deutscher Heimatschutz und Deutsche Heimatpflege. Rückblick und Ausblick," in Deutscher Heimatbund (ed.), *50 Jahre Deutscher Heimatbund* (Neuß, 1954), 47.

[77] Oberkrome, *Deutsche Heimat*, 160.

The Federation for Heimat Protection tried to regain the initiative in
early 1934 with a week of campaigning against outdoor advertising, a
topic always sure to arouse the conservationists.[78] But the campaign,
hastily announced in March 1934, ran into opposition from the advertising industry, and activism ceased as quickly as it had emerged; an agreement in the Fall of 1934 declared all nonadministrative action against
outdoor advertising illegal.[79] The ongoing campaign against Haverbeck
was more successful: Haverbeck was relieved from his duties as secretary on October 20, 1934, after an internal audit had revealed some
irregularities, and the RVH fell apart during the following months.[80]
With that, the issue of *Gleichschaltung* became dormant within the
conservation community, in spite of occasional rumors to the contrary.[81] The only exception was the bird protection community, where
a decree of September 1938 forced all associations in the field to join
Lina Hähnle's Bird Protection League, which by that time already ran
under the more imposing title "Reich League for the Protection of
Birds" (*Reichsbund für Vogelschutz*).[82] But even though the traumatic
threat of a confiscation of the organizations' assets never materialized,
the episode certainly did not foster the conservationists' sympathy for
the Nazis.

All in all, the first 2 years of Nazi rule provided a dismal balance for
the conservation movement. On the one hand, the associations had managed to fend off the attempt at *Gleichschaltung*, thus maintaining their
cherished autonomy. On the other hand, the early gestures of deference,
like membership in the NSDAP and the ideologically charged rhetoric
depicting conservation as a quintessential Nazi goal, had not provided a
positive return. The aborted campaign against outdoor advertising and

---

[78] See Frank Uekötter, *Naturschutz im Aufbruch. Eine Geschichte des Naturschutzes in
Nordrhein-Westfalen 1945–1980* (Frankfurt and New York, 2004), 37–56.
[79] See Scheck, *Denkmalpflege*, 225–8; Ditt, *Raum*, 225–30; and WAA Best. 717 Zug.
23/1999 Naturschutzverein, Landschaft Westfalen im Reichsbund Volkstum und Heimat
to member associations, March 21, 1934. See also Lindner, *Außenreklame*, 106–12, on
the legal status quo.
[80] See the proceedings in WAA LWL Best. 702 no. 184b vol. 1. See also Oberkrome,
Deutsche Heimat, 160; Scheck, *Denkmalpflege*, 232; Ditt, *Raum*, 215n; and Helmut Fischer, *90 Jahre für Umwelt und Naturschutz. Geschichte eines Programms* (Bonn, 1994),
38.
[81] See StAW Landratsamt Bad Kissingen no. 1237, Bund Naturschutz in Bayern to the Gruppenvorstände and Vertrauensmänner, November 14, 1935; and Schwenkel, *Taschenbuch*,
13.
[82] *Reichsministerialblatt der Forstverwaltung* 2 (1938), edition C: 353; StAD G 24 no. 1800
p. 7. See Wöbse, "Lina Hähnle," 316n; and Helge May, *NABU. 100 Jahre NABU – ein
historischer Abriß 1899–1999* (Bonn, n.d.), 16.

the meager results of the animal protection laws were stark reminders of the difficulties of pushing conservation concerns in the Nazi state. For a community with far-reaching goals and scores of fiery members thirsty for action – paraphrasing Lord Nelson, Hans Stadler once admonished his fellow conservationists that "Lower Franconia expects every man to do his duty"[83] – such a result was clearly disappointing. Thus, it is likely that if the story had continued in this way, the conservation movement would have developed what the German historian Martin Broszat has called *Resistenz*: a mental distance toward the Nazi regime based on a distinct set of thoughts and rules that imposed limits to Nazi rule and Nazi ideology but did not necessarily inspire open resistance. With this mindset, the conservation movement would have continued to do its own business while accepting that the Nazis did theirs.[84] But the distance between the two camps shrank dramatically in 1935, giving way to a strong affection, if not enthusiasm, for the Nazis. The event that defined this new stance more than anything else was the passage of the national conservation law (*Reichsnaturschutzgesetz*) on June 26, 1935.

Six days earlier, Victor Klemperer had noted in his diary, which would become one of the most important memoirs of the Nazi era, that popular opinion had recently undergone a significant transformation. Observing the people around him, he gained the impression "that many otherwise well-meaning people, dulled to injustice inside the country and in particular not properly appreciating the misfortune of the Jews, have begun to halfway acquiesce to Hitler."[85] Klemperer's account, which agrees with other descriptions of that time, shows a certain amount of sympathy for the Nazi regime (which was also visible in the conservation community) but it was a highly ambivalent type of sympathy. Many people had come to accept the Nazis' rule, but they were far from enthusiastic about it; the Hitler myth was still building up at that time.[86] Conservationists had

---

[83] StAW Landratsamt Ebern no. 1336, Der Geschäftsführer der Höheren Naturschutzstelle von Mainfranken to the Geschäftsführer der Unteren Naturschutzstellen, December 10, 1936, p. 1.

[84] See Martin Broszat, "Resistenz und Widerstand. Eine Zwischenbilanz des Forschungsprojekts," in Martin Broszat, Elke Fröhlich, and Anton Grossmann (eds.), *Bayern in der NS-Zeit* vol. 4 (Munich, 1981), 697.

[85] Victor Klemperer, *I Will Bear Witness. A Diary of the Nazi Years 1933–1941* (New York, 1998), 126n. Klemperer was Jewish and worked as a scholar of Romance languages and literature at Dresden University until his dismissal in 1935. Married to a non-Jewish wife, he narrowly survived the Holocaust and died in 1960.

[86] See Aly, *Hitlers Volksstaat*, 49; and Kershaw, *Hitler Myth*. See also *Deutschland-Berichte der Sozialdemokratischen Partei Deutschlands (Sopade) 1934–1940*, vol. 2, 1935 (Bad Salzhausen and Frankfurt, 1980), 651, 758, 896.

realized that Hitler had come to stay, at least for the foreseeable future, and that one could live with this government, but it would take a major event to transform this attitude into wholehearted and sustained support. With this background, it becomes clear why the law of 1935 was such an important watershed in conservation history: from now on, conservationists acted under the opinion that the Nazi regime, unlike the Weimar Republic, was fulfilling their long-held dreams.

Praise for the new law was almost universal, pertaining to both the law's general intentions and its specific provisions. A 1936 legal dissertation argued that the law was nothing short of "a masterpiece of legislative art," and an article in a legal weekly found that the new law "laid the foundation for a new perspective on our *Heimat* nature."[87] Even in the 1950s, Ludwig Finckh emphatically declared that this was a law "like no other country ever had it."[88] Typically for the Nazi regime, comments extolled not only the provisions of the law but also the show of intentions behind it: praise went hand in hand with expressions of gratitude that the highest ranks of the regime had bestowed attention and support upon the conservationists. "In 1935, the Führer gave us the national conservation law," a grateful Wilhelm Lienenkämper wrote.[89] If the national conservation law became a myth in conservation circles, as Jens Ivo Engels has argued, this was a result of not only the law's content but also the memory that, if only for a brief moment, their cause had been dear to the heart of the most powerful – a deeply impressive event for a group that had complained of being ignored by society for decades.[90] For example, the Bavarian Conservation League not only wrote that the law meant "a great leap forward" for the league's work but also took note that the second man in the state had taken its cause under his wing: "Now Göring has taken conservation into his strong hand; he gave the legislative backbone

---

[87] Karl Cornelius, *Das Reichsnaturschutzgesetz* (Bochum-Langendreer, 1936), 2; F. Kersten, "Naturschutz," *Juristische Wochenschrift* 64 (1935): 3603. See also Lekan, "It Shall," 78; and Mitzschke, *Das Reichsnaturschutzgesetz*, xv.

[88] Ludwig Finckh, *Der Kampf um den Hohenstoffeln 1912–1939* (Gaienhofen, 1952), 12.

[89] KMK Wilhelm Lienenkämper, Zehn Jahre Landschaftsstelle für Naturschutz Altena-Lüdenscheid (typewritten manuscript, 1942), p. 4. Similarly, WAA Best. 717 file "Reichsstelle (Bundesstelle) für Naturschutz (und Landschaftspflege)," Der Provinzialkonservator von Westfalen to the Reichs- und Preußischer Minister für Wissenschaft, Erziehung und Volksbildung, December 31, 1935, p. 7; and Künkele, "Naturschutz," 28.

[90] See Jens Ivo Engels, "'Hohe Zeit' und 'dicker Strich.' Vergangenheitsdeutung und -bewahrung im westdeutschen Naturschutz nach dem Zweiten Weltkrieg," in Radkau and Uekötter, *Naturschutz und Nationalsozialismus*, 383; and Uekoetter, "Old Conservation History," 178.

to our concerns."[91] For the conservationists of the Nazi era, the law was important both as a legal document and a pledge of support from the new regime. After 1945, conservationists would seek a distinction between the law's contents and the circumstances of its passage, but the dominant line of thinking during the Nazi era ran otherwise.[92] After 1935, conservationists could refer not only to the letter of the law but also to the will of the Nazi regime, and they did so frequently. When urging a more systematic enforcement of the conservation law in 1938, the regional conservation advisor for the state of Hesse wrote, "I specifically draw your attention to the fact that the national conservation law was created upon initiative of the Führer."[93]

The conservationists' enthusiasm was by no means unfounded. The law stood out internationally in several respects, making it, as Charles Closmann wrote, "one of the industrialized world's most wide-ranging conservation laws."[94] Of course, some of its provisions were not new in themselves, for most German states had already passed laws that allowed for the protection of natural monuments and nature reserves. But even in this regard, the national conservation law stood out in that it made provisions uniform in all of Germany, abolishing the previous "diversity and multiplicity of conservation provisions."[95] Also, the national conservation law reinforced preexisting legislation symbolically, and that was by

[91] StAW Landratsamt Bad Kissingen no. 1237, Bund Naturschutz in Bayern to the Gruppenführer and Vertrauensmänner, August 28, 1935.

[92] See Walther Schoenichen, *Natur als Volksgut und Menschheitsgut. Eine Einführung in Wesen und Aufgaben des Naturschutzes* (Ludwigsburg, 1950), 35; and Wilhelm Lienenkämper, *Schützt die Natur – pflegt die Landschaft* (Hiltrup, 1956), 5.

[93] StAD G 38 Eudorf no. 47, Landschaftsbund Volkstum und Heimat, Gau Hessen-Nassau to the Ortsringleiter, June 4, 1938. Similarly, Schwenkel, "Vom Wesen," 75.

[94] Closmann, "Legalizing," 18. Similarly, Lekan, *Imagining*, 12; Raymond H. Dominick, "The Nazis and the Nature Conservationists," *The Historian* 49 (1987): 508; Gerhard Olschowy, "Welche Bereiche der Landespflege sollen eine gesetzliche Grundlage erhalten?," *Jahrbuch für Naturschutz und Landschaftspflege* 20 (1971): 35; and Ivo Gerds, "Geschichte des Naturschutzes in Schleswig-Holstein," Ulrich Jüdes, Ekkehard Kloehn, Günther Nolof, and Fridtjof Ziesemer (eds.), *Naturschutz in Schleswig-Holstein. Ein Handbuch für Naturschutzpraxis und Unterricht* (Neumünster, 1988), 99. For an overview of international conservation in the interwar years, see G. A. Brouwer, *The Organisation of Nature Protection in the Various Countries* (Special Publication of the American Committee for International Wild Life Protection no. 9 [Cambridge, 1938]).

[95] Walther Emeis, "Der gegenwärtige Stand des Naturschutzes in Schleswig-Holstein," *Die Heimat* 48 (1938): 139. See also Closmann, "Legalizing," 20; and Ludwig Sick, *Das Recht des Naturschutzes. Eine verwaltungsrechtliche Abhandlung unter besonderer Berücksichtigung des preußischen Rechts mit Erörterung der Probleme eines Reichsnaturschutzgesetzes.* Bonner Rechtswissenschaftliche Abhandlungen 34 (Bonn, 1935), 71.

no means unimportant to the conservation community. The commentary on the law written by Walther Schoenichen and Werner Weber noted that although it had been possible to designate nature reserves on the basis of a clause inserted into the Prussian Field and Forest Police Law in 1920, this makeshift was "an undignified state of affairs in that it offered only a back door to the important cause of conservation."[96] Moreover, the law's provisions for the administrative structure of conservation were important even though they adhered to the traditional two-tiered system of consultation by honorary conservation advisors outside the bureaucracy and decision-making within the general administration. While it had previously been left up to each of the regional and provincial leaders whether to set up institutions for the enforcement of conservation provisions, the national conservation law now called for a comprehensive administrative network in all parts of Germany.[97]

However, the truly revolutionary part of the national conservation law was that it moved beyond the classic canon of German conservation to include landscape protection as a key goal of conservation. As mentioned above, there had been a growing interest in landscape planning during the late Weimar years, but the legislative response had been weak. Under Weimar, the drafts for a Prussian conservation law did not even include provisions pertaining to the landscape in general.[98] A draft for the Prussian Field and Forest Police Law amendment of 1920 had included "the face of the landscape" among the items under protection, but the parliament's judicial committee decided to take it out of the final draft.[99] In contrast, paragraph 19 of the national conservation law allowed for the "protection of parts of the countryside" to forestall measures that would "deface" or otherwise harm nature or the human experience of nature.[100] Moreover, paragraph 20 specified that "all government agencies are obliged to consult with the conservation administration before the approval of projects that may lead to significant alterations of the landscape."[101] Both provisions were unprecedented, and they made for the

---

[96] Schoenichen and Weber, *Reichsnaturschutzgesetz*, 3n.

[97] See *ibid.*, 37–54.

[98] See LASH Abt. 301 no. 4066, Der Preußische Minister für Wissenschaft, Kunst und Volksbildung to the Oberpräsidenten, the Regierungspräsidenten in Liegnitz, Lüneburg and Düsseldorf and the Verbandspräsident des Siedlungsverbandes Ruhrkohlenbezirk, September 3, 1923, and GStA HA I Rep. 90 A no. 1798 pp. 262–7, 287–91.

[99] *Sammlung der Drucksachen der verfassunggebenden Preußischen Landesversammlung, Tagung 1919/21*, vol. 8 (Berlin, 1921): 4235.

[100] Schoenichen and Weber, *Reichsnaturschutzgesetz*, 90.

[101] *Ibid.*, 97.

giant leap that the law constituted in the legal history of German conservation. Upon announcing the passage of the law, the head of the German Forest Service Walther von Keudell was particularly eager to stress this broadening of the conservationists' agenda: "We do not want to make Germany into a country with a whole host of little scenic spots." Rather, von Keudell declared that from now on, conservationists would have a say in everything that had an impact on the appearance of the countryside.[102]

With that, the competences of the nature protection community had grown dramatically. But at the same time, it was clear that in using these competences, the demands of conservation would often conflict with other kinds of land use. A number of legislative models had evolved to reconcile these divergent interests. For example, the Hessian conservation law of 1931 had included provisions on how to meet compensation claims from property owners, whereas a draft of the Prussian conservation law had urged refraining from measures if they implied disproportionate damage to another party.[103] But again, the national conservation law diverged markedly from this tradition in that paragraph 24 generally ruled out indemnity for measures taken in the execution of the law. In other words, the administration could now designate a nature reserve or prohibit alterations of the landscape, and the owners of the land would not have any chance to sue for monetary compensation.[104] This drastic approach was by no means coincidental. One of the Nazis' key motives in legal reform was the supremacy of collective interests, epitomized in the slogan "the common good above the individual good" (*Gemeinnutz vor Eigennutz*) in point 24 of the NSDAP's party platform of 1920.[105] The general goal behind this clause was to move beyond the tradition of Roman law, whose individualistic idea of property allegedly stood in contrast to the concept of common good inherent to the Germanic character. In its ultimate expression, this line of reasoning argued that the individual was not actually owner of a piece of property but merely holder of a title awarded to

---

[102] HStADd Best. 10702 no. 1426, *Frankfurter Zeitung* no. 328–9 of June 30, 1935.

[103] *Hessisches Regierungsblatt* no. 24 of December 28, 1931, p. 227n; GStA HA I Rep. 90 A no. 1798 p. 264. See also Schoenichen, *Naturschutz im Dritten Reich*, 85; Köttnitz, "Über ein Naturschutzgesetz," *Blätter für Naturschutz und Naturpflege* 16 (1933): 134; and Sick, *Recht*, 82–6.

[104] Schoenichen and Weber, *Reichsnaturschutzgesetz*, 112n; Kersten, "Naturschutz," 3603; Mitzschke, *Das Reichsnaturschutzgesetz*, xxi–ii.

[105] Walther Hofer, *Der Nationalsozialismus. Dokumente 1933–1945* (Frankfurt, 1957), 31. Therefore, it is doubtful whether the law could have been passed in identical form during the Weimar Republic, as Gröning and Wolschke-Bulmahn have argued: see Gröning and Wolschke-Bulmahn, *Liebe zur Landschaft Teil 1*, 200.

him by the collective *Volksgemeinschaft*, and the Nazis expected the individual to surrender this title immediately when the community of National Comrades called for it.[106] Paragraph 24 of the national conservation law was one of numerous expressions of this rationale during the Nazi era: Werner Weber reported that by September 1936, the Nazi regime had enacted forty-seven laws that ruled out indemnification for its provisions.[107]

However, the conservationists' enthusiasm over paragraph 24 had little to do with Germanic fantasies. Their line of reasoning was of a far more practical kind: the clause was, as the Bavarian Conservation League put it, "of great importance for future enforcement."[108] For decades, negotiations with property owners had been one of the most excruciating exercises that the German conservation community had to face. Government decrees had not been much help in this regard: a Bavarian decree of 1928 pointed conservationists to "amicable negotiations," unable to offer any legal tool to the conservation administration that could push property owners toward cooperation, whereas the Prussian deregulation directive of 1932 even asked for the property owners' consent in writing.[109] Of course, conservationists could try to purchase prospective nature reserves, but that was frequently a rather theoretical option. It is revealing that a county commissioner recommended using neutral middlemen in land purchases to avoid inflated prices, and Schoenichen's idea of a "Rhineland protection lottery" in 1929 provided a fitting demonstration of the conservationists' financial limitations.[110] However, all these problems became moot with publication of the

---

[106] See Michael Stolleis, *Gemeinwohlformen im nationalsozialistischen Recht* (Berlin, 1974), 30, 118n.

[107] Werner Schubert, "Zur Entwicklung des Enteignungsrechts 1919–1945 und den Plänen des NS-Staates für ein Reichsenteignungsgesetz," *Zeitschrift der Savigny-Stiftung für Rechtsgeschichte*, Germanistische Abteilung 111 (1994): 494. See also BArch R 2/4730 pp. 12–12r. A moderating clause for cases of hardship included in the law's original draft was deleted in the lawmaking process. (BArch R 2/4730 pp. 37, 56.)

[108] StAW Landratsamt Bad Kissingen no. 1237, Bund Naturschutz in Bayern to the Gruppenführer and Vertrauensmänner, December 4, 1935. See also BArch R 22/2117 p. 54.

[109] StAN Rep. 212/19ᵛᴵᴵ no. 2536, Regierung von Mittelfranken to the Bezirksamt Eichstätt, February 8, 1928, p. 3; LASH Abt. 301 no. 4065, Der Preußische Minister für Wissenschaft, Kunst und Volksbildung to the Regierungspräsidenten, March 21, 1932.

[110] WAA LWL Best. 702 no. 191, Provinzmittel für den Naturschutz. memorandum of the Sauerländischer Gebirgsverein, ca. 1934; HStAD Landratsamt Siegkreis no. 586, Der Direktor der Staatlichen Stelle für Naturdenkmalpflege in Preussen to the Minister für Wissenschaft, Kunst und Volksbildung, October 16, 1929, p. 4. Before World War I, several associations had used lotteries to raise funds for large nature reserves: see Schmoll, *Erinnerung*, 201, 218; and Lekan, *Imagining*, 42.

national conservation law: even if one generally refrained from confiscation of relevant property, as most conservationists did, negotiations with property owners were obviously much easier with the indemnity clause at hand.[111] In fact, German conservationists had been asking for such a provision for more than 20 years: when the principality of Schwarzburg-Rudolstadt, a miniature state in central Germany that became part of Thuringia in 1920, passed a conservation law in 1910 that ruled out indemnification by the state, a group of prominent German conservationists filed a petition with the other German state governments asking them to enact similar laws. However, it is revealing that the authors designated their petition as "confidential," and no law emerged in the following years.[112] When Fritz Koch, one of the signers of the petition, lobbied for such a law in Thuringia during the 1920s, the campaign resulted in public outrage and a crushing defeat.[113] Nonetheless, hope remained alive for such a provision: characteristically, Schoenichen's article in the *Völkischer Beobachter* of 1933 saw a "special task for the National Socialist movement" in the protection of areas in "private possession," invoking the principle of "the common good above the individual good."[114]

Therefore, it was no exaggeration when Schoenichen's and Weber's commentary on the law declared that the law "does justice to all significant demands of conservation" and that its passage meant "the fulfillment of a long-held wish."[115] But why did the Nazis enact such a stringent law? This question is all the more important because the first steps toward the national conservation law looked remarkably similar to the hapless efforts of the Weimar years. When the ministry of justice sent out the first draft of a national conservation law in February 1935, other departments voiced a whole host of objections.[116] The ministry of education was the most vociferous in its protest because the draft robbed it of its authority on conservation issues and gave it to the ministry of the interior; the minister of education argued that the justice department did not have the right to prepare such a draft at all.[117] Similarly, the minister of agriculture emphasized

---

[111] On the actual use of paragraph 24 in conservation practice, see pp. 142–5.

[112] GLAK Abt. 235 no. 48254, Eingabe an die deutschen Regierungen, undated (ca. 1913). Among the signers of the petition were Ernst Rudorff, Fritz Koch, Carl Fuchs, Ludwig Finckh, and Hermann Hesse.

[113] Oberkrome, *Deutsche Heimat*, 124–6.

[114] Schoenichen, "Naturschutz im nationalen Deutschland," 6.

[115] Schoenichen and Weber, *Reichsnaturschutzgesetz*, 1, 6

[116] BArch R 2/4730 p. 3.

[117] BArch R 22/2117 pp. 62–3, R 2/4730 pp. 14–15r.

his responsibility for the protection of birds and likewise showed no inclination to surrender his jurisdiction, pointing to a national law for the
protection of birds that he was working on.[118] The ministry of the interior stood to profit from the transfer of authority, but its statements were
remarkably unenthusiastic: it argued that the law would have to wait until
the issue of expropriation in general had been dealt with properly.[119] The
war department asked for a clause that permitted the secret suspension
of conservation regulations for military reasons, the Inspector General
for the German Roadways also wished to participate in the law-making
process, and even the minister of finance had a small but tricky objection:
although the law itself gave no reason for concern, he strongly objected
against the elevation of the Prussian Agency for the Protection of Natural
Monuments to an institution of the Reich because such a move meant a
violation of the cost-sharing agreement between Prussia and the Reich.[120]
All in all, the prospects looked dim for a national conservation law in
early 1935.

The situation changed dramatically when Hermann Göring adopted
the issue and pushed aggressively for the new law. In a phone call on the
evening of April 30, 1935, that would become legendary among conservationists, he pressured the minister of education, Bernhard Rust, into sur-
rendering authority over conservation to his own Forest Service (*Reichsforstamt*).[121] His experts went to work on a revised version of the law in
cooperation with the ministry of justice, and when a new draft emerged
on June 17, 1935, ministry officials shifted into high gear: Göring did
away with a final attempt of the ministry of the interior to claim jurisdiction in the field, agreed with the ministry of labor that inner-city parks
would not fall under the law, and ignored objections from the ministry of
trade and commerce against the indemnity clause; the *Wehrmacht* got an
exemption clause for military reservations.[122] On June 25, 1935, he submitted a revised draft for discussion at the cabinet meeting the next day
and asked for a preamble to be written only hours before the meeting.[123]

[118] BArch R 22/2117 p. 74.
[119] BArch R 2/4730 p. 18r, R 22/2117 p. 44r.
[120] BArch R 2/4730 pp. 21–2, R 22/2117 pp. 65, 75.
[121] Hans Günter Hockerts, Friedrich P. Kahlenberg (eds.), *Akten der Reichskanzlei. Die
   Regierung Hitler vol. II: 1934/1935, Teilband 1: August 1934–Mai 1935. Bearbeitet von
   Friedrich Hartmannsgruber* (Munich, 1999), 556n.
[122] BArch R 22/2117 p. 170, R 2/4730 pp. 39, 51, 53–4, R 43 II /227 p. 103, Schoenichen
   and Weber, *Reichsnaturschutzgesetz*, 34–6.
[123] BArch R 2/4730 pp. 62, 80. The hectic sequence of events was due to the upcoming
   cabinet meeting. Preparing the draft on time was important because of the decreasing

FIGURE 3.2. Hermann Göring, passionate hunter, father of the national conservation law, and supreme German conservationist since 1935 here seen in 1933 with a moose he had shot. Photo from SV-Bilderdienst.

Work on the last details continued even during the cabinet meeting, and the national conservation law was adopted as the last item of business.[124] On the same day, Hitler signed a decree that officially transferred the responsibility for conservation issues to Göring's Forest Service.[125]

The transfer of authority had nothing to do with issues of practicability and everything to do with Göring's stamp-collector attitude toward offices and titles. But unintendedly, the transfer seemed to offer new possibilities for the conservation movement. With the selection of Walter von Keudell as head of the German Forest Service, the *Dauerwald* concept had

number of cabinet meetings during the Nazi era. In 1935, only twelve cabinet meetings were held, compared with seventy-two meetings in 1933. The last cabinet meeting during the Nazi era took place on February 5, 1938: See Lothar Gruchmann, "Die 'Reichsregierung' im Führerstaat. Stellung und Funktion des Kabinetts im nationalsozialistischen Herrschaftssystem," in Günther Doeker and Winfried Steffani (eds.), *Klassenjustiz und Pluralismus. Festschrift für Ernst Fraenkel zum 75. Geburtstag* (Hamburg, 1973), 192.

[124] Hans Günter Hockerts and Friedrich P. Kahlenberg (eds.), *Akten der Reichskanzlei. Die Regierung Hitler vol. II: 1934/1935, Teilband 2: Juni–Dezember 1935. Bearbeitet von Friedrich Hartmannsgruber* (Munich, 1999), 652.

[125] *Reichsgesetzblatt 1935*, part 1: 826.

emerged as the official forestry doctrine of the Third Reich in 1934.[126] The
Dauerwald idea had been a minority position in the 1920s, which many
German foresters met with scornful disregard.[127] For more than a century,
most German foresters were adherents of clear-cutting, where trees of the
same age, preferably conifers, grew until they were ready for harvesting.
In contrast, the *Dauerwald* concept envisioned a continuous use of the
forests, with a mixture of age groups and even of species and a beneficial
effect on forest ecology. The reasons behind the Nazis' penchant for the
Dauerwald are not entirely clear: the depressed wood market of the early
1930s gave it a certain economic appeal, and Heinrich Rubner pointed
to the growing contacts between Göring and von Keudell in 1932, but
Michael Imort has argued "that the *Dauerwald* doctrine was proclaimed
mainly because it offered the Nazis an abundance of propagandistic analo-
gies between German forest and German *Volk*."[128] In his publications,
Schoenichen stressed the advantages that the more natural *Dauerwald*
had from the conservationists' point of view, and Klose later credited von
Keudell with creating a climate conducive to conservation issues within
the Forest Service.[129] In his press statement after the passage of the conservation law, von Keudell lashed out against traditional forestry, noting
that "in the quest for a maximum amount of wood, it has transformed
our country into a coniferous wasteland (*Nadelholzsteppe*)."[130] In a 1936
book, Vietinghoff-Riesch, a key proponent of forestry reform, stressed the
common ground between *Dauerwald* forestry and conservation, even suggesting at one point that they were essentially synonymous.[131] All in all,
it seemed that Göring's power play had incidentally fostered a promising
meeting of minds.

However, the nascent alliance never materialized. It is an irony of history that the *Dauerwald* concept went into a decline just at the time

[126] Michael Imort, "'Eternal Forest – Eternal *Volk*.' The Rhetoric and Reality of National
Socialist Forest Policy," in Brüggemeier, Cioc, and Zeller, *How Green*, 43, 48. See also
Aldo Leopold, "Deer and Dauerwald in Germany. I. History; II. Ecology and Policy,"
Journal of Forestry 34 (1936): 366–75, 460–6.
[127] See Bode and Hohnhorst, *Waldwende*, 89–97; and Rubner, *Deutsche Forstgeschichte*,
esp. pp. 24–9.
[128] Rubner, *Deutsche Forstgeschichte*, 53–5; Imort, "Eternal Forest," 44, 51.
[129] Walther Schoenichen, "Wie lässt sich im Rahmen der heutigen Zivilisation die Schönheit
der Landschaft erhalten?," in Union Géographique Internationale (ed.), *Comptes Ren-
dus du Congrès International de Géographie Amsterdam 1938* vol. 2 (Leiden, 1938), 276;
Schoenichen, *Biologie*, 111; Schoenichen, *Naturschutz als völkische und internationale
Kulturaufgabe*, 19; Closmann, "Legalizing," 31; Wettengel, "Staat und Naturschutz,"
386.
[130] BArch R 22/2117 p. 215.
[131] Vietinghoff-Riesch, *Naturschutz*, 67, 134, 145.

that the conservationists came under the wings of the Forest Service. In fact, the *Dauerwald* doctrine was never uncontested, even among the leaders of the Forest Service: at a conference in 1937, a high-ranking forester delivered a thinly veiled attack on the *Dauerwald* rules in the presence of von Keudell and received thunderous applause.[132] At the same time, the growing demand for wood evolved into the dominant motive of German forest policy from the mid-1930s, and von Keudell finally had to resign from his post in November 1937 when he proved unwilling to relax *Dauerwald* policies in the interest of increased wood production.[133] Forestry decrees continued to include references to the *Dauerwald* idea, and a Committee for the Rescue of Deciduous Forest (*Ausschuss zur Rettung des Laubwaldes*), led by Wilhelm Münker, proved widely popular even within the Forest Service.[134] But at the same time, the German war economy demanded ever-increasing amounts of wood, with cutting yields reaching 150 percent of sustainability as early as 1935.[135] And so it came about that the *Dauerwald* doctrine did not mean a merger of forestry and conservation but rather camouflaged the exploitation of Germany's forests, for the *Dauerwald* rules, as well as the more flexible concept of "natural" (*naturgemäß*) forest use that replaced *Dauerwald* as the universal buzzword in 1937, allowed a more inconspicuous form of forest overuse than traditional clear-cutting.[136] Clearly, Simon Schama mistook rhetoric for reality when he argued in his *Landscape and Memory* that "no German government had ever taken the protection of the German forests more seriously than the Third Reich and its Reichsforstminister Göring."[137]

---

[132] Rubner, *Deutsche Forstgeschichte*, 104.

[133] Wettengel, "Staat und Naturschutz," 386; Imort, "Eternal Forest," 57n. See also Paul Josephson and Thomas Zeller, "The Transformation of Nature under Hitler and Stalin," in Mark Walker (ed.), *Science and Ideology: A Comparative History* (London and New York, 2003), 127.

[134] HStAD NW 72 no. 531 p. 118; WAA Best. 717 file "Provinzialbeauftragter," Niederschrift über die Tagung des Ausschusses zur "Rettung des Laubwaldes" im Deutschen Heimatbund vom 23.–25. Oktober 1941 im Sauerland und Bergischen Land.

[135] Imort, "Eternal Forest," 57; Josephson and Zeller, "Transformation," 127–9. For an overview on forest overuse during the Nazi era, see Rolf Zundel and Ekkehard Schwartz, *50 Jahre Forstpolitik in Deutschland (1945 bis 1994)* (Münster-Hiltrup, 1996), 14.

[136] See Hansjörg Küster, *Geschichte des Waldes. Von der Urzeit bis zur Gegenwart* (Munich, 1998), 214; and Peter Michael Steinsiek and Zoltán Rozsnyay, *Grundzüge der deutschen Forstgeschichte 1933–1950 unter besonderer Berücksichtigung Niedersachsens. Aus dem Walde*. Mitteilungen der Niedersächsischen Landesforstverwaltung 46 (Hannover, 1994), 277.

[137] Simon Schama, *Landscape and Memory* (London, 1995), 119. Also, Schama mistakenly speaks of a *ministry* of forestry; Göring's official title was *Reichsforstmeister*.

With this development, nature protection was basically trapped in a department increasingly committed to a purely utilitarian view of forests, and conservationists were essentially unanimous after 1945 that working within the Forest Service under Göring had been an unpleasant experience.[138] Nature protection clearly ranked low on its agenda, stowed away in a subdivision until an internal reorganization in 1941.[139] Michael Imort reported that whereas the forestry and hunting branch included seventy-one academics, the number of academics dealing with the protection of nature was four.[140] It is telling that Lutz Heck, who took charge of nature protection within the Forest Service in 1938, devoted only part of his time to conservation work because he retained his job as director of the Berlin zoo.[141] Heck usually comes across badly in environmental history, if he is mentioned at all; in his seminal article on the conservation administration in the Third Reich, Michael Wettengel mentions nothing but Heck's bad relationship with Klose.[142] However, Heck was in a strong position because of his close ties to Göring: he had helped to create the bison reserve in Göring's cherished Schorfheide nature reserve, and Heck went to Göring's Carinhall estate personally whenever the young lions that Göring liked to keep as pets had grown too big.[143] Thus, Heck could start an initiative that moved even beyond the generous provisions of the national conservation law: a drive for the designation of national parks. At a conference in June 1939, he laid out his plans for large parks in different parts of Germany, stressing the parks' importance for popular recreation and *Heimat* education. In fact, he even named a number of potential sites like the Lüneburg Heath and the Grossglockner area in the Austrian Alps.[144] But when Heck finally made his plans public in March 1940,

---

[138] Günter W. Zwanzig, "50 Jahre Reichsnaturschutzgesetz," *Natur und Landschaft* 60 (1985): 276.

[139] Walter Mrass, *Die Organisation des staatlichen Naturschutzes und der Landschaftspflege im Deutschen Reich und in der Bundesrepublik Deutschland seit 1935, gemessen an der Aufgabenstellung in einer modernen Industriegesellschaft* (Stuttgart, 1970), 30; Lutz Heck, "Die derzeitige Gliederung des deutschen Naturschutzes," *Naturschutz* 23 (1942): 74.

[140] Imort, "Eternal Forest," 62.

[141] BArch R 2/4730 p. 252.

[142] Wettengel, "Staat und Naturschutz," 387.

[143] Rubner, *Deutsche Forstgeschichte*, 130. See also Knopf and Martens, *Görings Reich*, 54.

[144] StAD G 15 Friedberg B 101, Niederschrift über die Arbeitsbesprechung und Bereisung am 19. und 20. Juni 1939 in Frankfurt a.M. und Umgebung, p. 1. Gröning and Wolschke-Bulmahn have falsely depicted the national park project as an outgrowth of war conditions: see Gröning and Wolschke-Bulmahn, *Liebe zur Landschaft Teil 1*,

with an article in the *Völkischer Beobachter*, World War II had begun and the plan was shelved "until the peaceful work of the German people resumes."[145] Few conservationists remembered the plan after 1945, in spite of occasional references in the literature.[146]

Conservationists usually paid most of their attention to the Reich Conservation Agency, the former Prussian Agency for the Protection of Natural Monuments that was transformed into a national institution in 1935. The national conservation law meant a massive increase in work for the agency: in 1938, the network of conservation advisors comprised 55 institutions on the regional and some 880 on the local level.[147] With many of its members newly appointed, the national agency faced a deluge of questions on a wide range of issues, from important legal details to trivialities like the proper procedure for the protection of a scenic tree that happened to stand right on the border between Germany and Czechoslovakia.[148] It is illustrative of the new kind of challenges for the conservation agency that doubts emerged almost immediately about whether Schoenichen was still the right man for the job.[149] Schoenichen finally resigned in 1938, to be replaced by Hans Klose, a former school teacher who had worked on conservation issues in the Forest Service since 1935.[150] For Lutz Heck, Klose's appointment was a chance to get rid of a rival within the Forest Service,[151] but with

209; and Gert Gröning, "Naturschutz und Nationalsozialismus," *Grüner Weg 31 a 10* (December 1996): 16.

[145] Lutz Heck, "Neue Aufgaben des Naturschutzes. Nationalparks für Großdeutschland," *Völkischer Beobachter, Norddeutsche Ausgabe* 53, 73 (March 13, 1940): 3n. However, it should be mentioned that this was by no means the first initiative to create a national park in German history. For example, there had been plans to designate a national park in the Königssee area near Berchtesgaden almost since the first protection decree in 1910. The Bavarian government finally created Berchtesgaden national park in 1978: see Hubert Zierl, "Geschichte des Berchtesgadener Schutzgebietes," in Walter Brugger, Heinz Dopsch, and Peter F. Kramml (eds.), *Geschichte von Berchtesgaden. Stift – Markt – Land*, vol. 3 part 1 (Berchtesgaden, 1999), 617–20.

[146] See Hans Klose and Herbert Ecke (eds.), *Verhandlungen deutscher Landes- und Bezirksbeauftragter für Naturschutz und Landschaftspflege. Zweite Arbeitstagung 24.–26. Oktober 1948 Bad Schwalbach und Schlangenbad* (Egestorf, 1949), 17; and Walther Schoenichen, "Naturschutz im Rahmen der europäischen Raumordnung," *Raumforschung und Raumordnung* 7 (1943): 146.

[147] BArch R 2/4730 p. 248.

[148] HStADd Best. 10747 no. 2251, Der Reichsforstmeister und Preußische Landesforstmeister to the Reichsstatthalter in Sachsen, Landesforstverwaltung, November 24, 1937.

[149] See WAA LWL Best. 702 no. 184, Kühl to Hartmann, October 30, 1935.

[150] Mrass, *Organisation*, 11.

[151] Oberkrome, *Deutsche Heimat*, 182.

his reputation as a "very energetic man" – in contrast to Schoenichen, whom many saw as "too soft"[152] – he was the able manager that the conservationists' network needed most at that time.[153] A skillful tactician, he had a realistic conception of the conservationists' range of options and their limitations. When plans emerged after 1945 to reopen the quarry at the Hohenstoffeln Mountain, closed in 1939 after almost 3 decades of campaigning, Klose dismissed calls for strict opposition and proposed to negotiate, arguing that "politics is the art of the possible" – in a way, the credo of his life.[154] Incidentally, the shift at the top also showed that political considerations did not necessarily reign supreme in Nazi Germany. Charles Closmann has rightly pointed out that Schoenichen was a "more committed Nazi" than Klose, whom he describes as "a consummate opportunist"; unlike Schoenichen, Klose never joined the NSDAP.[155] After the national conservation law, the call was for managerial skills, not the literary activity that Schoenichen had cherished so much. Schoenichen complained after his resignation that Klose was ill qualified to "continue the consolidation and deepening of conservation ideology," but he was almost alone with this critique. A clear ideological profile was no longer what the conservation community needed most.[156]

The consolidation of the conservation advisors' network also spelled the end of the conflicts between state and party officials that had existed in some regions during the first years of Nazi rule. In several cases, NSDAP members had challenged the government's authority over conservation issues with attempts to do conservation work on the Nazi Party's authority. The issue at stake was power: none of the party members pursued an agenda that differed markedly from the conservationists' mainstream. The most aggressive party conservationist was Hans Stadler, whose appeals to subordinates stood out for their militarist choice of words and frequent references to the support of the regional *Gauleiter*.[157] In Nuremberg, Karl Hoepfel acted as the NSDAP's Curator for Heimat Affairs (*Gauheimatpfleger*), but his agenda was more modest than Stadler's: one of his major projects was the designation of hiking trails.[158] A third

---

[152] StAR Nachlass Ludwig Finckh II a folder 36, Ludwig Finckh to the Reichsführer SS Chefadjutantur, March 30, 1935.
[153] StAW Landratsamt Ebern no. 1336, Stadler to Hoch, July 13, 1935.
[154] BArch B 245/3 p. 60. On the Hohenstoffeln conflict, see Chapter 4, Section 1.
[155] Closmann, "Legalizing," 34; BArch B 245/3 p. 54r.
[156] BArch B 245/11 p. 52.
[157] See his correspondence in StAW Landratsamt Bad Kissingen no. 1233 and Landratsamt Ebern no. 1336.
[158] StAN Rep. 212/19[VII] no. 2535, Nationalsozialistische Deutsche Arbeiterpartei, Kreisleitung Weißenburg to the Bezirksamt Weißenburg, November 16, 1936.

example was Gau Cultural Leader (*Gaukulturwart*) Hermann Bartels of Münster, who tried to move into conservation issues with his network of party officials for cultural affairs, but his work soon met with resistance from the well-organized Westphalian conservation community.[159] Bartels made sure that the appointment of conservation advisors became subject to party approval, to the consternation of Schoenichen, but after that, Bartels quickly abandoned conservation issues.[160] Resistance from the bureaucracy was also strong in Franconia, culminating in a decree by the Bavarian ministry of the interior of 1937 that declared Stadler's conservation decrees invalid. As a result, Stadler was forced to resubmit applications for a number of natural monuments with the administration, a humiliating amount of paperwork for an activist who liked to think of conservation in terms of "counterattacks" and "front duty."[161] The rift between party-based and state-based conservation ended when Hoepfel and Stadler joined the state's network after the passage of the national conservation law, becoming conservation advisors in their respective regions in 1936.[162] For all the chaos that reigned in conservation circles during the Nazi era, there was at least a consensus that conservation was a task of the government and not of the party.

Whereas the conservation administration could easily fend off the challenge from the Nazi Party, it had more trouble in the competition with other groups over authority for landscape preservation. In this field, the Reich Conservation Agency had a powerful rival in the network of Landscape Advocates that Fritz Todt set up as Inspector General for the German Roadways. Created for the construction of the Autobahn,

---

[159] WAA Best. 717 file "Reichsstelle (Bundesstelle) für Naturschutz (und Landschaftspflege)," Gaukulturwart Bartels, Aufruf an die Mitarbeiter des Naturschutzes, November 9, 1933.

[160] See proceedings in WAA Best. 702 no. 184b vol. 1. Refusal did not necessarily show a democratic mindset, however: Bartels dismissed a candidate for the Iserlohn district because he had been a member of the *Stahlhelm*, the militant right-wing servicemen's association founded in 1918. (*Ibid.*, Gaukulturamt to the Kommissar für Naturdenkmalpflege der Provinz Westfalen, July 11, 1934.)

[161] StAW Landratsamt Obernburg no. 210, Regierung von Unterfranken und Aschaffenburg to the Bezirksverwaltungsbehörden, March 23, 1937; StAW Landratsamt Ebern no. 1336, Der Regierungsbeauftragte für Naturschutz in Unterfranken to the Bezirksbeauftragten, April 2, 1937. See *ibid.*, Der Gauheimatpfleger und Beauftragte für Naturschutz der NSDAP Mainfranken to the Bürgermeister, November 1, 1937; Der Regierungsbeauftragte für Naturschutz in Unterfranken to the Bezirksbeauftragen für Naturschutz, March 12, 1937; and *Blätter für Naturschutz und Naturpflege* 19 (1936): 138.

[162] StAN Rep. 212/17^IV no. 101, Regierung von Oberfranken und Mittelfranken to the Oberbürgermeister der Stadtkreise and the Bezirksämter, April 17, 1936; StAW Landratsamt Bad Kissingen no. 1234, Regierung von Unterfranken und Aschaffenburg to the Bezirksverwaltungsbehörden, April 16, 1936.

the Inspector General was a showcase for the polycentric dynamism of the Nazi state. Established outside the Reich Transport Administration (*Reichsverkehrsministerium*), the Inspector General stood directly under Hitler's command, making for enormous leeway in the design of construction projects. In fact, Todt's efficient work in Autobahn construction spurred his career until he became minister for weapons and munitions in 1940, effectively putting him in charge of the German war economy until his mysterious death in a plane crash in 1942.[163] The work of Todt's Landscape Advocates won considerable praise from conservationists, much of which was because of Alwin Seifert, the group's energetic leader and "Reich Landscape Advocate" (*Reichslandschaftsanwalt*) from 1940, who rose from obscurity to become a charismatic leadership figure.[164] As a "politically savvy environmentalist," Seifert enjoyed protection not only from Fritz Todt but also from Rudolf Hess, the Deputy Leader of the Nazi Party.[165] But in spite of his dependence on these Nazi leaders, Seifert maintained a great degree of intellectual autonomy during the Nazi era and even instigated controversial public discussions. Going through his publications, one is torn between admiration for his independent thinking and relief that one did not have to work with him. Seifert was a proponent of organic farming and acted "as a go-between for the Anthroposophic Society and the Nazi state," a delicate role given the uncertain standing of anthroposophy in Nazi Germany.[166] After Rudolf Hess' flight to England in 1941, Seifert was under surveillance by the secret police, and though he was never arrested, his power base clearly eroded during the war.[167] Still, he kept receiving his monthly salary of 2,000 Reichsmarks plus 500 Reichsmarks for office expenses until the last months of the war.[168] In 1937, by way of comparison, the average monthly salary in Germany was 155 Reichsmarks.[169]

Thomas Zeller, the leading expert on Seifert's life and work, has described him pointedly as "the Nazis' environmental court jester and

---

[163] Wehler, *Deutsche Gesellschaftsgeschichte vol. 4*, 627.

[164] Thomas Zeller, "'Ganz Deutschland sein Garten.' Alwin Seifert und die Landschaft des Nationalsozialismus," in Radkau and Uekötter, *Naturschutz und Nationalsozialismus*, 273n.

[165] Zeller, "Molding," 148; Zeller, "Ganz Deutschland," 297.

[166] Zeller, "Molding," 157. See also Uwe Werner, *Anthroposophen in der Zeit des Nationalsozialismus (1933–1945)* (Munich, 1999), esp. pp. 88, 111, 267–8.

[167] Zeller, *Straße, Bahn, Panorama*, 88.

[168] BArch Berlin Document Center Speer Listen Best. 8461 E 0104 pp. 32–68.

[169] Frank Bajohr, *Parvenüs und Profiteure. Korruption in der NS-Zeit* (Frankfurt, 2001), 235.

Cassandra rolled into one."[170] Seifert's career was indeed unique, and his role had no resemblance to any other in the German conservation community. Seifert dealt with a wide range of issues, and he always expressed his views with a firmness that many perceived as arrogant. One of his specialties was writing directions for landscape planning after a 1-day visit: a typical example was his statement on the Wutach conflict, which was reportedly based on a 90-minute field trip.[171] In at least one case, even Todt felt that he could not tolerate Seifert's presumptuous style without a conciliatory addition: transmitting Seifert's report on the Schluchsee project in the Black Forest, Todt apologized for "the drastic style," arguing that it was "a direct personal statement" where one could only wish for "a blunt description."[172] Seifert's most controversial assertion was that Germany was in great danger of "desertification" (*Versteppung*) due to the drainage of fields, the cultivation of previously unused land and the regulation of rivers. His article on the topic, published in 1936, in Todt's own journal *Deutsche Technik* (German Technology), resulted in a flurry of comments.[173] Pointing to the Dust Bowl in the contemporary United States, he lashed out against the hydrological engineers' "mechanistic" approach and called for a holistic view that gave sufficient attention to the interconnectedness of nature.[174] His argument for a "natural" design of rivers remained vague, and Seifert actually refused to elaborate on his ideas in scholarly journals, seeing himself above all as a practitioner, but *Versteppung* became a popular buzzword that conservationists came to use even in other contexts; Wilhelm Lienenkämper evoked the theme in a critique of the one-sided use of field and forest, and a hunting official from the Rhineland saw Seifert's argument as a general warning "that there is a limit to all kinds of manipulations in nature that we may not transgress."[175] Seifert also tried to convince the Nazi regime to implement

[170] Zeller, "Molding," 160.
[171] GLAK Abt. 237 no. 50599, Reichslandschaftsanwalt Alwin Seifert to the Generalinspektor für Wasser und Energie, September 7, 1942. See also HStAS EA 3/102 no. 29, Gutachten der Landesnaturschutzstelle Baden, November 30, 1942, p. 12.
[172] StAF Landratsamt Neustadt Best. G 19/12 no. 3060, Der Beauftragte für Technik und deren Organisation to the Direktion des Schluchseewerks, September 25, 1935.
[173] See Alwin Seifert, "Die Versteppung Deutschlands," in Alwin Seifert, *Im Zeitalter des Lebendigen. Natur, Heimat, Technik* (Planegg, 1942), 24–50.
[174] For a more thorough discussion of Seifert's argument, see Zeller, "Ganz Deutschland," 282–7. On the Dust Bowl in the United States, see Donald Worster, *Dust Bowl. The Southern Plains in the 1930s* (Oxford, 1979).
[175] WAA LWL Best. 702 no. 184b vol. 2, Wilhelm Lienenkämper, Das Naturschutz-ABC, p. 11. See also HStAD Landratsamt Siegkreis no. 434, Der Kreisjägermeister des Siegkreises to "alle Behörden, die auf die Landeskulturmassnahmen einen Einfluss haben," February 6, 1937.

organic farming on a grand scale, even though his argument ran directly against the views of the hostile agricultural science community of the 1930s.[176] But Seifert also dealt with other, seemingly marginal, topics: in 1939, Seifert urged Todt to give special attention to unsightly power lines in alpine power projects.[177] Seifert also criticized the use of human feces as fertilizer, arguing that it would drive the German "master race" (*Herrenvolk*) into degeneration.[178]

Seifert did not shy away from Nazi rhetoric, as his reference to the Germans as a "master race" shows. With Heinrich Wiepking-Jürgensmann, his arch rival in the landscape architects' profession, he even competed as to who was the greater anti-Semite.[179] Still, Zeller has pointed out that Seifert was not "a fanatical Nazi longing for Hitler's rise to power"; fittingly, Seifert did not join the NSDAP until 1937, and his membership had probably less to do with deep convictions than with his professional crisis during that year.[180] Moreover, his understanding of human races differed from the official Nazi doctrine: he adhered to the theory of race of Friedrich Merkenschlager, a Nazi party member who was ostracized after a press dispute with Richard Walther Darré in 1933, and even tried to win Hess and Todt for Merkenschlager's reading in 1940.[181] Seifert was clearly much too eclectic in his thinking and far too independent intellectually as to become a narrow-minded believer in the Nazi doctrine. More than with other people, it is important to look at the time

[176] Zeller, "Molding," 160. On the conflict between biodynamic agriculture and the agricultural science establishment, see Frank Uekötter, "Know Your Soil. Transitions in Farmers' and Scientists' Knowledge in the Twentieth Century," in John McNeill and Verena Winiwarter (eds.), *Soils and Societies: Perspectives from Environmental History* (Cambridge, 2006), 320–38; and Gunter Vogt, *Entstehung und Entwicklung des ökologischen Landbaus* (Bad Dürkheim, 2000), 117–27.

[177] Helmut Maier, "'Unter Wasser und unter die Erde.' Die süddeutschen und alpinen Wasserkraftprojekte des Rheinisch-Westfälischen Elektrizitätswerks (RWE) und der Natur- und Landschaftsschutz während des 'Dritten Reiches,'" in Günter Bayerl and Torsten Meyer (eds.), *Die Veränderung der Kulturlandschaft. Nutzungen – Sichtweisen – Planungen* (Münster, 2003), 165.

[178] Alwin Seifert, "Über die biologischen Grenzen der landwirtschaftlichen Verwertung städtischer Abwässer," *Deutsche Wasserwirtschaft* 35 (1940): 163.

[179] See Thomas Zeller, "'Ich habe die Juden möglichst gemieden.' Ein aufschlußreicher Briefwechsel zwischen Heinrich Wiepking und Alwin Seifert," *Garten + Landschaft* 8 (1995): 4–5. For an ill-fated attempt to whitewash Seifert, see Reinhard Falter, "Alwin Seifert (1890–1972). Die Biographie des Naturschutz im 20. Jahrhundert," *Berichte der Bayerischen Akademie für Naturschutz und Landschaftspflege* 28 (2004): 69–104.

[180] Zeller, "Ganz Deutschland," 281; NSDAP Membership no. 5774652, from May 1, 1937.

[181] Charlotte Reitsam, "Das Konzept der 'bodenständigen Gartenkunst' Alwin Seiferts. Ein völkisch-konservatives Leitbild von Ästhetik in der Landschaftsarchitektur und seine fachliche Rezeption bis heute," *Die Gartenkunst* 13 (2001): 279n.

and context of his statements. For example, Seifert became increasingly radical in his attacks on nonnative species, eventually designating the blue spruce as "public enemy number one." But his stance originally derived from contemporary plant sociology, and Seifert draped his convictions in Nazi rhetoric only after he had faced enormous difficulties in the realization of his ideas.[182] Tellingly, Seifert offered two different conceptual drafts to Todt when he first contacted him in 1933, one with emphasis on native species and one without.[183] Calling Seifert a "dedicated advocate of Nazi blood-and-soil ideology," as some have done, reveals little more than thinking in clichés.[184]

Seifert's greatest accomplishment was perhaps that he came across in public as a powerful and influential conservationist, although his position within the Inspector General's Autobahn project remained weak and highly controversial. From the selection of the Landscape Advocates to work in the field, Seifert's was a story of perpetual compromises, an experience that strongly contributed to his own radicalization. The Landscape Advocates were always limited to a consultative function, confined to their own persuasive skills without a legal provision that would force anyone to heed their advice, and the engineers in charge turned out to be overwhelmingly reluctant to listen. Todt had created the institution of Landscape Advocates, but he was of little help in their daily conflicts: "Todt almost never stipulated what specific advice, opinion, or reports he preferred. Rather, he used his power to reward or ignore the expertise provided."[185] It was indicative of the Landscape Advocates' difficult standing that Todt cut their hourly salary rate in 1936. The conflict finally reached its peak in 1937 when Alwin Seifert resigned from his work for the Autobahn project for 9 months; at that time, some 600 miles of Autobahn were already open to the public, and construction was under way for even more than that. From the outset, Seifert had advocated a road design that stressed smooth curves, as opposed to the straight lines and sharp corners that most engineers favored, but Seifert's proposal did not become dominant until the late 1930s, and by that time, the greater part of the Autobahn project had already moved beyond the planning stage.[186] "It is time to abandon the myth of an exemplary reconciliation of nature and technology in the Autobahn project,"

---

[182] See Zeller, *Straße, Bahn, Panorama*, 165–87 (quotation p. 175).
[183] Zeller, "Ganz Deutschland," 276.
[184] Gröning and Wolschke-Bulmahn, *Grüne Biographien*, 362.
[185] Zeller, "Molding," 152.
[186] This account is based on Zeller's exhaustive discussion of the Autobahn project. See Zeller, *Straße, Bahn, Panorama*, 91–198.

Zeller wrote.[187] Authors like Schoenichen and Schwenkel extolled the Autobahn as "a magnificent example of landscape design," but if the Autobahn pleased the conservationists' eyes, it did so in spite of the Landscape Advocates' influence rather than because of it.[188]

The Landscape Advocates tried to use their position to move into other fields, but they never gained a monopoly over landscape issues. Seifert managed to block his longtime rival Wiepking-Jürgensmann from work with the Autobahn project, but Wiepking-Jürgensmann won the prestigious landscaping project for the Berlin Olympic Games in 1936 and maintained a presence in the field as a professor of horticulture at the Berlin Agricultural College in 1934.[189] These standing conflicts won a new quality after 1939, when the occupation of Poland opened a new playing field for the landscape planning profession. In the quest for the unique chance of planning on a grand scale, Wiepking-Jürgensmann generally won the upper hand. The Inspector General for the German Roadways published temporary guidelines for landscaping along the main roads in the newly occupied area, thus defining roadways, as in Germany proper, as a special terrain off-limits to other conservationists.[190] But it was Wiepking-Jürgensmann who joined Heinrich Himmler's Reich Commissariat for the Strengthening of German Nationality (*Reichskommissariat für die Festigung des deutschen Volkstums*), where he drew up plans that presumed the expulsion of the resident population.[191] In May 1942, Wiepking-Jürgensmann also assumed a post within the Forest Service, thus linking conservation and landscape planning institutionally. Responsibility for landscape protection within the German heartland remained with Hans Schwenkel.[192] Klose's Reich Conservation Agency mostly lost

---

[187] Zeller, "Ganz Deutschland," 306. Similarly, Erhard Schütz and Eckhard Gruber, *Mythos Reichsautobahn. Bau und Inszenierung der "Straßen des Führers" 1933–1941* (Berlin, 1996).

[188] Schwenkel, *Taschenbuch*, 37 (quotation); Schwenkel, "Aufgaben," 134; Schoenichen, *Naturschutz als völkische und internationale Kulturaufgabe*, 32; Künkele, "Naturschutz," 21; Walter Hellmich, *Natur- und Heimatschutz* (Stuttgart, 1953), 10; Schütz and Gruber, *Mythos Reichsautobahn*, 7.

[189] Zeller, *Straße, Bahn, Panorama*, 101; Ursula Kellner, *Heinrich Friedrich Wiepking (1891–1973). Leben, Lehre und Werk* (Ph.D., Hannover University, 1998), 271.

[190] Zeller, "Ganz Deutschland," 300.

[191] See Gert Gröning and Joachim Wolschke-Bulmahn, "1. September 1939. Der Überfall auf Polen als Ausgangspunkt 'totaler' Landespflege," *Raumplanung* no. 46/47 (December, 1989): 149–53.

[192] See Lutz Heck, "Behördliche Landschaftsgestaltung im Osten," *Naturschutz* 23 (1942): 61–2. Hartenstein pointed out that the corresponding arrangement between the Reich Commissariat and the Forest Service spelled the end of plans to set up a "National

out in this struggle for power in Eastern Europe, but a number of initiatives showed that he was not immune to the air of omnipotence that accompanied conquest. In March 1943, Hans Klose even proposed an inventory of nature reserves in the Caucasus region, a region from which the *Wehrmacht* had just fled.[193] The planners' work in Eastern Europe will be discussed more extensively in Chapter 5, but it should be mentioned from the outset that it was here that conservation and racism finally met in a way that was more than sheer rhetoric, resulting in ghastly plans that, though never realized, displayed a shocking degree of inhumane thinking.[194] A frequently quoted sentence from Wiepking-Jürgensmann's landscape planning book of 1942, where he speaks of "the murders and cruelties of the Eastern races" being "engraved, razor-sharp, into the grimaces of their native landscapes," provides a sobering reminder of the profession's implication in crimes against humanity.[195]

All in all, it is clear that the German conservation community never merged into a forceful alliance during the Nazi era. Instead, it was a rather chaotic set of actors with three centers of gravity: the Landscape Advocates under Alwin Seifert's charismatic leadership, a second group of landscape planners around Heinrich Wiepking-Jürgensmann, and the Reich Conservation Agency under Schoenichen and Klose, with its vast network of conservation advisors in all parts of Germany. This fragmentation becomes even more apparent if one takes a final look at other issues that are today a common part of the environmental agenda. To be sure, some links did exist: Schoenichen listed air and water pollution among the conservationists' concerns in his book of 1942.[196] But experience had

Landscape Office" (*Reichslandschaftsamt*) pursued by Konrad Meyer, Wiepking-Jürgensmann, and Erhard Mäding. (Hartenstein, *Neue Dorflandschaften*, 55.)

[193] BArch B 245/214 p. 147.

[194] See Klaus Fehn, "'Artgemäße deutsche Kulturlandschaft.' Das nationalsozialistische Projekt einer Neugestaltung Ostmitteleuropas," Kunst- und Ausstellungshalle der Bundesrepublik Deutschland (ed.), *Erde* (Cologne, 2002), 559–75; Fehn, "Lebensgemeinschaft"; and Wolschke-Bulmahn, "Violence as the Basis of National Socialist Landscape Planning in the 'Annexed Eastern Areas,'" in Brüggemeier, Cioc, and Zeller, *How Green*, 243–56.

[195] See Klaus Fehn, "Rückblick auf die 'nationalsozialistische Kulturlandschaft.' Unter besonderer Berücksichtigung des völkisch-rassistischen Mißbrauchs von Kulturlandschaftspflege," *Informationen zur Raumentwicklung* no. 5/6 (1999): 283; and Stefan Körner, *Theorie und Methodologie der Landschaftsplanung, Landschaftsarchitektur und Sozialwissenschaftlichen Freiraumplanung vom Nationalsozialismus bis zur Gegenwart* (Berlin, 2001), 27. Most recently, this quotation has been used in Douglas R. Weiner, "A Death-Defying Attempt to Articulate a Coherent Definition of Environmental History," *Environmental History* 10 (2005): 412.

[196] Schoenichen, *Naturschutz als völkische und internationale Kulturaufgabe*, 19n.

shown that pollution issues usually ranked low on their list of priorities. During the war, a plan for an ore refinery near the Porta Westfalica, the scenic passage of the Weser River through a mountain range toward the north German lowlands, resulted in a wave of protests not only from regional leaders but also from Fritz Todt.[197] However, this sudden outburst of activity also revealed the conservation community's indifference to pollution issues in general: the issue at stake at the Porta Westfalica was the damage to a scenic area, not pollution damage per se. The same held true for the increasing importance of recycling efforts during the Nazi era: the driving force was the Nazis' quest for autarky in preparation for war, and few people realized that these efforts could also have merit from a different perspective. It took the conservation community until 1943 to realize that a scrap metal collection drive could be a good occasion for a campaign against outdoor advertising.[198] The conservation community of the Nazi era was limited not only in its powers but also in its view of contemporary problems.

[197] WAA LWL Best. 702 no. 184, Reichsminister Fritz Todt to the Regierungspräsident Minden, October 6, 1941. See also BArch B 245/55, Regierungspräsident Minden to the Oberbergamt Clausthal-Zellerfeld, February 7, 1941. For a more intensive discussion of air pollution policy in Nazi Germany, see Frank Uekoetter, "Polycentrism in Full Swing: Air Pollution Control in Nazi Germany," in Brüggemeier, Cioc, and Zeller, *How Green*, 101–28.

[198] StAW Landratsamt Obernburg no. 209, Landrat Obernburg to the Bürgermeister, September 18, 1943. See also Friedrich Huchting, "Abfallwirtschaft im Dritten Reich," *Technikgeschichte* 48 (1981): 252–73; Gerhard Lenz, "Ideologisierung und Industrialisierung der Landschaft im Nationalsozialismus am Beispiel des Großraumes Bitterfeld-Dessau," in Bayerl and Meyer, *Veränderung der Kulturlandschaft*, 195n; Peter Münch, *Stadthygiene im 19. und 20. Jahrhundert. Die Wasserversorgung, Abwasser- und Abfallbeseitigung unter besonderer Berücksichtigung Münchens* (Göttingen, 1993), 280n; and Anton Lübke, *Das deutsche Rohstoffwunder. Wandlungen der deutschen Rohstoffwirtschaft*, 6th edition (Stuttgart, 1940), 527–32.

4

Conservation at Work: Four Case Studies

In 1931, the Netherlands Committee for International Nature Protection published a worldwide overview on the organization of nature protection. In spite of the deficiencies of the German conservation bureaucracy during the Weimar years, this book portrayed it favorably: "There is nowhere else in Europe such an extensive organisation for nature protection as among our neighbors to the east," the Dutch conservationists declared.[1] It is tempting to speculate what the author would have said about the system of the late 1930s: the 55 regional and 880 county institutions in all parts of Germany. In all likelihood, this was the most comprehensive network for the protection of nature of its time – an array of manpower for conservation purposes that no other country could muster. But manpower is only one requirement for a successful conservation policy. It is difficult, if not impossible, to judge the relative worth of the German conservation administration by laws and institutions alone. After the previous chapter, the general ambivalence should be clear: on the one hand, paragraph 20 of the National Conservation Law meant that the conservationists had veto power over every project that affected the landscape, at least in theory. On the other hand, the final decision on conservation issues remained in the hands of Hermann Göring, and it was clear that conservation concerns ranked lower on Göring's agenda than the military buildup that he chaired as head of the Four Year Plan Agency. Inevitably, the conservation administration became entangled in a Darwinian struggle with other institutions and causes, and the outcome would depend on much more than the letter of the law.

[1] Brouwer, *The Organisation*, 31.

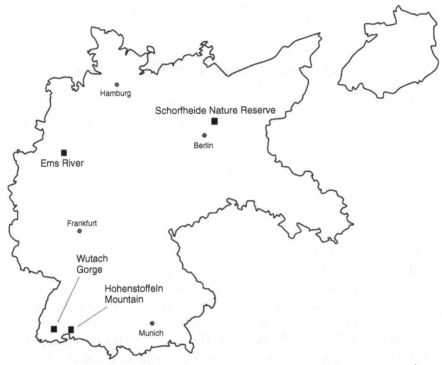

FIGURE 4.1. Four case studies in conservation: Hohenstoffeln Mountain, the Schorfheide National Nature Reserve, the Ems River, and Wutach Gorge. Map courtesy of Simona Grothues.

The following four case studies provide an idea of the opportunities and the limits of conservation work in Nazi Germany. Of course, the selection of four cases brings up the question of the criteria for this choice. After all, there were many more conflicts during the 12 years of Nazi rule that deserve attention, and one can be almost certain that future research will reveal further, heretofore unknown incidents. In addition, it seems there is no typical story: the issues at stake and the lines of conflict differed considerably from case to case. Therefore, the first important criterion for selection was geographical: the case studies come from different parts of the country. The regulation of the Ems River took place in the northwestern part of Germany, whereas the Schorfheide nature reserve was close to Berlin, some 250 miles to the east. The Wutach River and the Hohenstoffeln Mountain are both in the southern German state of Baden, in the vicinity of the Swiss border, but this proximity was intentional: as the narrative will show, the Wutach story was in some ways a follow-up to the Hohenstoffeln conflict. The second criterion was that the conflicts should cover different periods, thus allowing a glimpse at changes over time. The third and most important criterion was that the case studies should be as different as possible, thus mirroring the inherent diversity of conservation work in Nazi Germany. Thus, the following case studies open up perspectives on a wide range of issues: river regulation, hydroelectric power, quarrying, hunting, tourism, expropriation, racism and anti-Semitism and their relative importance, the conflict between economic and conservation interests, the limits of public protest during the Nazi era, agricultural policy, and government corruption. The range of parties involved is equally wide, from the Labor Service to the Gestapo. The Nazi leaders who played a role in the following stories include Hermann Göring, Fritz Todt, and Heinrich Himmler.

The Hohenstoffeln Mountain

In the mid-1930s, the southern German novelist Ludwig Finckh published a book on his home region. Entitled *The Unknown Hegau*, it sought to reveal the beauty of a region that many people had missed, mostly the result of the nearness of other, more scenic, rivals. Lying close to Lake Constance, the Black Forest, and the Rhine Valley between Constance and Basel, the Hegau usually ranked low on the itinerary of tourists who came to the southwestern corner of Germany. "The German does not know his fatherland yet," Finckh wrote and urged his fellow countrymen to come and see the Hegau rather than travel abroad. His book offered an emphatic description of the Hegau region, whose main scenic peculiarity was a number of cone-shaped mountains of volcanic origin. "The Hegau is sacred land. Every stone tells of the making of the earth." His narrative spoke of the face and the land and the human history that it mirrored. But when he came to speak on the Hohenstoffeln Mountain, one of the former volcanoes, his elated style suddenly broke, and Finckh lapsed into a tragic mode: "it is painful to speak of this mountain."[2]

By that time, more than 2 decades had passed since the opening of a stone quarry on the slopes of the Hohenstoffeln, and quarrying had

---

[2] Ludwig Finckh, *Der unbekannte Hegau* (Bühl, 1935), 5, 7, 20. The Hohenstoffeln conflict has been subject to two essays in a regional history journal. (Volker Ludwig, "Die Entstehung des Naturschutzgebietes 'Hohenstoffeln,'" *Hegau* 42 [1997/1998]: 153–90; Kurt Oesterle, "Doktor Faust besiegt Shylock. Wie Ludwig Finckh den Hohenstoffel rettete und wie der Reichsführer-SS Heinrich Himmler als sein Mephisto ihm dabei half," *Hegau* 42 [1997/1998]: 191–208.) However, the following interpretation differs markedly from the authors' interpretation on a number of points.

changed the face of the mountain significantly. Conflicts over quarries are among the classic controversies of German conservation, going back to the protection of the Rock of the Dragon (*Drachenfels*) in the Rhine Valley in 1836, an event that conservationists liked to remember as the first German nature reserve.[3] For a movement with strong feelings for scenic landscapes, quarries stood out as an eyesore, a wound in the land that was difficult, if not impossible, to heal.[4] The scenic argument gained even more weight when there were remnants of a castle on the mountain top, though the ruins on the Hohenstoffeln were already reported to be "in total decay" in the mid-nineteenth century.[5] But at the same time, the owners and operators of quarries had proven to be difficult foes. In many cases, the only acceptable solution from the conservationists' point of view was the immediate termination of all quarrying operations, making conflicts of this kind a life-or-death dispute from the businessmen's point of view. In addition, the cycles of business were usually averse to the protection of nature. During an economic upswing, stone material was in high demand, and the conservationists had to stop a booming enterprise, whereas a depression made the jobs at stake especially precious. The Hohenstoffeln quarry, whose basalt made good road-building material, was no exception.[6]

It was a testament to the strength of conservation sentiment that when the plan to open a quarry on the Hohenstoffeln emerged shortly before World War I, protest came from a wide range of parties. One of the first petitioners was the Natural History Association of Baden (*Badischer Landesverein für Naturkunde*), which feared that a quarry would destroy the mountain within a matter of years.[7] The State Geological Survey soon agreed, assuming that the basalt would be exhausted quickly, and "while the public will only profit from the quarry in a small way, the mountain will be disfigured for all time."[8] Protest also came from the Tourist Association of Lake Constance (*Bodensee-Verkehrs-Verein*),

[3] Wettengel, "Staat und Naturschutz," 358. On the myth of the "first German nature reserve" and its nationalist implications, see Schmoll, *Erinnerung*, 132–8.

[4] Schmoll, *Erinnerung*, 197.

[5] GLAK Abt. 235 no. 16725, Auszug aus dem Bericht des Regierungsdirectors in Constanz über die Visitation des Bezirksamts Blumenfeld, September 30, 1854.

[6] See Fischer, "Heimatschutz und Steinbruchindustrie," esp. p. 70.

[7] GLAK Abt. 235 no. 16725, Bezirksamt Engen to the Ministerium des Kultus und Unterrichts, December 7, 1911.

[8] Ibid., Direktion der Geologischen Landesanstalt to the Ministerium des Innern, February 13, 1912, p. 3.

which bristled at the thought of an unsightly quarry, even though the Hohenstoffeln was some 10 miles from the lakeshore.[9] But the Hohenstoffeln quarry soon ceased to be a purely local issue. As early as April 1913, a newspaper in Mannheim spoke of a truly national affair, "for the mountains of the Hegau are German mountains, not only mountains of the state of Baden."[10] A resolution by the Federation for Heimat Protection underscored this assertion, as did a passionate plea to the owner of the mountain, Baron Ferdinand von Hornstein, a hapless novelist living in Munich. The signers of this petition included Ernst Rudorff, Carl Fuchs, and Fritz Koch, all leading figures in the Federation for Heimat Protection; Hermann Hesse, who later won the Nobel Prize for Literature; and Ludwig Finckh.[11]

Even on the local level, the prospect of jobs did not erase worries over the project's environmental impact, and county officials were wondering as early as 1911 "if and how we can stop the prospective destruction."[12] However, a look at the laws in force produced a disappointing result: "In our judgment, it will not be possible to prohibit basalt mining on the Hohenstoffeln," the ministry of the interior of Baden declared in 1912, adding that "appeals to the owner" would be the only way to forestall the "very regrettable defacement of the landscape."[13] At the same time, explorations into the geology of the Hohenstoffeln produced a highly favorable result: the Hohenstoffeln's basalt was of excellent quality, and it would be easy to mine.[14] With that, the start of mining operations was only a question of time, and the authorities in charge, though aghast about the prospect of scarring the Hohenstoffeln, were at a loss to prevent it. In March 1913, shortly before the start of quarrying operations, the operators of the quarry pledged "to ensure the conservation and preservation

---

[9] *Ibid.*, Bodensee-Verkehrs-Verein to the Ministerium des Kultus und Unterrichts, June 17, 1913.

[10] *Mannheimer Tageblatt* no. 97 of April 10, 1913.

[11] GLAK Abt. 235 no. 16725, Der Geschäftsführende Vorstand des deutschen Bundes Heimatschutz to the Ministerium des Innern, June 4, 1913, and petition to Freiherr Dr. Ferdinand von Hornstein, undated.

[12] *Ibid.*, Bezirksamt Engen to the Ministerium des Kultus und Unterrichts, December 7, 1911. Hans Klose's later assertion that officials did not give much thought to the environmental impact was clearly wrong. (Hans Klose, "Corona imperii," *Naturschutz* 19 [1939]: 36.)

[13] GLAK Abt. 235 no. 16725, Ministerium des Innern to the Ministerium des Kultus und Unterrichts, February 23, 1912.

[14] *Ibid.*, Bezirksamt Engen to the Ministerium des Kultus und Unterrichts, March 21, 1912.

of the mountain's historic ruins," but time would show that this promise was worth little more than the paper it was printed on.[15]

Quarrying continued through the 1920s and so did the conservationists' protest against it. A meeting in December 1921 drew representatives from half a dozen associations, among them the Heimat League of Baden (*Verein Badische Heimat*), the Black Forest Association of Baden (*Badischer Schwarzwaldverein*), the *Naturfreunde* tourist association, and two leagues of artists from Lake Constance and Karlsruhe, the state's capital.[16] In fact, it turned out that quarrying was not undisputed even within Baron von Hornstein's family: the owner's cousin, Karl von Hornstein, was against the project, though for rather selfish reasons – it threatened his own forests and hunting reserves.[17] However, this family dispute did not stop the exploitation of the stone reserves, and neither did the conservationists' continuing protest, which reached its peak with a resolution of the first National Conservation Conference (*Naturschutztag*) in Munich in 1925.[18] At that time, the state authorities still had a great deal of sympathy for the conservationists' cause. Whereas the state of Baden was the operators' key ally during the 1930s, statements during the 1920s were almost unanimous in its opposition. The ministry of finance imposed a ban on state purchases from the Hohenstoffeln quarry in 1925, and a ministry official from the department of labor, writing in his capacity as a member of the Heimat League of Baden, asked the conservationists "to arouse the public's conscience" and even pushed them to declare "that it is a command of public decency not to support this company through the purchase of stone material" – a thinly veiled plea for a boycott.[19] However, the legal situation had not changed, and the passage of a state conservation law would not have helped: after all, the forced closure of the quarry would inevitably have brought up damage claims. "It is very much in doubt whether parliament, given the state's current finances, will provide the necessary funds, especially since a look at the size of the investment

---

[15] *Ibid.*, Basaltwerke Immendingen & Hohenstoffeln to the Bezirksamt Engen, March 10, 1913, p. 2.
[16] GLAK Abt. 237 no. 36121, Vermerk über die Begehung des Hohenstoffeln, December 15, 1921.
[17] *Ibid.*, letter of the Amtsvorstand Engen, November 21, 1921.
[18] GLAK Abt. 237 no. 36122, Landesausschuß für Naturpflege in Bayern to the Badisches Staatsministerium, September 24, 1925. Volker Ludwig erroneously dates this resolution to the year 1926. (Ludwig, "Entstehung," 160.)
[19] GLAK Abt. 237 no. 36122, Finanzministerium to the Badische Wasser- und Straßenbaudirektion, March 2, 1925; Abt. 237 no. 36121, Stürzenacker to the Verein Badische Heimat, July 7, 1924.

and the number of workers shows that it will be no small amount," a memorandum of the ministry of education noted regretfully in 1925.[20] Even the chairman of the Heimat League of Baden became resigned after a visit to the quarry, conceding in 1926 "that there is no way to close an enterprise that has invested some 800,000 Reichsmarks, employs a large number of people and produces high-quality basalt gravel."[21]

It was during the 1920s that Ludwig Finckh slowly moved into a leading position in the fight for the Hohenstoffeln. To be sure, he had been active on the Hohenstoffeln almost from the beginning, but only as one of a multitude of voices. However, it is revealing that Finckh was the first to speak at the meeting in December 1921, and his emphatic critique of the "desecration of the *Heimat*" set the tone for the rest of the speakers.[22] By 1925, his pivotal role was so clear that a newspaper referred to the conservationists as "a group of *Heimat*-loving campaigners, with Ludwig Finckh, our cherished local poet, leading the way."[23] At the same time, Finckh's literary fortunes declined, and the novel *The Rose Doctor (Der Rosendoktor)*, published in 1905, remained his only literary success.[24]

However, Finckh's leadership not only meant that an energetic person with great stamina was now in the movement's vanguard. With Finckh, the campaign slowly changed from a politically neutral one, where support came from the Heimat League of Baden as well as the social democratic *Naturfreunde* tourist association, into a campaign with a distinct rightist touch. A virulent anti-Semite, Finckh was sued and fined during the Weimar years when one of his articles on the Hohenstoffeln included a

[20] GLAK Abt. 235 no. 16725, memorandum of the Ministerium des Kultus und Unterrichts, June 24, 1925. Similarly, Abt. 237 no. 36121, Arbeitministerium to the Deutscher Bund Heimatschutz, January 31, 1922. On the range of options in the 1920s, see also StAR Nachlass Ludwig Finckh II a folder 1, Verschönerungs-Verein für das Siebengebirge to Ludwig Finkh, December 13, 1921.

[21] GLAK Abt. 235 no. 16725, memorandum of October 22, 1926.

[22] GLAK Abt. 237 no. 36121, Vermerk über die Begehung des Hohenstoffeln, December 15, 1921, p. 2.

[23] *Neue Badische Landeszeitung* no. 101, February 24, 1925. See also GLAK Abt. 235 no. 16725, Entschließung des Bezirkslehrervereins (Bad. Lehrerverein) Radolfzell-Singen und Engen und Konstanz zum Hohenstoffelnschutz, January 1925. In the 1930s, Finckh himself even noted in a private letter, "The mountain is my fate. The mountain, that's me." (StAR Nachlass Ludwig Finckh II a folder 15, Ludwig Finckh to Erb, September 11, 1934.)

[24] Oesterle, "Doktor Faust," 191; Manfred Bosch, *Bohème am Bodensee. Literarisches Leben am See von 1900 bis 1950* (Lengwil, 1997), 46. His novel on the Hohenstoffeln conflict is a sound demonstration that environmental activism is not necessarily conducive to good writing. (Ludwig Finckh, *Der Goldmacher* [Ulm, 1953].)

reference to the Jew Shylock.[25] In 1932, he was deeply impressed by a speech of Hitler's in his hometown, Reutlingen, stating in a private letter that "he said nothing different from what I have been writing for eleven years."[26] In a chronicle of the Hohenstoffeln conflict published after the war, Finckh spoke of "decline" in the years from 1919 to 1932, and it was obvious that this referred not only to the Hohenstoffeln conflict but also to the Weimar Republic: "discord, party politics, one lawsuit over corruption after another, ... it was hard to still believe in honesty."[27]

After the lawsuit, Finckh was clearly eager to keep a low profile in ideological terms. But after the Nazis' seizure of power, he could speak openly, and Finckh delved into Nazi ideology in a way that made the publications of Schoenichen or Schwenkel pale in comparison. "Two worldviews are clashing here, the worldview of 1913 and the spirit of 1933. The representatives of purely monetary business are standing on the one side, and on the other side all those men who know higher values," Finckh declared in 1933.[28] Furthermore, Finckh tried to cash in on the Nazis' cult of Albert Schlageter, a Freikorps fighter and activist in the anti-Allied resistance in 1923 whom the French had executed during the occupation of the Ruhr region.[29] With the Nazis celebrating Schlageter as a martyr to the German cause, Finckh asserted that Schlageter had visited the Hohenstoffeln in 1922 and carved his initials into a tree – and as it happened, this tree was just at that time standing on the quarry's rim, about to fall if the work progressed.[30] Thinking that the Hohenstoffeln's twin peaks called for two martyrs, Finckh's campaign also referred to Horst Wessel, a prominent member of the Nazi SA units who had been killed by communists in 1930; a poem of Wessel's became the unofficial anthem of Nazi Germany.[31] "Dedicate the Hohenstoffeln as a national monument for Southern Germany, as a memorial to Schlageter and Horst Wessel,"

---

[25] See StAR Nachlass Ludwig Finckh II a folder 1; BArch B 245/3 p. 68r; and Hugo Geißler, "Ludwig Finckhs Kampf um den Hohenstoffeln," *Tuttlinger Heimatblätter* no. 31 (1939): 13. See also DLA Nachlass Ludwig Finckh, Konvolut Material den Hohenstoffel im Hegau betreffend, Ludwig Finckh, Privatbericht, February 14, 1923; and Bosch, *Bohème*, 47n.

[26] DLA Nachlass Will Vesper, Ludwig Finckh to Will Vesper, August 2, 1932.

[27] Finckh, *Kampf um den Hohenstoffeln (1952)*, 4, 6.

[28] BArch B 245/3 p. 399. Similarly, StAR Nachlass Ludwig Finckh II a folder 2, Ludwig Finckh to Wilhelm Kottenrodt, November 8, 1933.

[29] See Elisabeth Hillesheim, *Die Erschaffung eines Märtyrers. Das Bild Albert Leo Schlageters in der deutschen Literatur von 1923 bis 1945* (Frankfurt, 1994).

[30] See Ludwig, "Entstehung," 169.

[31] See Thomas Oertel, *Horst Wessel. Untersuchung einer Legende* (Cologne, 1988).

Finckh demanded in February 1934, proposing "national celebrations" on the Hohenstoffeln that should "advertise the Third Reich" and "the Germany of Adolf Hitler."[32] A memorandum on the Hohenstoffeln, written by Werner Kornfeld of the German Heimat League in collaboration with Ludwig Finckh, spoke of the Hegau's "heroic German landscape" whose destruction would be "completely incomprehensible" under a regime that had broken with the liberalist past: "it is an absurdity to destroy the most eminent mountain of the Hegau in the Third Reich, in an era of reference to the ancestors, of blood and soil and race."[33] On several occasions, Finckh suggested that the lack of popularity of his books was the result of a Jewish conspiracy.[34]

With that, Finckh had moved closer to Nazi ideology than most other conservationists. Finckh not only transformed the Hohenstoffeln campaign into a right-wing crusade, but he also moved toward personal attacks – in other words, toward denunciation. A letter of April 8, 1935, included a number of charges that, if taken seriously, could have inflicted serious harm during the Nazi era. Finckh wrote that a key ally of the mining company was a former "Bolshevik" (*Rätebolschewist*) who had worked "under the Jew Kurt Eisner," the murdered prime minister of Bavaria during the revolution of 1918/1919. Even more, he asserted that the two leaders of the mining company were Freemasons, a group who experienced systematic prosecution during the early years of the Nazi regime. For Finckh, the situation was as follows: "If the Freemasons seek to ruin a person standing in their way because he wants to save a mountain of his *Heimat*, they welcome the use of any creature, no matter how degenerate."[35] Finckh even repeated this assertion in letters that he sent to *Reichsführer-SS* Heinrich Himmler later that year.[36] At the same time, Finckh started an inquiry into the owners' Aryan origins.[37] Fortunately, nobody took Finckh's charges seriously, and the quarry's operators were

[32] BArch B 245/3 p. 381. See also *ibid.*, pp. 287, 382, 397; and GLAK Abt. 237 no. 36122, Ludwig Finckh to the Ministerpräsident in Stuttgart, 12. Hartung [sic] 1934.

[33] BArch Berlin Document Center RSK II no. I 107 p. 1576.

[34] See DLA Nachlass Will Vesper, Ludwig Finckh to Will Vesper, March 22, 1933; and BArch Berlin Document Center RSK II no. I 107 p. 2070.

[35] GLAK Abt. 237 no. 36123, Ludwig Finckh to the Reichsstatthalter Robert Wagner, April 8, 1935.

[36] BArch Berlin Document Center RSK II no. I 107 pp. 1696, 1700; StAR Nachlass Ludwig Finckh II a folder 15, Ludwig Finckh to the Reichsführer SS, September 9, 1934. See also *ibid.* folder 14, Karl F. Finus, Bericht über die Unterredung Dr. Udo Rousselle – Dipl. Landw. Finus in Seeshaupt, September 1, 1934.

[37] StAR Nachlass Ludwig Finckh II a folder 5, Ludwig Finckh to the Ortsgruppenleiter der NSDAP Frankfurt, June 5, 1934.

FIGURE 4.2. "Stofflio" – the trademark greeting of the followers of Ludwig Finckh in their fight for the Hohenstoffeln Mountain, here seen on Finckh's letter paper. Printed with permission from the Ludwigh Finckh papers at the Reutlingen city archive.

never prosecuted, but that does little to excuse either the words or the intention. In resorting to denunciations, Finckh clearly crossed yet another threshold.[38]

But with 230 employees in 1933, the mining company was still an important factor for the local economy, and especially so at the time of the Great Depression.[39] Therefore, the local mayors generally supported the company, and other institutions like the German ministry of trade and commerce and the *Deutsche Arbeitsfront*, the workers' representation in Nazi Germany, likewise opposed the quarry's closure.[40] But it was not only jobs that made for the reservations of some Nazi leaders toward Finckh: it was even more disturbing from the Nazis' point of view that Finckh's work clearly took the form of a public campaign – for that, from the Nazis' standpoint, was synonymous with stirring up unrest and discontent. In April 1934, Ludwig Finckh published a petition entitled "German landscape in peril" with a long list of signatories that read like a "Who's Who" of German conservation; the most prominent names

[38] Ironically, Finckh also suspected Karl Asal, conservation official in the ministry of education, to be a Freemason and warned his allies not to discuss plans with him. (StAR Nachlass Ludwig Finckh II a folder 36, Stoffelfunk of March 22, 1935.)

[39] GLAK Abt. 237 no. 36122, Der Präsident des Badischen Gewerbeaufsichtsamtes to the Finanz- und Wirtschaftsminister, October 3, 1933. For more detailed employment figures, see Ludwig, "Entstehung," 162.

[40] *Ibid.*, Vermerk über die Begehung des Steinbruchs Hohenstoffeln on May 26, 1934, Deutsche Arbeitsfront to the Ministerium der Finanzen und der Wirtschaft, September 30, 1933, and July 5, 1934, Der Reichswirtschaftsminister to the Reichsminister des Innern, June 29, 1934.

were Paul Schultze-Naumburg, Martin Heidegger, Walther Schoenichen, Karl Johannes Fuchs, Hans Schwenkel, Lina Hähnle, Paul Schmitthenner, Ludwig Klages, Wilhelm Münker, Konrad Günther, Werner Lindner, Werner Haverbeck, and Fritz Todt.[41] In June 1934, Finckh went even further when he used a convention of the German Hiking and Mountain Climbing Association (*Deutscher Wander- und Bergsteigerverband*) in Berlin to fight for his cause, thus transforming the assembly into a rally for the Hohenstoffeln's rescue.[42] With that, Finckh had clearly overstepped the limits of legitimate conservation work during the Nazi era, and the Nazis finally intervened: the regional newspapers were advised not to report on the event, and internal remarks indicate that the administration's patience was running out.[43] "This extraordinary activism of Dr. Finckh is at odds with our official line of reasoning which refuses any kind of agitation in the general public," the prime minister of Baden wrote immediately after the conference, arguing "that one can and should deal with this question without stirring the passion of the public." Two months later, he urged "a containment of public discussions over the problem of the mountain's rescue."[44] In December 1934, Robert Wagner, the Reich Commissioner (*Reichsstatthalter*) for the state of Baden, wrote a furious letter to Finckh, informing him that he was "tired and sick" of the issue and "advising" Finckh to "exercise restraint" in the future.[45]

It would have been easy for the Nazis to stop the movement to save the Hohenstoffeln. All that it would have taken to decapitate the efforts was the arrest of Ludwig Finckh – and the Nazis were not known for being picky about arrests. In fact, Finckh was under surveillance by the Gestapo in May 1935, though it is not clear whether this was related to Robert Wagner's outburst of anger; the Gestapo thought that Finckh's complaints over the Third Reich's inaction, voiced in a private letter, included "some critical remarks against the Nazi state."[46] However, Finckh was never

---

[41] GLAK Abt. 237 no. 36122, Deutsche Landschaft in Gefahr, April 1934. Also BArch B 245/3 pp. 323–4, 354–7.

[42] BArch B 245/3 pp. 286, 291. See StAR Nachlass Ludwig Finckh II a folder 5, Reichsverband deutscher Gebirgs- und Wandervereine, June 1934, for the convention's annoucement.

[43] GLAK Abt. 237 no. 36122, Landesstelle Baden des Reichsministeriums für Volksaufklärung und Propaganda to Ministerpräsident Walter Köhler, June 18, 1934.

[44] *Ibid.*, Badisches Staatsministerium, Der Ministerpräsident, to the Reichsminister des Innern, June 26, 1934; GLAK Abt. 237 no. 36123, Der Ministerpräsident to the Stellvertreter des Führers, Reichsminister Heß, September 21, 1934.

[45] StAR Nachlass Ludwig Finckh II a folder 29, Der Reichsstatthalter in Baden to Ludwig Finckh, December 1, 1934; BARch B 245/3 p. 16.

[46] GLAK Abt. 237 no. 36123, letter of the Landeskriminalpolizei Konstanz, Geheime Staatspolizei, May 25, 1935.

arrested, though he did face an investigation as a party member from a NSDAP county board – yet another turn in a strangely convoluted tale.[47] More than any other story, the Hohenstoffeln campaign shows the confusion that the polycentric administrative structure of Nazi Germany could produce: economic interests and jobs, the protection of nature, and the Nazis' censure of public agitation came together in a plot that, though rational in its own terms, objectively bordered on the absurd. There were a lot of things for which one could blame Ludwig Finckh, but disloyalty to the Nazi regime was certainly not one of them.[48]

As a result, it is surprisingly difficult to define clearly Finckh's role in the Hohenstoffeln conflict. Of course, he was the central figure in the entire conflict from the mid-1920s, but defining the precise nature of his centrality and the true character of his leadership is tricky. He phrased his protest in a distinctly Nazi way, and yet he was walking on thin ice politically. He kept the issue alive through his tireless campaigning, and yet it is doubtful whether his rhetoric always helped his cause. Even for a person sympathetic to his concerns, it was taxing to receive a constant flow of letters that laid out the mountain's plight in Finckh's pathetic, long-winded, and frequently aggressive style. Finckh could get his views published in the *Völkischer Beobachter*, the Nazis' leading newspaper, in September 1933, but a few months later, newspapers were banned from reporting on his Berlin rally.[49] He received support from some Nazi leaders, whereas others brusquely advised him to shut up. Paradoxes abounded, and they did so because the Hohenstoffeln campaign revealed the tension between Nazism's totalitarian ideals and its polycentric reality. In a way, Finckh was successfully doing the impossible: he was running a conservation campaign in a state that claimed a monopoly on political campaigns.

However, Finckh found not only resistance among Nazi leaders but also sympathy, and that probably saved him from prosecution. Although Finckh's campaign was eyed suspiciously, the cause itself touched a nerve

---

[47] BArch Berlin Document Center RSK II no. I 107 p. 1700. See also StAR Nachlass Ludwig Finckh II a folder 40, Karl Model to the Gauleitung der Nationalsozialistischen Deutschen Arbeiterpartei, Abteilung Parteigericht in Radolfzell, February 2, 1936.

[48] Asked for its opinion when Finckh appeared on the Gestapo's radar screen, the police confirmed that Finckh "stood completely and totally behind the government," citing the mayor of Gaienhofen, Finckh's hometown, as witness. (GLAK Abt. 237 no. 36123, Gendarmerie-Station Wangen to the Bezirksamt Geheime Staatspolizei Konstanz, June 5, 1935.)

[49] See Ludwig Finckh, "Der Kampf um den Hohenstoffeln," *Völkischer Beobachter, Norddeutsche Ausgabe* 46.264 (September 21, 1933): 9.

in some circles, and a rapid succession of measures was the result. Ironically, the first success was a financial one: the mining company agreed to pay 3,000 Reichsmarks per year to the ministry of education of Baden to compensate for the scenic damage it was inflicting.[50] Of course, such a materialist fix did little to silence an idealistic movement – Karl Ferdinand Finus, a close ally of Finckh, spoke bluntly of "blood money"[51] – and a new measure followed within a matter of months. But now, the initiative was with the Reich agencies in Berlin, rather than the state ministries in Karlsruhe, mirroring a centralization of decisions that was typical of the Nazi state. In November 1934, the German ministry of the interior ordered a halt to all operations on the upper part of the quarry, effectively putting the mountain top under protection. In the absence of a state conservation law, it was a daring decree in judicial terms, but when challenged to produce a proper legitimation, the ministry of the interior found a creative one: the decree referred to the constitution of Weimar! As mentioned above, article 150 of the Weimar constitution defined the protection of natural monuments as the duty of the state, and because the Nazis had never formally suspended the constitution, the article made for a suitable point of reference – at least for a regime that cared more about action than the letter of the law. The travesty of the rule of the law becomes complete when one looks at the decree's date: it was enacted on November 9, 1934, the anniversary of Hitler's failed 1923 putsch and the highest holiday in Nazi Germany.[52] However, the decree was obviously seen as a mere makeshift, and within days of the passage of the national conservation law, the Reich Forest Service and Schoenichen's conservation agency were working on a new decree that rested on sounder footing. After a visit on July 20, 1935, the German Forest Service came up with a compromise in its ensuing decree. It created a nature reserve on the Hohenstoffeln, but limited it to the upper stretches of the mountain: protection ended 300 feet below the summit. With that, the Forest Service sought to preserve the face of the mountain while avoiding a closure of the quarry.[53]

---

[50] GLAK Abt. 237 no. 36122, Der Minister des Kultus, des Unterrichts und der Justiz to the Finanz- und Wirtschaftsminister, November 8, 1933; Abt. 235 no. 6548, memorandum of the Minister des Kultus, des Unterrichts und der Justiz, January 8, 1934.

[51] StAR Nachlass Ludwig Finckh II a folder 14, Karl F. Finus, Bericht über die Unterredung Dr. Udo Rousselle – Dipl. Landw. Finus in Seeshaupt, September 1, 1934, p. 3.

[52] BArch B 245/3 pp. 256–56r.

[53] GLAK Abt. 237 no. 36123, Der Reichsforstmeister to the Badischer Finanz- und Wirtschaftsminister, August 24, 1935.

The decree explicitly referred to the "unpleasant fights" since 1933 over the Hohenstoffeln and was clearly written with the intention of ending the previous strife. This seemed to meet with success, for the bitterness of the earlier fights mostly disappeared and many parties were content with the compromise. The Inspector General for the German Roadways rescinded a ban on supplies from the Hohenstoffeln that Fritz Todt had previously imposed, and Schoenichen's conservation agency began to work on a plan for planting the quarry to bring it into a more natural state; an article in a regionalist journal already celebrated the movement's ultimate success.[54] However, Ludwig Finckh saw the continuation of mining operations as a defeat, and the economic boom of the late 1930s was working in his favor. With unemployment in steady decline, the mining company found it more and more difficult to find people willing to do the dangerous work: in September 1938, it employed only ninety-eight workers, sixteen of whom were Italians.[55] And Finckh finally found a way to repeal the 1935 decree. With Werner Kornfeld of the German Heimat League and Wolfram Sievers of the *SS-Ahnenerbe* research division to relay his concern, he successfully urged Heinrich Himmler to send a letter to Hermann Göring calling for the quarry's closure.[56] Presumably, it was the Hohenstoffeln's "great historic past" that inspired the *Reichsführer-SS* to react: Himmler's letter spoke of a "Germanic fortress" on the mountain top.[57] Göring followed suit and ordered to close the Hohenstoffeln quarry with a telegram on Christmas Eve, 1938.[58] In spite of protests from the company and the chamber of commerce, mining operations finally ceased on the Hohenstoffeln by the end of 1939.[59]

---

[54] GLAK Abt. 237 no. 41672, Der Generalinspektor für das deutsche Straßenwesen to the Badisches Finanz- und Wirtschaftsministerium, February 12, 1936, and Der Direktor der Staatlichen Stelle für Naturdenkmalpflege in Preußen to the Badisches Ministerium des Kultus und Unterrichts, September 27, 1935; W. Pfeiffer, "Wie steht es um den Hohenstoffeln?," *Schwäbisches Heimatbuch* 1936: 118. See also Abt. 237 no. 36122, memorandum of the Badisches Finanz- und Wirtschaftsministerium, June 16, 1934.

[55] GLAK Abt. 237 no. 41672, Süddeutsche Basaltwerke to the Badisches Finanz- und Wirtschaftsministerium, September 18, 1938.

[56] See proceedings in BArch Berlin Document Center RSK II no. I 107 and BArch NS 21/99.

[57] BArch Berlin Document Center RSK II no. I 107 p. 1586. See also Finckh's corresponding remarks in StAR Nachlass Ludwig Finckh II a folder 36, Ludwig Finckh to the Reichsführer SS Chefadjutantur, March 30, 1935.

[58] GLAK Abt. 235 no. 48275, telegram to the Höhere Naturschutzbehörde Baden, December 24, 1938.

[59] GLAK Abt. 455 Zug. 1991/49 no. 1356, Der Minister des Kultus und Unterrichts to the Landrat Konstanz, August 21, 1939. For the futile protests of industry, see Abt. 237 no. 41672.

With this success after almost three decades of campaigning, Ludwig Finckh was jubilant, and he celebrated his victory with a fawning magazine article: "It was a symbol: the Führer's principles are not simply written on paper, they become a fact, a truth, they lead towards realization."[60] In an interview shortly after the announcement of the closing, Finckh was even more outspoken: "I see this as a victory of the German law over the Roman-Jewish literal interpretation of the law."[61] "The German spirit has won over the American one," a party official from Freiburg emphatically declared, whereas the more sober Hans Klose spoke of "a milestone in the history of nature protection." Gotthold Wurster even published a booklet with excerpts from the letters of congratulations that reached Finckh and his allies.[62] The fate of the workers was not of much concern to the conservationists, and in fact had never been. Finckh rarely dealt with economic and social issues, and if he did, his statements smacked of arrogance. In a letter to the journal *Bodenreform* (Land Reform) in 1933, he argued for the protection of the Hohenstoffeln on social grounds: "excessive quarrying has transformed the sons of peasants into industrial workers; they shall return to their native soil."[63] Two years later, Finckh declared that although "one cannot expect much understanding" for the needs of conservation among workers so far, that would change when "we educators of the people" have done the necessary work "for the soul of the nation."[64]

Incidentally, the loss of jobs did not become a problem for the Hegau region because the war effectively ended unemployment in Germany. However, a second problem did not solve itself: how should the state deal with the costs that its decision implied for the mining company? During the 1920s, Finckh had still spoken of the necessity of compensation, once proposing a "public 'mountain protection' lottery" to the ministry

[60] Ludwig Finckh, "Der Kampf um den Hohenstoffel," *Schwaben* 11 (1939): 219.

[61] *Der Führer. Hauptorgan der NSDAP Gau Baden* 13.16 (January 16, 1939): 4. Similarly, Ludwig Finckh, "Die Entscheidung am Hohenstoffeln," *Schwäbisches Heimatbuch* 1939: 174.

[62] BArch B 245/3 p. 176; Klose, "Corona imperii," 38; Gotthold Wurster (ed.), *Der Hohenstoffeln unter Naturschutz 1939. Widerhall und Dank des deutschen Volkes* (Heidenheim, n.d.).

[63] *Bodenreform* 44 (1933): col. 295.

[64] GLAK Abt. 237 no. 36123, letter of Ludwig Finckh, March 15, 1935. Tellingly, a list of alternative work projects that Finckh compiled in 1934 included the cultivation of wasteland as the first item, an activity that conservationists in all parts of Germany unanimously abhorred. (StAR Nachlass Ludwig Finckh II a folder 29, Ludwig Finckh, Arbeitsbeschaffungsplan für den Fall einer Betriebseinschränkung am Hohenstoffeln, December 5, 1934.)

of education.[65] However, his radicalization after 1933 quickly rendered ideas of this kind obsolete, and Finckh was silent on the issue during the Nazi era. In a 1934 letter to his lawyer, Finckh directly called for the expropriation of Baron von Hornstein because "owners who surrender the mountain of their forefathers have forfeited their property right."[66] Interestingly, it was Hans Klose who pointed to the need for some kind of indemnification: "as much as I was in favor of rescuing the Hohenstoffeln, I am at a loss to completely agree with one-sided measures, for they would be nothing but expropriation."[67] But with the company's loss exceeding one million Reichsmarks, the costs of indemnification were prohibitive, and the German ministry of finance pointed out that the company was not entitled to compensation according to the National Conservation Law.[68] Internal discussions continued until far into the war, but to no avail.[69] After brief talk of reopening the quarry after 1945, the issue fell dormant.

Ultimately, Ludwig Finckh had won, but it was an ambivalent victory in retrospect. After all, his success implied enormous costs to the mining company, which was effectively robbed of its property, and to the conservation movement, in the form of right-wing ideology, which became intrinsically linked to the cause. However, Finckh did not show signs of remorse in either regard after the war. Recalling the fight in a letter of 1949, Finckh pictured himself as the leader of an innocent band of conservationists that somehow managed to prevail against insurmountable powers: "we were a small, impoverished, but undeterred group of *Heimat* friends. But our call was full of strength, and it found resonance in the entire German nation."[70] Interestingly, Hans Klose mostly agreed, even though he had not been involved personally in the contacts with Himmler and the *Ahnenerbe*.[71] In fact, it seems that Klose, ever the power broker, tacitly admired the way Finckh had managed to mobilize the *Reichsführer-SS*: "Given the situation in 1938, it was a very clever move of the Hohenstoffeln's friends to use the influential Herr Himmler as an instrument for a good cause. Nobody will want to blame us for that."[72] He was clearly

---

[65] GLAK Abt. 235 no. 16725, Ludwig Finckh to the Ministerium für Kultus und Unterricht, July 23, 1925.
[66] StAR Nachlass Ludwig Finckh II a folder 15, Ludwig Finckh to Erb, September 11, 1934.
[67] GLAK Abt. 235 no. 48275, Der Direktor der Reichsstelle für Naturschutz to Ministerialrat Asal of the Ministerium des Kultus und Unterrichts, May 7, 1940.
[68] BArch R 2/4731 pp. 41–2, 45.
[69] BArch B 245/3 pp. 80–2, 85–6, R 2/4731 pp. 43, 57–8, 64, 69.
[70] BArch B 245/3 p. 11.
[71] *Ibid.* p. 126.
[72] *Ibid.* p. 54r.

FIGURE 4.3. The Hohenstoffeln Mountain today. Note the sharp decline on the left slope, the site of the former quarry. Photo by author.

wrong on the second point and certainly naïve on the first one. From a strictly tactical view, one might indeed speak of a "clever move." But was it not advisable, after 1945, with knowledge of the full horror of the Nazi regime, to add a moral dimension to such a perspective? After all, it was well known in 1946 that Himmler was not only the head of the German police state but also the chief organizer of the Holocaust. And this was not the last time that he became involved in conservation issues.

The Schorfheide National Nature Reserve

On the evening of April 30, 1935, Hermann Göring took charge of German conservation through his famous telephone call with Bernhard Rust. After he hung up, Göring's thoughts drifted to a related issue on which he elaborated for the rest of the meeting: the future of the Schorfheide. This wooded area with a number of beautiful lakes, some forty miles from downtown Berlin, was clearly dear to his heart, and the officials present must have sensed that Göring's true motivation on conservation issues lay in his concern for this area. Göring was not sure whether the Schorfheide should find a place in the national conservation law that he had just set on its tracks. He reasoned that a separate law probably better suited his ideas. However, the general direction for the Schorfheide was clear in Göring's remarks: he sought to create a special nature reserve, "similar in its design to the national parks in North America."[73]

Göring was not the first of the powerful to feel a deep affection for the Schorfheide's treasures. In fact, the romance of the powers-that-be with the Schorfheide's forests dated back to the twelfth century, when members of the nobility first went to hunt in the area.[74] Hunting continued to be the Schorfheide's prime use for centuries, and monarchs guarded the area's wildlife carefully. Around 1590, the Elector of Brandenburg ordered the construction of a fence of some 30 miles length along the Schorfheide's border to the Uckermark to prevent big game from leaving to the north.[75] With the construction of a special hunting lodge in the mid-nineteenth century, named Hubertusstock after the patron saint of hunting, royal visits grew more frequent, and Emperor Wilhelm II visited the Schorfheide at least once every year during his reign.[76] In his famous descriptions of the Brandenburg region, Theodor Fontane praised the rich game population and even spoke of a "unique" area where the Prussian monarchs would hunt only on special days to make an impression on their guests.[77] In the summer of 1885, the Russian Tsar Alexander III took up residence in the Hubertusstock lodge.[78]

Royal hunting could be taxing on the environment, but after some excesses during the nineteenth century, Wilhelm II imposed a ban on large-scale hunting that remained in effect until 1945.[79] For the Schorfheide's game, the most difficult times in the early twentieth century were probably the revolutionary years of 1919 and 1920, when a great deal of illegal

---

73 *Akten der Reichskanzlei* vol. 2.1, 557.
74 Erwin Nippert, *Die Schorfheide. Zur Geschichte einer deutschen Landschaft*, 2nd edition (Berlin, 1995), 65.
75 Hannelore Kurth-Gilsenbach, *Schorfheide und Choriner Land* (Neumanns Land-schaftsführer, Radebeul, 1993), 18. On the issue of fencing and other environmental implications of early modern hunting, see Martin Knoll, "Hunting in the Eighteenth Century: An Environmental History Perspective," *Historical Social Research* 29, 3 (2004): 9–36.
76 Nippert, *Schorfheide*, 70, 73.
77 Theodor Fontane, *Wanderungen durch die Mark Brancenburg. Zweiter Band: Das Oder-land* (Munich, 1960), 429n.
78 Knopf and Martens, *Görings Reich*, 24.
79 Erwin Buchholz and Ferdinand Coninx, *Die Schorfheide. 700 Jahre Jagdrevier* (Stuttgart, 1969), 109, 114.

hunting led to a sharp decline of red deer.[80] However, the game population soon rebounded, and the regional government put a large part of the Schorfheide under protection in 1930.[81] German politicians continued to show a penchant for the area during the Weimar years, and the first German president, Friedrich Ebert, repeatedly came to the Hubertusstock lodge for recreation.[82] Somewhat unusual for a Social Democrat, Ebert was also interested in hunting, as was his successor Paul von Hindenburg, a World War I general who became president of the Weimar Republic in 1925. Hindenburg's presidency has often been described as conducive to the decline of the republic, but his behavior in the Schorfheide was impeccable. He applied in writing for a license to kill one stag during each season, and when, after several days of stalking, he once encountered a prime specimen that happened to stand on the border between two forestry districts, he refused to shoot because he only had a license for one of the districts.[83]

Thus, it was by no means surprising that Göring showed an interest in the Schorfheide. Moreover, Göring's interest grew out of the same penchant for hunting that had long been a privilege of the rulers in the region. Göring made his first hunting trips to the Schorfheide during the late 1920s and quickly fell in love with the area.[84] He did not hesitate to reserve a place for himself in the Schorfheide as soon as he could: being the prime minister of Prussia and the state's supreme forester, he arranged for some 300 acres to be set aside for his lifetime use in early 1933. At the same time, Hitler created a special fund that Göring could use at his pleasure.[85] With these means at hand, Göring ordered the construction of a mansion in the Schorfheide's forests, and within 10 months, work was complete on the best-known and most pompous of Göring's many residences: Carinhall.[86] The name paid tribute to Göring's deceased wife Carin, whose remains rested in a mausoleum that Göring built with the

---

[80] Max Rehberg, "Pflanzenkleid, Tierwelt und Naturschutz," in Max Rehberg and Max Weiss (eds.), *Zwischen Schorfheide und Spree. Heimatbuch des Kreises Niederbarnim* (Berlin, 1940), 42.

[81] BArch B 245/233 p. 78. Even in some recent publications, the legend persists that the nature reserve originated in Göring's initiative: e.g., Andreas Kittler, *Hermann Görings Carinhall. Der Waldhof in der Schorfheide* (Berg, 1997), 56; and Gröning and Wolschke-Bulmahn, *Liebe zur Landschaft Teil 1*, 210.

[82] Nippert, *Schorfheide*, 83.

[83] Buchholz and Coninx, *Schorfheide*, 111n.

[84] Nippert, *Schorfheide*, 17.

[85] Knopf and Martens, *Görings Reich*, 25; Mosley, *Reich Marshal*, 180.

[86] See Knopf and Martens, *Görings Reich*, 7.

house. Göring turned the mausoleum's inauguration, in June 1934, into a pompous celebration that took the form of an act of state. It was the only time during his tenure that Hitler paid a visit to the Schorfheide.[87]

Construction on the Carinhall residence continued almost constantly through the Nazi era, and the complex soon earned an ambiguous reputation in the population at large. In their book on the Carinhall complex, Volker Knopf and Stefan Martens estimate that the total costs of Göring's building activities in the Schorfheide amounted to 7,512,155 Reichsmarks – this at a time when a house for one family cost about 10,000 Reichsmarks.[88] But Göring's interest always extended beyond Carinhall's security barriers to the Schorfheide in general. Already in 1933, government minutes recorded Göring's intention to halt all kinds of development in the area.[89] Thus, it was only natural that the national conservation law included a provision aimed specifically at the Schorfheide, the only German nature reserve that was mentioned by name in the official comment to the law's draft.[90] Paragraph 18 of the national conservation law provided for the creation of national nature reserves (*Reichsnaturschutzgebiete*).[91] A look at the implementation of this clause shows that the guiding thought was to accommodate Göring's penchant for hunting: all four national nature reserves – the Schorfheide, the Darß in West Pomerania, the Rominten in East Prussia, and the delta of the Memel River in the same province – offered rich game populations to a privileged group of hunters.[92] National nature reserves were allowed only on state property, and the law provided for the creation of a special state body for land purchases within the Forest Service (*Reichsstelle für Landbeschaffung*). Interestingly, the national nature reserves were excluded from the law's indemnity clause, and confiscation was allowed only with "proper compensation" – though one may doubt that the payments were on a par with market prices.[93] The Schorfheide became a national nature reserve in early 1937; in 1939, the area under protection grew from 125,000 to 141,200 acres.[94]

[87] Mosley, *Reich Marshal*, 180–4; Nippert, *Schorfheide*, 26.

[88] Knopf and Martens, *Görings Reich*, 107n.

[89] See BArch B 245/233, pp. 48, 142.

[90] BArch B 2/4730 p. 77.

[91] Schoenichen and Weber, *Reichsnaturschutzgesetz*, 87.

[92] See Reinhard Piechocki, "'Reichsnaturschutzgebiete' – Vorläufer der Nationalparke?" *Nationalpark* 107 (2000): 28–33.

[93] See Schoenichen and Weber, *Reichsnaturschutzgesetz*, 28, 87–9; and Piechocki, "Reichsnaturschutzgebiete," 29.

[94] BArch B 245/233 pp. 50, 74.

FIGURE 4.4. Hermann Göring leading a group of visitors through the Schorfheide National Nature Reserve. The people to the right of Göring are Lutz Heck, director of the Berlin zoo and in charge of nature protection within the forest service since 1938; Max Esser, a sculptor; and Water von Keudell, head of the German forest service until 1937. Photo from Ullstein Bild.

During the Nazi era, the Schorfheide National Nature Reserve won a special reputation through attempts to reintroduce previously extinct species. For Göring, a true German wilderness would be home to a number of animals that had long disappeared from the German heartland, thus almost unlimited resources were available for a number of reintroduction projects.[95] With the help of the Berlin zoo and its director, Lutz Heck, a bison reserve was set up in the Schorfheide, and the bison population had grown to some seventy animals by 1940.[96] The gamekeepers also tried to breed wild horses in the Schorfheide, with some Przewalski horses from zoological gardens among them, but the herd comprised only sixteen specimens by the end of the war.[97] The breeding of moose

[95] See Buchholz and Coninx, *Schorfheide*, 79.
[96] Nippert, *Schorfheide*, 121n; Horst Siewert, "Die Schorfheide," in Rehberg and Weiss, *Zwischen Schorfheide und Spree*, 232.
[97] Kurth-Gilsenbach, *Schorfheide*, 22; Nippert, *Schorfheide*, 123.

turned out to be even more difficult, and the integration project ultimately failed: the Schorfheide's forests provided neither the food nor the space that the moose enjoyed in their traditional homelands.[98] In the summer of 1942, a moose found its way into the Carinhall estate and started to eat the park's flowers; Göring sent out a full company of soldiers to catch the animal and release it in a different part of the Schorfheide, but the moose returned to Carinhall within a matter of days and finally had to be shot. The last remaining moose was killed in 1943 while roaming the outskirts of Berlin.[99] Further reintroduction efforts dealt with mufflons, beavers, and eagle-owls.[100] In 1935, a well-funded research institute on game issues (*Forschungsstätte Deutsches Wild*) opened in the eastern part of the Schorfheide reserve.[101]

For Göring, the reintroduction of these species was not only the realization of archaic fantasies but also a question of prestige. Thus, Göring tried to put on a show when a bull from Canada arrived at the bison reserve. Ten days before Carinhall's pompous inauguration, Göring invited some forty guests, with the ambassadors of France, Britain, Italy, and the United States among them, to a special ceremony in the Schorfheide reserve. Arriving late in an open sports car, Göring explained his intentions for the Schorfheide and then led his guests to the bison reserve, where a number of bison cows were about to meet the bull. Spontaneously baptizing the bull "Ivan the Terrible," Göring ordered the bull's transport box opened, and the Reich's second-in-command learned that there were limits to his powers: "Ivan" took a few timid steps into his new home, took an unenthusiastic glance at the females, turned around, and, to the gamekeepers' consternation, tried to get back into his box.[102] "This part of the programme... did not fulfil our expectations," the British ambassador Sir Eric Phipps wrote in his memorandum. Phipps had gotten used to a more proactive type of bull during a previous assignment in Spain, and his report provided a scathing description of Göring's regime in the Schorfheide. "The whole proceedings were so strange as at times to convey a feeling of unreality," Phipps noted about the event, which also included an exhaustive tour of the Carinhall residence and the mausoleum. "The chief impression was that of the almost pathetic naïveté of General Göring, who showed us his toys like a big, fat, spoilt child." But the report closed

[98] Ulrich Scherping, *Waidwerk zwischen den Zeiten* (Berlin and Hamburg, 1950), 84.
[99] Buchholz and Coninx, *Schorfheide*, 86; Scherping, *Waidwerk*, 85.
[100] See Buchholz and Coninx, *Schorfheide*, 79–89.
[101] Kurth-Gilsenbach, *Schorfheide*, 22; Buchholz and Coninx, *Schorfheide*, 126n.
[102] Knopf and Martens, *Görings Reich*, 37.

on a gloomy note, for Phipps felt that the seemingly harmless spectacle revealed a deeper, more worrisome truth: "And then I remembered there were other toys, less innocent, though winged, and these might some day be launched on their murderous mission in the same child-like spirit and with the same childlike glee."[103] The confidential report, soon to be nick-named the "bison dispatch," became so popular among its readers that even Göring ultimately learned of it, and Göring's relations with Phipps cooled as a result.[104] However, the general public showed more inter-est in Göring's animal farm: opened in 1936, a game reserve with some 200 animals on display drew more than 100,000 visitors during its first year and a half.[105]

Because of the size of the area, the Schorfheide's popularity never came into conflict with ceremonies and acts of state in Carinhall. In fact, Göring sought to promote the area's attractiveness to the general public through a special Schorfheide Foundation (*Stiftung Schorfheide*). Brought into being by a law of January 25, 1936, the foundation was designed "to awake and deepen a sense of connectedness with nature, especially among the urban population"; at the same time, the foundation was to create "a protected reserve" for threatened plants and animals.[106] With funding from the Prussian state, the foundation was made responsible for an area roughly identical with that of the national nature reserve. Paul Körner initially chaired the foundation's work, to be succeeded by Erich Gritzbach, the author of a servile Göring biography.[107] However, the foundation also served another purpose, which becomes clear from its list of expenses for 1936: the foundation's budget reserved no less than 225,000 Reichsmarks for hunting expenses![108] There can be no doubt that this huge sum was the result of Göring's expensive hunting excursions, and it would not be surprising if the foundation's money also covered some other expenses; after all, Göring was notorious for his waste of money even during the Nazi era.[109] There are no financial records available for the foundation

---

[103] E. L. Woodward and Rohan Butler (eds.), *Documents on British Foreign Policy 1919–1939*, 2nd series, vol. 6 (London, 1957), 749–51.

[104] Knopf and Martens, *Görings Reich*, 38.

[105] Siewert, "Schorfheide," 235. Gritzbach reported 140,000 visitors in 1936 alone. (Gritzbach, *Hermann Göring*, 110.)

[106] Mitzschke, *Das Reichsnaturschutzgesetz*, 72.

[107] Knopf and Martens, *Görings Reich*, 34.

[108] BArch R 2/4730 p. 157. See also Andreas Gautschi, *Die Wirkung Hermann Görings auf das deutsche Jagdwesen im Dritten Reich* (Ph.D. dissertation, Göttingen University, 1997), 115, 236–8.

[109] Bajohr, *Parvenüs*, 67.

during the following years, but given that it provided a budget outside the normal administration, and given that Göring's extravagant style assured a constant flow of bills to be paid, it seems likely that a good part of the foundation's revenues went into sustaining Göring's lifestyle. With the Schorfheide Foundation, conservation provided camouflage for governmental corruption.

In a way, this abuse of conservation had its own logic. After all, Göring's conservation policy had always served a double purpose: the same nature reserve that provided a haven for animals and plants was also a perfect backdrop to the Carinhall residence and a playground for the dedicated hunter. And this was not the only case during the Nazi era where conservation and corruption went hand in hand. For example, Hamburg's *Gauleiter* Karl Kaufmann suddenly discovered his penchant for the protection of nature when it provided a pretense for the occupation of a proper hunting reserve. Being, like so many *Gauleiters*, a dedicated hunter, Kaufmann had to contend with the limited means of the city-state of Hamburg, which offered neither large forest areas nor a significant stock of game within its borders. However, when the city-state grew considerably after the passage of the Greater Hamburg Law in 1937, Kaufmann jumped into action. Having his eyes on the Duvenstedter Brook on the northern outskirts of the greater Hamburg, he assured the area's designation as a nature reserve, fenced it off at state expense, declared the area off-limits to the general public, and had the state government transfer the hunting rights to him. Stocking the area with a sizable red deer population, he finally had the hunting reserve that he had been craving.[110] Ironically, the frustration of the area's residents was shared by Martin Bormann, the powerful chief of the Nazi Party's chancellery, who discovered after a *Gauleiter* meeting in early 1942 that many of the participants were so eager to tell their hunting stories that Bormann found it impossible to touch on other topics of greater political significance.[111]

However, extravagances of this kind did not jeopardize the position of either Göring or Kaufmann. Göring did gradually fall from grace with Hitler, but that had more to do with political failures than with his wasteful reign in the Schorfheide: Göring's boastful pledge as head of the

---

[110] Hans Walden, "Zur Geschichte des Duvenstedter Brooks," *Naturschutz und Landschaftspflege in Hamburg* 46 (1995): 17; Hans Walden, "Untersuchungen zur Geschichte des Duvenstedter Brooks," *Mitteilungen zum Natur- und Umweltschutz in Hamburg* 3 (1987): 26–32. For the official legitimation of the Duvenstedter Brook nature reserve, see BArch B 245/196 pp. 405–7.

[111] Bajohr, *Parvenüs*, 72.

Luftwaffe that no Allied plane would ever reach Berlin became symbolic of his ineptitude. To compensate for his declining fortunes, Göring spent more and more time in his beloved Schorfheide, and Carinhall eventually became the official headquarters of the German Air Force.[112] Within his realm in the Schorfheide, Göring continued to act like an absolute ruler. When a forest fire raged there in the summer of 1942, Göring appeared at the scene when the fire was already under control and pestered fire fighters with calls to guard the fence of the bison reserve, which had suffered from the fire, ignoring protestations that the bison had fled from the fire into other parts of the 1,500 acre reserve. Months later, Göring still prided himself on having forestalled a potential disaster with his swift reaction.[113] Authorities also continued to purchase land for conservation purposes, and in 1942 a government decree enlarged the Schorfheide national nature reserve from 141,200 to 185,500 acres.[114] In January 1945, with the Allied troops at the German borders preparing for the battle that would end the war, guests at Göring's birthday party could admire, if they were in the mood, his plans for yet another expansion of the Carinhall estate. A Hermann Göring Museum, with a central building of some 1,000 feet length, was scheduled for opening on Göring's sixtieth birthday, January 12, 1953.[115]

The events of the following months spoiled these glamorous dreams. Göring spent the last weeks of the war in Carinhall, busy with the shipment of the art treasures he had acquired during the previous 12 years.[116] During that time, Göring also ordered his beloved bisons shot. The Carinhall estate, which experienced neither bomb attacks nor artillery fire for the entire duration of the war, was mined and finally blown up on April 28, 1945, when the first Red Army patrols appeared in the vicinity.[117] It took some 10 years to clean the ruins from the area, though attentive visitors can still discover some slabs of concrete at the location.[118] The Schorfheide's plants and animals did not fare much better after 1945,

---

[112] Nippert, *Schorfheide*, 59.

[113] Buchholz and Coninx, *Schorfheide*, 45n.

[114] *Reichsministerialblatt der Forstverwaltung* 6 (1942): 316. For the decree's draft, see BArch R 2/4731 pp. 46–7.

[115] Knopf and Martens, *Görings Reich*, 118.

[116] Nippert, *Schorfheide*, 62n.

[117] Kurth-Gilsenbach, *Schorfheide*, 22; Knopf and Martens, *Görings Reich*, 128.

[118] Knopf and Martens, *Görings Reich*, 150n; Kurth-Gilsenbach, *Schorfheide*, 34; Annett Gröschner, "Auf Carinhall, Schorfheide," in Stephan Porombka and Hilmar Schmundt (eds.), *Böse Orte. Stätten nationalsozialistischer Selbstdarstellung – heute* (Berlin, 2005), 103.

with heavy cutting reducing the area's forest reserves and Red Army soldiers decimating the game population. According to Erwin Buchholz and Ferdinand Coninx, the Red Army employed tanks to drive the game out of the forests and then used machine guns for the kill, extinguishing the last of the wild horses in the process.[119] Ironically, the Nazis' reintroduction efforts failed with the majestic species, the bison and the moose, and succeeded with the less conspicuous ones, the beaver and the mufflon. The later was the only type of animal that had never before lived in the Schorfheide area.[120]

The Schorfheide continued to serve as a hunting reserve during the following decades, marking some strange similarities between the Nazi regime and the socialist GDR. Just like Göring, the East German government started reintroduction efforts when the Soviet ambassador donated a herd of moose in 1964, and the attempt failed once again; the surviving moose were transferred to the Friedrichsfelde animal park.[121] After his fall from power, Erich Honecker, the secretary-general of East Germany's socialist party between 1976 and 1989, took pride in the preservation of the Schorfheide's natural beauty to distract from the GDR's environmental toll.[122] However, the socialist rulers did not follow Göring's hunting practice because they favored a different type of hunting with severe environmental implications: seeking a large bag above all, the state foresters had to increase the game population at all costs, and the inflated deer herd inflicted massive damage on the Schorfheide forests.[123] Göring had been more selective in his hunting: he showed little interest in small game and concentrated his energies on the deer population, displaying a jealousy of trophies that became legendary in his lifetime. When the Hungarian prime minister Julius Vités Gömbös, a strong admirer of Nazi Germany, shot a magnificent stag during a state hunt in the Rominten national nature reserve, Göring chastised the foresters in charge immediately after Gömbös' departure because he had previously shot a much less impressive specimen in Hungary; at times, Göring boasted of his intention to shoot "the strongest stag in Europe."[124] For the Schorfheide's flora, the

[119] Nippert, *Schorfheide*, 153; Buchholz and Coninx, *Schorfheide*, 129.
[120] Buchholz and Coninx, *Schorfheide*, 79, 81, 88, 122n; Kurth-Gilsenbach, *Schorfheide*, 22.
[121] Thomas Grimm, *Das Politbüro privat. Ulbricht, Honecker, Mielke & Co. aus der Sicht ihrer Angestellten* (Berlin, 2004), 123n.
[122] Reinhold Andert and Wolfgang Herzberg, *Der Sturz. Erich Honecker im Kreuzverhör* (Berlin and Weimar, 1991), 387.
[123] Nippert, *Schorfheide*, 188n; Kurth-Gilsenbach, *Schorfheide*, 19; Gautschi, *Wirkung*, 369.
[124] Nippert, *Schorfheide*, 52, 56n.

implications were favorable: foresters sought to reduce an excessive game population during the Nazi era, focusing on the development of a strong but limited deer population. In his memoirs, Ulrich Scherping, who was in charge of the state hunt during the Nazi era, spoke of a "very tame hunting business" in the Schorfheide, in spite of a large number of special guests.[125] However, it was clear that this was an accidental by-product of Göring's hunting preferences rather than the result of a clear environmental policy. After all, the encounter with "Ivan the Terrible" gave sufficient proof that the autonomous dynamic of nature did not have a place in Göring's worldview.

Regulating the Ems River

Since the eighteenth century, the promotion of agriculture has ranked among the major tasks of government in Germany. One way to increase agricultural production was the regulation of the water flow on arable land, and projects for the irrigation and drainage of farmland have always been a fixture of agricultural policy. One of the most famous eighteenth-century projects was the draining of the Oderbruch in Brandenburg, where a water project that shortened the flow of the Oder River reclaimed some 140,000 acres of farmland.[126] However, there were also numerous other projects, state-run as well as private, that sought to achieve the same goal on a more modest scale. In the west German region of Westphalia, water projects became common during the nineteenth century, transforming moors and heaths, which previously had been used only extensively, if at all, into land for intensive agricultural use. Many of these projects focused on the watershed of the Ems, a river that runs west through the province and turns north near Münster, the provincial capital, ultimately flowing into the North Sea on the Dutch–German border. However, many of these projects had produced disappointing results, especially before the widespread use of mineral fertilizer boosted agricultural productivity in the late nineteenth century. Also, the regulation of the water flow often turned out to be more difficult than expected, caused mostly by

---

[125] Siewert, "Schorfheide," 230; Scherping, *Waidwerk*, 120n. This situation is all the more remarkable because Aldo Leopold found the German forests generally "overstocked with deer." (Leopold, "Deer and Dauerwald," 366.)

[126] See Bernd Herrmann with Martina Kaup, *"Nun blüht es von End' zu End' all überall." Die Eindeichung des Nieder-Oderbruches 1747–1753* (Münster, 1997); Reinhard Schmook, "Zur Geschichte des Oderbruchs als friederizianische Kolonisationslandschaft," *250 Jahre Trockenlegung des Oderbruchs. Fakten und Daten einer Landschaft* (n.l., 1997), 41.

unexpected side effects and the internal dynamic of the watershed. Many projects that seemed at the time to be the ultimate fix looked more like one more chapter in an endless struggle a few years later.[127]

In the 1920s, another round opened in this enduring battle when a number of summer floods inflicted significant damage on many farms along the Ems River. During the farm year 1924/1925, flood damage amounted to 150,000 Reichsmarks for one county alone, whereas damage in 1927 amounted to 220,000 Reichsmarks on 3,850 acres of arable land. On the tributaries of the Ems, farmers reported an additional loss of some 400,000 Reichsmarks.[128] Farmers were quick to blame the hydrology of the Ems River, arguing that the Ems had become unable to contain the excess water after heavy rainfall. The situation was to a large extent a product of previous hydrological projects: while these projects shunted water away from the fields and into the river more quickly, the Ems itself had remained a long, winding river with strong sedimentation – an island of untamed nature in a region that bore the marks of intensive agricultural use. Therefore, a call emerged for regulation of the river flow, and an assembly of the local farmers' associations, held on October 4, 1926, specifically to discuss water issues, passed a resolution to that effect.[129] The Prussian Hydrological Office (*Kulturbauamt*) in Minden heeded the cry and got to work on a comprehensive plan for the mitigation of the flooding problem. In spring 1928, the Hydrological Office presented a plan for the regulation of some eighty miles from the source of the Ems to a point near Greven, a town close to the northern outskirts of Münster. Beyond that point, the Ems was a river of the first category, meaning that Reich agencies, not Prussian officials, had jurisdiction over it.[130]

Environmental historians have long recognized hydrological engineers as a special kind of experts, and the Ems River project would attest to

---

[127] See Rita Gudermann, *Morastwelt und Paradies. Ökonomie und Ökologie in der Landwirtschaft am Beispiel der Meliorationen in Westfalen und Brandenburg (1830–1880)* (Paderborn, 2000).

[128] WAA LWL Best. 305 no. 46, Niederschrift über die Besprechung der Frage der Emsregulierung im Sitzungssaale der Landwirtschaftskammer zu Münster, October 18, 1930, p. 5; and KAW Landratsamt Warendorf B 775, Der Kreisausschuss des Kreises Wiedenbrück, April 14, 1925.

[129] KAW Landratsamt Warendorf B 775, Entschließung des Westfälischen und Emsländischen Bauernverein of October 4, 1926. See also Barbara Köster, *Das Warendorfer Emstal gestern und heute* (Warendorf, 1989), 80.

[130] WAA LWL Best. 305 no. 47, Allgemeiner Plan des Preußischen Kulturbauamts Minden, April 13, 1928.

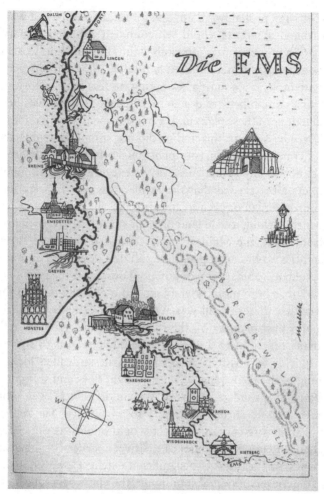

FIGURE 4.5. An overview chart from a 1958 book. During the Nazi era, the regulation project focused mostly on the stretch between Greven and Wiedenbrück. Map by Waldemar Mallek, printed in Sten Woelm, *Das Bilderbuch von der Ems* (Münster, 1956).

their peculiarity. With command over significant resources and closely aligned to the state, hydrological engineers wielded a considerable degree of power, and they were usually not averse to using it. In fact, Karl August Wittfogel argued in his famous theory of hydrological societies that centralized command over water resources was tantamount to despotism.[131]

---

[131] See Karl August Wittfogel, *Die orientalische Despotie. Eine vergleichende Untersuchung totaler Macht* (Frankfurt, 1977).

The plan of 1928 probably did not aim for total power, but it was, like so many hydrological reports, a bold, self-confident statement. It started with a confirmation of the farmers' previous claims that the Ems was unable to handle the amount of water after heavy rainfall. Next, the report reviewed previous attempts at a solution. Counting no less than twenty-six plans since the first comprehensive design in 1852, the hydrologists bemoaned the fact that none of these plans had been implemented with the stringency required. Needless to say, this finding did not stimulate doubts about the wisdom of comprehensive master plans but rather led to a warning that there must not be any compromise in the execution of plan number 27. The planners also stressed that the farmers themselves were unable to develop a proper plan or even to cooperate at all: recounting horror stories of farmers seeking to win land on their side of the river while eroding the opposite bank, the engineers claimed that only impartial expertise could point the way to an appropriate solution. Seeking a uniform grade and the systematic obliteration of potential obstacles, the plan envisioned a waterway that bore more resemblance to a channel than to the wild, scenic river that the Ems still was. With a geometric, trapeziform cross section and robust planting on the river banks, the engineers reduced a river of many functions to a ditch whose only task was to siphon away water as quickly as possible. Also, the new design called for a radical streamlining of the river's course, with straight lines and soft curves taking the place of meanders. Between Warendorf and Greven alone, the river's length was to shrink from 32.3 to 23.1 miles. The report mentioned that some stretches of the river would qualify as a "wilderness," but it did not discuss the changes to the river's scenery or other kinds of environmental implications to a significant extent. However, it was clear that from the conservationists' standpoint, the plan's consequences would be profound.[132]

The plan came with an impressive price tag: all in all, the hydrologists estimated that regulation would cost some ten million Reichsmarks. Nevertheless, the plan quickly won friends within the administration. "A regulation of the Ems River is an absolute necessity," the county commissioners from the three affected counties stressed, adding that "any kind of red tape must not stand in the project's way."[133] The farmers

---

[132] See WAA LWL Best. 305 no. 47, Allgemeiner Plan des Preußischen Kulturbauamts Minden, April 13, 1928, esp. pp. 1, 8, 12n, 47, 72n, 105, 111.

[133] WAA LWL Best. 305 no. 46, Niederschrift über die durch Erlass des Preußischen Landwirtschaftsministers angeordnete Besprechung über die Emsregulierung on April 13, 1928, p. 4.

likewise embraced the plan, even stating that river regulation was an issue of economic life or death for farming in Westphalia.[134] The latter statement may sound like an undue dramatization in retrospect, but it needs to be seen in the context of the dismal situation of farmers at that time. In the late 1920s, a growing tax burden, rising debt caused by increased mechanization and a decline of commodity prices came together in a secular crisis, and the political radicalization of the farming community in some parts of northern Germany spurred government agencies into action.[135] At the same time, the farming crisis made any thought of a significant contribution from the farmers' coffers illusory, and farmers were eager to point out that "the state or some other body will need to shoulder the costs."[136] As it turned out, the regulation of the Ems River was indeed free to the main beneficiaries: whereas farmers along the river banks profited from the project, state agencies on different levels paid for it.[137]

However, the farmers did not always pursue a uniform interest in the regulation project. The most vociferous proponents always came from the upper stretches of the river where the impact of flooding had been particularly severe. In 1931, the county commissioner of the upstream Wiedenbrück County even spoke of the project as if there were a natural right to river regulation: "For years, we have been talking about the Ems regulation project, and for years we have been waiting for its execution. After all, the regulation of the Ems is not any kind of river regulation."[138] However, farmers downstream were somewhat more reluctant, not least because they feared that river regulation in the Wiedenbrück area would

---

[134] *Ibid.*, Niederschrift über die Besprechung der Frage der Emsregulierung im Sitzungssaale der Landwirtschaftskammer zu Münster, October 18, 1930, p. 9.

[135] See Ulrich Kluge, *Agrarwirtschaft und ländliche Gesellschaft im 20. Jahrhundert* (Munich, 2005), 20–6. On different aspects of the contemporary crisis of farming in Westphalia, see Burkhard Theine, *Westfälische Landwirtschaft in der Weimarer Republik. Ökonomische Lage, Produktionsformen und Interessenpolitik* (Paderborn, 1991); Peter Exner, *Ländliche Gesellschaft und Landwirtschaft in Westfalen 1919–1969* (Paderborn, 1997); and Helene Albers, *Zwischen Hof, Haushalt und Familie. Bäuerinnen in Westfalen-Lippe 1920–1960* (Paderborn, 2001).

[136] WAA LWL Best. 305 no. 46, Niederschrift über die Besprechung der Frage der Emsregulierung im Sitzungssaale der Landwirtschaftskammer zu Münster, October 18, 1930, p. 5. Similarly, KAW Landratsamt Warendorf B 775, Entschließung des Westfälischen und Emsländischen Bauernverein of October 4, 1926.

[137] WAA LWL Best. 305 no. 53, Gutachtliche Äusserung der Landesbauernschaft zum Emsausbau, June 27, 1938.

[138] StAT C 2303, Niederschrift über die Verhandlungen betreffend den Emsausbau on March 4, 1931, p. 4n.

cause the floods to drown their land.[139] Also, calculations showed that the economics of regulation differed markedly depending on the section of the river. Above the village of Einen between the towns of Warendorf and Telgte, regulation promised protection to some 21,600 acres of land, implying costs of 230 Reichsmarks per acre with prospective costs of five million Reichsmark for the entire project. However, the area at stake below Einen comprised only 3,100 acres, whereas regulation would likewise cost five million Reichsmarks, and a tally of 1,600 Reichsmarks per acre was "unjustifiable" by itself.[140] Typically, the farmers' meeting in 1930 ended with a call for unity and a "comprehensive view" on the project: "damage below Warendorf must not increase due to the start of construction on the upper stretches under any circumstances."[141] However, such a statement merely masked the divergent interests without solving the fundamental dilemma.

All in all, it seems that the fate of the project was still undecided in the early 1930s.[142] What tilted the scale in the project's favor was the sudden availability of cheap labor as a result of the Great Depression. With the government setting up labor projects to curb mass unemployment, the costs of labor shrunk dramatically.[143] Moreover, the project suddenly looked like a win–win scenario: farmers would profit from higher and more secure yields, unemployed workers would find jobs, even if low-paid ones, and the hydrological experts would get a chance to implement their design. The only faction that would not win was the conservation community, for the project was almost identical to the scenario that Schoenichen condemned in his "Appeal of the German Landscape to the Labor Service." "The work of the Labor Service must under no circumstances lead to a German landscape full of geometry and concrete," he wrote, warning

139 WAA LWL Best. 305 no. 46, Niederschrift über die Besprechung der Frage der Emsregulierung im Sitzungssaale der Landwirtschaftskammer zu Münster, October 18, 1930, p. 1.
140 StAT C 2303, Niederschrift über die Verhandlungen betreffend den Emsausbau on March 4, 1931, p. 2.
141 WAA LWL Best. 305 no. 46, Niederschrift über die Besprechung der Frage der Emsregulierung im Sitzungssaale der Landwirtschaftskammer zu Münster, October 18, 1930, p. 9.
142 See KAW Kreisausschuss Warendorf B 267, *Die Glocke* of November 2, 1932.
143 See StAT C 2303, Niederschrift über die Verhandlungen betreffend den Emsausbau on March 4, 1931, p. 9; StAT C 1978, Der Vorsitzende des Kreisausschusses, memorandum of September 7, 1933, p. 2; WAA LWL Best. 305 no. 46, Niederschrift über die Besprechung der Frage der Emsregulierung im Sitzungssaale der Landwirtschaftskammer zu Münster, October 18, 1930, and Entschließung der Zentrumsfraktion, Münster, April 21, 1931; and WAA LWL Best. 305 no. 50, 55, 65.

of "replacing a river's meander with a straight, canal-like bed."[144] The Westphalian planners had favored robust plants over concrete, but other than that, Schoenichen's remarks described quite precisely the plan that was now about to move from the drawing board toward realization.

With the combination of agricultural interests, job creation, and an enticing master plan, the project quickly gained momentum, and the first stretches of the river were "corrected," as a convenient euphemism had it, in 1932.[145] However, these early efforts did not prevent the Nazis from staging an "official" inauguration for the Ems regulation project in March 1934. Choosing a site where a 40-foot channel eliminated a bend of more than half a mile, the event showed the Nazis' skill in transforming a rather banal act into an impressive festivity. With flags and other decoration dotting the area, the ceremony drew a large number of attendants. The regional *Gauleiter* Alfred Meyer and Karl Friedrich Kolbow, the head of the provincial administration, both used the opportunity to address their subjects and praise the project that was getting underway. Upon command, the Labor Service comrades took "their weapon, the spade," as the local newspaper reported, and got to work. The paramilitary character of the Labor Service project was perfectly clear.[146]

Up to this point, the project had evolved without significant input from the conservation community. In fact, the first statements from the community did not emerge until the summer of 1933, even though the local newspapers had reported on earlier steps.[147] Part of the reason was judicial: there was no legal requirement to inform the conservationists of upcoming projects before the national conservation law of 1935 made the consultation of the conservation administration mandatory. However, the conservationists' occupation with other projects certainly played a role as well. The late 1920s were a boom time for Westphalian conservation, and conservationists were busy purchasing or renting tracts of land and designating them as nature reserves, leading to a total of fifty-six nature reserves within the provincial boundaries by 1933.[148] By contemporary

---

[144] Schoenichen, "Appell," 146n.

[145] Köster, *Emstal*, 85.

[146] *Marienbote* [Telgte] 17/12 (March 25, 1934). On the paramilitary character of the German Labor Service, see Patel, *Soldaten*, 336n.

[147] See Thorsten Kaatz and Christian Schulze-Dieckhoff, "Wenn die Ems ihr Bett verläßt... Beitrag zum Wettbewerb Deutsche Geschichte um den Preis des Bundespräsidenten" (February, 1987), 53n.

[148] WAA Best. 717 file "Provinzialbeauftragter," Liste der Naturschutzgebiete der Provinz Westfalen, aufgestellt vom Kommissar für Naturdenkmalpflege der Provinz Westfalen nach dem Stande vom 1. Oktober 1933.

standards, that was certainly an impressive number, and Thomas Lekan spoke of "the most effective regional nature conservation organ in Prussia."[149] However, a closer look reveals the limits of conservation work during the Weimar years: about half of these nature reserves comprised less than 10 acres.[150] In short, the focus was on small areas of special value from a conservation standpoint, whereas the impact of large-scale projects, like the one under way along the Ems, was mostly beyond the conservationists' purview. The goal was the preservation of isolated spots rather than comprehensive land management.

Thus, when the Heimat League of Westphalia (*Westfälischer Heimatbund*) finally voiced some concerns in 1933, its protest was of a rather low-key kind: the league asked for "a conservationist approach wherever possible." The motives were twofold: the league pointed to "the landscape's peculiar scenic beauty" but also mentioned the value of the Ems valley "as a recreational area for the residents of Münster."[151] Three days after the league's petition, Gau Cultural Leader Bartels filed his own letter supporting this concern, demonstrating that the competition between state and party conservation was still alive in Westphalia.[152] In fact, the competition was probably instrumental for the Heimat League's intervention because 2 weeks earlier, the Gütersloh local branch of the Nazi Cultural Alliance (*NS-Kulturbund*), a member institution of Bartels' party conservation network, had discussed the issue and called for conservation as "a völkisch obligation." Invoking the Nazi principle of "the common good above the individual good," the alliance had asked to put the entire upper Ems valley under protection: "The time will soon be past when the precious treasures of nature were seen from a purely utilitarian perspective as an object of exploitation, for here, as in so many fields, the ideology of National Socialism will enlighten the people."[153]

The government's response was ambivalent. On the one hand, the provincial administration stressed the importance of keeping the interests of conservation in view. In fact, the administration even promised "to do everything possible to protect property owners along the Ems from summer floods as well as preserve the Ems as a recreational area for the people

---

[149] Lekan, "It Shall," 75.

[150] WAA Best. 717 file "Provinzialbeauftragter," Liste der Naturschutzgebiete der Provinz Westfalen, aufgestellt vom Kommissar für Naturdenkmalpflege der Provinz Westfalen nach dem Stande vom 1. Oktober 1933.

[151] WAA LWL Best. 305 no. 54, Westfälischer Heimatbund to the Landeshauptmann der Provinz Westfalen, September 1, 1933.

[152] *Ibid.*, Nationalsozialistische Deutsche Arbeiterpartei, Gauleitung Westfalen-Nord, Der Gaukulturwart to the Landeshauptmann der Provinz Westfalen, September 4, 1933.

[153] *Ibid.*, *Die Glocke* of October 21, 1933.

of Münster." On the other hand, the government was evasive in that it did not discuss the critical points in any detail and in fact refrained from any concrete promise. The administration promised to hear conservation advisors even in the absence of a legal requirement, but it was clear that it saw their suggestions as nonbinding advice.[154] Therefore, one could read the administration's letter in two ways: as an indication that the issue was taken care of and that there was no need for further activism from the conservationists or as a sign that concerns over the changes in the land were welcome within the administration. Conservationists clearly favored the latter reading, and a groundswell of protest developed in the following months. A local league of artists (*Freie Künstlergemeinschaft Schanze*) filed a petition in November 1933 that expressed "strong concerns" regarding the transformation of the Ems and the Werse, a tributary of the Ems on the eastern outskirts of Münster. The letter was somewhat sharper than the Heimat League's statements: whereas the latter took the project in general for granted, the artists' petition asserted "that cultural values rank higher than economic advantages" and asked for the declaration of "an inviolable nature reserve" as an alternative to river regulation. In fact, the letter even alluded to Hitler's mountain retreat on the Obersalzberg, though it cautiously spoke of a "symbolic comparison": just as the Führer was seeking "rest and recreation" in "secluded, untouched nature," many people of Westphalia would cherish the Ems landscape "as an inexhaustible source of refreshment and strength."[155] Again, the provincial administration answered in a polite fashion: "it might be useful to assemble all circles with an interest in conservation issues at a meeting in order to discuss the plan and collect ideas."[156]

With the petition of the artists' league, the concern over the regulation of the Ems had clearly extended beyond the core groups of the conservation community. The next petition followed up on this tendency in that it included a number of different parties. Filed in January 1934, Albert Kreiss, a novelist from Münster, figured as its main author, with half a dozen other residents signing as "coauthors": Clemens Brand, the director of the city's land survey office, a professor of biology from Münster University, a geographer, a hunter, and representatives of the city's anglers and canoeists. However, the breadth of these perspectives was not the only

---

[154] *Ibid.*, Der Landeshauptmann der Provinz Westfalen to the Westfälischer Heimatbund, September 21, 1933.

[155] *Ibid.*, Freie Künstlergemeinschaft Schanze to Landeshauptmann Kolbow, November 27, 1933.

[156] *Ibid.*, Der Landeshauptmann der Provinz Westfalen to the Freie Künstlergemeinschaft Schanze, December 21, 1933.

innovation of this petition. Starting with emphatic praise for the river's "primeval character" and "the love of the *Heimat*," the memorandum moved toward a comprehensive reevaluation of the entire project. The authors took issue with the "canal-like profile" of the future Ems and asked to preserve its winding course, two revendications that ran directly counter to the project's general thrust. In fact, the memorandum suggested that the current meandering may be advantageous for flood prevention in that it retained water rather than sending it away quickly with unknown repercussions downstream. The memorandum also took issue with the farmers' damage claims that underlay the entire project. Given that the farmers' grassland was usually much too dry, many property owners were actually profiting from flooding: "so far, significant flood damage has been limited to a few, isolated farmers." Furthermore, the memorandum pointed to the internal dynamic of nature: a quicker flow of the river would inevitably lead to unintended side effects, and the lower water table, an almost certain result of the project, would have a very negative impact on land cultivation. Finally, the memorandum pointed to the maintenance costs that a canallike design would imply. All in all, the petition called for a fundamental reorientation of the entire regulation project.[157]

It is instructive to compare this memorandum with the earlier voices from the conservation community. In its sentimental beginning, the memorandum was in line with the previous statements of the Heimat League, the parallel Bartels network, and the artists' league. But after that, the memorandum's line of reasoning differed markedly. Whereas the conservation community merely pointed to recreational and aesthetic considerations to demand their incorporation into the overall project, the memorandum touched on further issues and challenged the fundamental pillars of the project. Ultimately, the memorandum implied a basic reassessment of the entire design, leading to a new vision for the project. With that, it provided an instructive perspective on the contemporary conservation sentiment: whereas statements from the conservation community displayed a constrained approach that took the project's general merits for granted, the memorandum's authors argued that the economic advantages were themselves open to question. The truly explosive nature of this approach becomes clear when one realizes that it linked up with earlier doubts among key proponents of the project. For example, an official

---

[157] See WAA Best. 717 no. 59, Gedanken zum geplanten Ausbau der Ems, January 1934, esp. pp. 1, 3–6. For the original draft of the petition, which was even sharper in its critique, see WAA Best. 717 no. 60.

from the Prussian ministry of agriculture mentioned the heavy rainfall of the previous 4 years in a meeting in 1928, stressing that with less rain in the upcoming years, "the prospective regulation measures will not be profitable."[158] In that context, the memorandum could have been the starting point for a new, holistic approach that saw the Ems not simply as a water main – it could have, if the memorandum had been discussed openly.

Within days after the first copies of the memorandum began to circulate, the president of the provincial administration, Karl Friedrich Kolbow, moved to suppress the nascent discussion. The regional conservation advisor Paul Graebner received a harsh letter asking him "to prevent the spread of the memorandum" because of its "completely false and distorted content."[159] More importantly, the local newspapers received instructions from Kolbow "to consult with Münster's county commissioner or myself *before* publishing letters or articles on the topic to prevent the spread of erroneous ideas and unnecessary concerns in the general public over the consequences of the river's regulation for the Ems scenery."[160] When Bartels proposed organizing a lecture on the prospective changes of the Ems River a few months later, Kolbow asked *Gauleiter* Meyer to step in "in order to prevent a new wave of concern in the public at large." On that occasion, Kolbow also spoke of the conservationists as "a small band of self-important people."[161] When Schoenichen expressed worries over the preservation of hedgerows in the context of river regulation, the county of Münster "took exception to this kind of reporting" and argued that the intervention "only sought to bring the Ems regulation project into discredit."[162] With these sharp reactions, the issue quickly dropped from the agenda, and silence prevailed.

The rapid shift of the government's stance calls for explanation. Why did it seek to quench protest from a group that it was planning to invite to

---

[158] WAA LWL Best. 305 no. 46, Niederschrift über die durch Erlass des Preußischen Landwirtschaftsministers angeordnete Besprechung über die Emsregulierung on April 13, 1928, p. 6.

[159] WAA Best. 717 no. 103, Der Oberpräsident der Provinz Westfalen to the Kommissar für Naturdenkmalpflege, February 13, 1934.

[160] WAA LWL Best. 305 no. 54, Der Landeshauptmann der Provinz Westfalen to the Schriftleitung der Nationalzeitung, the Münsterischer Anzeiger, the Münstersche Zeitung, the Deutsches Nachrichtenbüro Münster and the Westfälische Provinzialkorrespondenz Werland, January 22, 1934. Emphasis in the original.

[161] WAA Best. 717 no. 59, Der Landeshauptmann der Provinz Westfalen to the Gauleitung Westfalen Nord, May 24, 1934.

[162] WAA Best. 717 no. 103, Der Kreisausschuss des Landkreises Münster to the Regierungspräsident Münster, July 14, 1934.

an official hearing only a few weeks earlier? The approaching festivities certainly played a role in the swift reaction. With a spectacular ceremony planned for March 1934, the last thing that one might need was a group of disgruntled conservationists disturbing the show of unanimity. Also, the authors certainly touched some nerves with their bold assertion that the preservation of the Ems scenery was in the spirit of Adolf Hitler. "There is no greater friend of nature, and no one who keeps the triad of fatherland, *Heimat* and nature more sacred, than the Führer," the memorandum declared – a daring claim before the passage of the national conservation law, and especially so in a critique of a Labor Service project.[163] However, the key motivation was probably that the conservationists' critique had crossed a certain threshold. For the government, the conservation community had always been a group with limited ambitions that could be appeased with small adjustments and small-scale changes, and the government's pledge to consult with the conservation community was presumably made on the assumption that their demands would again be confined to minor issues. With such a mindset, it was out of the question to place conservationists on a par with Labor Service officials or to review the entire project from a conservation standpoint. And with the conservationists' campaign slowly gathering momentum, the government saw a quick and decisive intervention as the best way to forestall future trouble.

As a result, there were essentially two Ems regulation projects since 1934: one in the propaganda of the Nazi regime and another one in the real world. Nazi leaders took pride in their commitment to conservation in their public remarks. To give just one example, Kolbow declared in his speech at the March 1934 ceremony "that the character of the Ems landscape will not be destroyed."[164] But the actual work along the river banks revealed little in the way of an environmental ethic. The new riverbed was usually characterized by straight lines and a rigid geometrical design, and a monotonous, canallike appearance took the place of the picturesque scenery.[165] To maximize the workload, the use of machinery was kept to a minimum, and earthwork was done exclusively by shoveling.[166] Labor Service workers prevailed until the advent of World War II, when Polish prisoners of war were used for a limited time.[167] The project was finally

---

[163] WAA Best. 717 no. 59, Gedanken zum geplanten Ausbau der Ems, January 1934, p. 2.
[164] *Marienbote* [Telgte] 17, 12 (March 25, 1934).
[165] See Köster, *Emstal*, 85–90.
[166] Ansgar Kaiser, *Zur Geschichte der Ems. Natur und Ausbau* (Rheda-Wiedenbrück, 1993), 110.
[167] See WAA LWL Best. 305 no. 55, Angabe an das Arbeitsamt, June 11, 1940.

FIGURE 4.6. The Ems River before and after regulation. Pictures taken by Bernhard Rensch, conservation advisor for the province of Westphalia. Printed with permission of the Westfälisches Archivamt Munster.

abandoned because of the demands of the war economy in 1941.[168] By that time, regulation had changed the face of the river for about 53 miles.[169]

Newspaper articles continued to touch on the conservationists' concerns, but because of government censorship, they generally served to soothe the public's worries. For example, an article in the daily *Münsterischer Anzeiger* mentioned the possibility that "natural attractiveness" might suffer from the straightening of the river's run but quickly moved to dispel all corresponding fears: "more than ever, we can be confident that, given the loving compassion of our current German leadership for everything of relevance to the *Heimat* soil and its peculiarity, one will avoid the mistakes that an earlier materialist era did permit."[170] Of course, words of this kind could not appease the conservation community, and the enduring groundswell of discontent reemerged in 1938 when river regulation touched on property belonging to the city of Münster at the confluence of the Ems and Werse Rivers. On the surface, the city's protest sought to preserve a spot of special value for recreation and the fostering of traditions (*Brauchtumspflege*).[171] However, the true motivation was already apparent in the person behind the initial protest: the initiative lay with the director of the land survey office of the city of Münster, Clemens Brand, a cosigner of the memorandum of 1934. Thus, it should come as no surprise that the protest soon took on a more general character. "There must not be any change to the area around the mouth of the Werse River," Paul Graebner declared in August 1938.[172] The provincial conservation advisor Bernhard Rensch used the opportunity to launch a detailed critique of the transformation of the Ems.[173] However, this initiative soon reached an inglorious end when the conservationists were forced to withdraw their objections during a meeting in October 1938.[174]

[168] Kaiser, *Geschichte*, 115.

[169] Martin Arens and Paul Otto, "Die Wasserwirtschaft des Emsgebietes," in Edgar Sommer (ed.), *Die Ems. Unsere Heimat – Unsere Welt. Deutsche Flüsse in Wort und Bild* 1 (Burgsteinfurt, 1956), 121.

[170] *Münsterischer Anzeiger* 83/754 (July 22, 1934).

[171] WAA LWL Best. 305 no. 54, Der Oberbürgermeister, Stadtvermessungsamt Münster to the Kulturamt Münster, July 12, 1938.

[172] *Ibid.*, Der Beauftragte für Naturschutz im Regierungsbezirk Münster to the Oberpräsident der Provinz Westfalen, August 16, 1938.

[173] *Ibid.*, Der Beauftragte für Naturschutz in der Provinz Westfalen to the Oberpräsident der Provinz Westfalen, July 19, 1938.

[174] See WAA Best. 717 no. 60, Niederschrift über die Besprechung vom 24.10.38 wegen Forderungen des Naturschutzes beim Emsausbau, October 27, 1938.

Brand continued to voice his concerns, using Bernhard Flemes, a writer from the town of Hameln, to relay a memorandum to Hans Klose, and the Reich Conservation Agency agreed that "there can be no doubt that the present form of river regulation will mean the ruin of the Ems landscape."[175] However, that was little more than despair in the face of the inevitable.

The conservationists' quick defeat was in part because of the internal dynamic of river regulation. Simply exempting a short stretch from modification was certain to spell disaster from a hydrological standpoint because a flood would inevitably rampage through this bottleneck. The traditional strategy of German conservation, to pick a number of scenic spots and forget about the rest, was clearly reaching its limits in this case. However, the key argument against the conservationists' objections was that the planners had already consulted with the conservation administration on a regular basis "and that as a result, conservation will need to accept the full responsibility for the result."[176] The planners had indeed been in touch with conservation advisors even before paragraph 20 of the national conservation law made their consultation mandatory.[177] However, the conservation advisors were usually heard only after the plans had been drawn up, and the minutes of these consultations reveal the stunning marginality of their role. At times, they asked for a quick planting of trees and bushes or the selection of native species, but any more general critique was clearly off-limits.[178] In fact, it seems that the conservation advisors did not even try to raise these issues.

Thus, the story of river regulation along the Westphalian Ems demonstrates the dialectics of paragraph 20 of the national conservation law. Because conservationists were not involved in the discussion of the project between 1928 and 1933, the master plan gave no attention to the concerns of nature protection. But with its involvement on a routine basis

---

[175] BArch B 245/23 pp. 87, 90–1.

[176] WAA Best. 717 no. 60, Niederschrift über die Besprechung vom 24.10.38 wegen Forderungen des Naturschutzes beim Emsausbau, October 27, 1938, p. 2.

[177] See WAA LWL Best. 305 no. 54, notes of November 20, 1933, and February 7, 1934; WAA Best. 717 no. 59, Der Landeshauptmann der Provinz Westfalen to the Gauleitung Westfalen Nord, May 24, 1934; and WAA Best. 717 no. 60, Wasserstraßenamt Rheine to the Beauftragten für Naturschutz Münster, July 31, 1939.

[178] See WAA LWL Best. 305 no. 64, Niederschrift über die Emsbegehung von der Eisenbahnbrücke Westbevern bis zur Schiffahrt und von der Brücke Heinrichmann unterhalb der Schiffahrt bis nach Gimbte on February 1, 1937; and WAA LWL Best. 305 no. 54, Der Beauftragte für Naturschutz im Regierungsbezirk Münster to the Oberpräsident der Provinz Westfalen, November 27, 1941.

after 1933, the conservation community became obliged to accept the project in general, whereas their impact remained confined to marginal issues. In other words, the conservation community was caught in a difficult situation: it was clearly discouraged by the conservation advisors' marginal role, but it did not have a chance to launch a more general critique of the project. To be sure, the conservationists were clearly willing to challenge major components of the overall design and may have dreamed of blocking the project in its entirety, but the Nazi regime clearly constrained their political options. Public protest was practically impossible after the suppression of the 1934 memorandum, and the hydrologists could easily quash internal criticism. If the conservationists' work looked inconsistent, if not incompetent in this case, it was for lack of an alternative.

All the while, the general public clearly entertained a considerable degree of sympathy for the conservationists' concerns. In fact, the worries remained so strong that in November 1937 the hydrologists finally sent one of their engineers to a *Heimat* rally in the town of Telgte to assuage local worries over the project's environmental impact.[179] However, when district conservation advisor Dr. Beyer spoke at the same meeting the following year, it became clear that the success had been a partial one at best. In some respects, the meeting on November 13, 1938, took place in a gloomy atmosphere: it was the week of the infamous "Kristallnacht," when dozens of Jews were killed, some 30,000 interned, and hundreds of synagogues burned and destroyed; one of them lay within the confines of Telgte.[180] But suppressing uncomfortable thoughts was a common sport in Nazi Germany, and so just a few blocks away from a synagogue in ruins, the local population embraced the protection of the beloved *Heimat* nature. Beyer's speech painted a dismal picture at times, speaking of "damage that cannot be remedied" and many "sinful" acts "in previous years." But in line with the government's desire for moderation, Beyer tried to close on an optimistic note: "there is hope that at least some stretches of the Ems in the vicinity of Telgte may remain in their original state." His remarks on "the conflict between romanticism and technology" were notably vague, and his intention to preserve scenic areas "here and there" had just received a crushing defeat, but Beyer's hopeful

[179] *Münsterländische Nachrichten* 12/214 (November 11, 1937).
[180] See Gregor Rüter, Rainer Westhoff, *Geschichte und Schicksal der Telgter Juden 1933–1945* (Telgte, 1985), 62–78.

remarks nonetheless won thunderous applause.[181] In that moment, the conservation movement's popularity was as apparent as its hapless situation.[182]

The Wutach Gorge

In 1925, Christmas was rainy in southern Germany. The weather bureau of the state of Baden reported an endless sequence of rainclouds moving over the country from the west, essentially drowning the holidays in lousy weather. At the same time, temperatures rose above the freezing point, and those who had hoped to go skiing over Christmas watched the dwindling snow in dismay. With continuous rain and melting snow, an unusually large amount of water fed into the rivers of the Black Forest. Soon, reports of flooding came in from the major rivers in the region, and residents who had been hoping for a few calm days at the end of the year found themselves busy fighting the high water. It was an unlikely moment for the birth of a nature reserve.[183]

One of the rivers with significant flood damage was the Wutach, a river in the southern Black Forest that starts on the Feldberg, the highest mountain in southwest Germany, and feeds into the Rhine between Constance and Basle, descending some 3,000 feet on its short run. The task of writing the flood damage report fell to Hermann Schurhammer, head of the building department for roads and waterways in the nearby town of Bonndorf. Schurhammer emphasized the difficult conditions for hydrological projects along the Wutach, especially in the section near Bonndorf, where the Wutach had carved a deep valley over the millennia, thus forming a scenic gorge. In this valley, the Wutach proved that it did not earn its name for nothing: the first syllable, *Wut*, means "fury" in German, and Wutach translates as "raging river." The Wutach Gorge was the result of erosion, and the violent river shifted its course erratically. Schurhammer recounted the story of three bridges that were torn down after a flood in 1919 changed the river's path but that could have served their purpose again by the mid-1920s because another flood had caused the river to return to its former bed. Against the background of these

---

[181] *Münsterländische Nachrichten* 13/268 (November 17, 1938).

[182] After 1945, regulation efforts along the Ems continued along the lines defined in the Nazi era for several decades. For that story, see p. 172.

[183] See *Freiburger Zeitung* no. 354 (December 29, 1929), p. 9 and no. 355 (December 30, 1925), p. 2.

tricky conditions, Schurhammer outlined a different approach: instead of repairing the damage of the Christmas flood at significant cost, he proposed "to leave the Wutach valley mostly to itself and thus make the first step towards the creation of a nature reserve."[184]

Coming from a hydrologist, it was an odd proposal, but the conditions along the Wutach made it rather easy from a water management perspective. Unlike the Ems River, farming interests were not affected to a significant extent, and commercial traffic usually ran across the gorge, rather than along its banks; most of the damage from the Christmas flood pertained to hiking paths. Therefore, the common hydrologists' quest for control of the water was little more than an empty gesture in the Wutach Gorge. The proposal spurred Schurhammer's career in conservation circles until he became one of Seifert's Landscape Advocates – the only engineer on such a post[185] – and conservation advisor for the entire state of Baden in 1939, but the original impulse came from a sober calculation of costs and benefits from a hydrological perspective.[186] However, conservationists were more interested in the scenic Wutach Gorge than in Schurhammer's motives, and his plan quickly won their sympathy. The State Natural History Association (*Badischer Landesverein für Naturkunde und Naturschutz*) organized an excursion through the gorge on July 4, 1926, and the participants were clearly charmed by the Wutach's natural treasures. "In a rare coincidence, the area unites limited economic importance with exciting geological phenomena and a rich plant and animal world. Therefore, the idea of creating a nature reserve deserves every support," an official from the ministry of education noted in his memorandum on the visit.[187] In January 1927, the state's conservation community published a petition in support of the nature reserve. In a show of unanimity, the signers included the Black Forest Association of Baden, the *Naturfreunde* tourist association, the State Natural History Association, and the Heimat League of Baden.[188] In September 1928, the state parliament of Baden unanimously passed a resolution in support of the nature reserve.[189]

---

[184] GLAK Abt. 235 no. 48295, Baurat Schurhammer to the Badisches Forstamt Bonndorf, February 12, 1926, p. 7.

[185] Zeller, "Ganz Deutschland," 293.

[186] GLAK Abt. 235 no. 6549, Der Minister des Kultus und Unterrichts to the Reichsforstmeister, August 7, 1939.

[187] *Ibid.*, memorandum of the Ministerium des Kultus und Unterrichts, July 16, 1926.

[188] HStAS EA 3/102 no. 29, resolution of January 1927.

[189] GLAK Abt. 237 no. 49495, Badischer Landtag, 64th session of September 13, 1928, p. 2915.

The conservationists' keen reaction was in part the result of a second conflict that played out in the region at that time. In 1924, plans emerged to build a hydroelectric power plant on the nearby Lake Schluchsee, some 6 miles west of the Wutach Gorge. Using the steep drop on the Black Forest's southern slope, the project promised to generate electricity at times of peak demand, a crucial function in every large electric power grid.[190] The plans drew widespread protest far beyond the conservation community, and when it became clear that the commercial merits of the Schluchsee project were so overwhelming and political support so strong that it was impossible to stop, the idea of a trade galvanized the conservationists' interest. If the transformation of the scenic Lake Schluchsee was inevitable, then at least another area of scenic value, the Wutach Gorge, should be set aside as a nature reserve. The ministry of education first aired this proposal in a memorandum of April 1928, and the idea quickly gathered momentum.[191] The resolution of Baden's parliament later that year also included a reference to the Schluchsee project.[192]

However, the prospective nature reserve on the Wutach was not without enemies. The forestry division of the ministry of finance lashed out against the plan in 1927, chastising "a fanciful penchant for nature, for virgin woods and primeval forests especially in lay circles." The plan did not offer any clear advantages, the foresters argued.[193] Also, the mayor of the upstream town of Neustadt expressed doubts about the plan, asserting that except for "some botanists and geologists," "foreigners will be fully satisfied after one visit to the gorge."[194] The mayor was also fearful that conservation officials would harass the paper mill in his town, which had been polluting the Wutach's water for decades.[195] Finally, the classic compensation problem made for a significant obstacle because private forest

[190] See Hans Allmendinger, *Die elektrizitätswirtschaftliche Erschliessung des Schluchseegebietes und ihre allgemeinen Zusammenhänge* (Ph.D. dissertation, University of Cologne, 1934), esp. pp. 12, 36n, 53n.

[191] GLAK Abt. 235 no. 48254, Der Minister des Kultus und Unterrichts to the Minister der Finanzen, April 19, 1928; GLAK Abt. 235 no. 48295, Badischer Landesverein für Naturkunde und Naturschutz to the Ministerium des Kultus und Unterrichts, April 24, 1928.

[192] Badischer Landtag, Sitzungsperiode 1927/28, Drucksache no. 92b.

[193] GLAK Abt. 235 no. 48295, Ministerium der Finanzen, Forstabteilung to the Minister des Kultus und Unterrichts, January 7, 1927, esp. p. 6 (quotation).

[194] GLAK Abt. 237 no. 49495, Der Bürgermeister Neustadt to the Landtagsabgeordnete Duffner, Maier and Martzloff, November 8, 1928, p. 3.

[195] See GLAK Abt. 235 no. 48254, Forst- und Domänendirektion Karlsruhe to the Ministerium des Kultus und Unterrichts, May 18, 1914.

owners were unwilling to accept restrictions on forest use if the state did not provide for some kind of indemnification.[196]

As a result, the administration pursued the plan at a rather leisurely pace until the passage of the national conservation law in 1935. With the appointment of Hermann Schurhammer as the government's special deputy for the creation of the Wutach Gorge in early 1936, the project finally shifted into high gear.[197] The forestry division made its peace with the nature reserve during the same year, and private property owners were obliged to adhere to limited forest use; the waste water issue was shelved out of consideration for the paper mill's 400 workers.[198] In August 1938, the ministry of education submitted to the Reich Forest Service the draft of a decree for the protection of 1,430 acres along the Wutach River; obviously overworked, it took the supreme German conservation authority almost a year to send its approval.[199] With the publication of the decree in August 1939, just days before the German invasion of Poland, the designation finally became official.[200]

But all the while, the Wutach nature reserve stood under a sword of Damocles: the hydroelectric project on the nearby Schluchsee. Hydroelectric utilities are notorious for their thirst for water, and the Schluchsee-werk, a subsidiary of two large utilities, the Badenwerk and the powerful Rheinisch-Westfälisches Elektrizitätswerk (RWE), set up for the development of water power in the southern Black Forest, was no exception.[201] A 1938 plan for the Schluchseewerk did not mention the Wutach as a prospective tributary, but that was clearly a tactical move.[202] When asked about the tributaries at an internal meeting, a key official declared in November 1938 "that they have been left out in order to avoid unrest

---

[196] See GLAK Abt. 237 no. 49495, memorandum of the Forstabteilung des Finanzminis-teriums, June 21, 1932, p. 2.

[197] *Ibid.*, Der Minister des Kultus und Unterrichts to the Geschäftsführer der Bezirks-naturschutzstelle für den Amtsbezirk Neustadt, March 6, 1936.

[198] GLAK Abt. 235 no. 48295, Badischer Finanz- und Wirtschaftsminister to the Minister des Kultus und Unterrichts, February 5, 1936, p. 1; GLAK Abt. 237 no. 49495, Badischer Finanz- und Wirtschaftsminister, Forstabteilung to the Finanz- und Wirtschaftsminister, January 28, 1936.

[199] GLAK Abt. 235 no. 48295, Minister des Kultus und Unterrichts to the Reichsforstmeis-ter, August 25, 1938; BArch B 245/6 p. 224.

[200] GLAK Abt. 235 no. 48295, Amtsblatt of August 12, 1939, pp. 180–1.

[201] Sandra Lynn Chaney, *Visions and Revisions of Nature. From the Protection of Nature to the Invention of the Environment in the Federal Republic of Germany, 1945–1975* (Ph.D. dissertation, University of North Carolina at Chapel Hill, 1996), 186.

[202] StAF E 34/1 no. 4, Schluchseewerk to the Bezirksamt Waldshut, June 30, 1938.

among downstream residents because the inclusion of these tributaries will follow only in a few years."[203] The planners even had a rough timetable in mind: when a small power plant on the Wutach River near Stallegg applied for a permission to raise its dam by 7 feet in 1937, the government approved the project under the condition that it might rescind its decision after 15 years "in order to make room for a hydroelectric project of greater economic significance."[204] In fact, the utility even considered the use of water from the Danube River, a project that would have required an underground duct at least 10 miles long across the continental watershed, until a closer investigation found that the costs of the Danube's diversion were prohibitive.[205]

The uncertainty over the dimensions of the Schluchseewerk system remained until the plans were finalized in the spring of 1942; from then on, it was clear that the project included a tall dam within the confines of the nature reserve and the diversion of the lion's share of the Wutach's water.[206] However, Schurhammer had already learned of the plan to use Wutach water, and he voiced his reservations about the planners' intentions as early as May 1941. Needless to say, the events of 1941 were clearly unconducive to an effective conservation drive: with the German invasion of the Soviet Union on June 22, 1941, World War II entered a new phase, and the defeat before Moscow toward the end of the year signaled the German army's declining fortunes. Nevertheless, the ministry of education for the state of Baden sustained Schurhammer's doubts in a letter to the ministry of finance and commerce on July 4, 1941.[207] In September 1941, the Inspector General for Water and Energy gave priority to the Schluchseewerk project. [208] However, the Inspector General's decree also ruled that the project had to adhere to the usual licensing procedures, and that provided an opportunity for the conservation administration to voice its concerns. On January 21, 1942, Hermann Schurhammer pointed

[203] GLAK Abt. 237 no. 50599, memorandum on negotiations in Karlsruhe on November 9, 1938, p. 2.
[204] GLAK Abt. 237 no. 48408, Entschließung des Bezirksamts Neustadt of March 30, 1938.
[205] GLAK Abt. 237 no. 50599, Baurat Henninger to Oberbaurat Köbler, April 1941.
[206] See proceedings in GLAK Abt. 237 no. 50599, esp. Finanz- und Wirtschaftsminister to the Abteilung für Landwirtschaft und Domänen, April 27, 1942.
[207] HStAS EA 3/102 no. 29, Minister des Kultus und Unterrichts als Höhere Naturschutzbehörde to the Finanz- und Wirtschaftsminister, Abteilung für Landwirtschaft und Domänen, July 4, 1941.
[208] *Ibid.*, Der Generalinspektor für Wasser und Energie to the Schluchseewerk, September 30, 1941.

out that the Schluchseewerk's plans had to be filed with him pursuant to paragraph 20 of the national conservation law.[209]

Historians have repeatedly argued that enforcement of paragraph 20 was highly deficient and that the obligation to consult with conservation officials in every project that affected the landscape was "frequently ignored."[210] However, the conflict over the Wutach Gorge shows that the letter of the law sometimes held force even if that implied the suspension of a war economy project, for that was the ultimate effect of Schurhammer's stance.[211] Sustained by the ministry of education in June 1942, Schurhammer's objections meant a ban on that part of the project, at least until he changed his mind or a higher authority decided otherwise, and that in turn blocked progress on the entire Schluchseewerk project.[212] To be sure, the start of construction in the Wutach Gorge was not imminent because the Wutach diversion belonged to the final phase of the project, but the design of the project depended on precise figures for the available water; and with the Wutach scheduled to deliver some 30 percent of the total water, it was impossible to order adequate machinery before reaching a final decision.[213] And simply ignoring the conservationists' objection was out of the question: in December 1942, the ministry of the interior ruled that such a move would be "detrimental to the administration's prestige."[214] During the same month, the German public nervously followed events on the eastern front: since November 22, 1942, the German Sixth Army had been trapped at Stalingrad.

It is not difficult to understand that this situation frayed the planners' nerves. Within days after the ministry of education's decree, representatives of the Schluchseewerk were in touch with Schurhammer seeking

---

[209] *Ibid.*, Landesnaturschutzstelle Baden to the Wasserwirtschaftsamt Waldshut, January 21, 1942.

[210] Wettengel, "Staat und Naturschutz," 390. See also Klueting, "Regelungen," 97.

[211] See StAF C 30/1 no. 1268, memorandum of the Badische Naturschutzstelle, March 20, 1942, p. 5, and Badische Naturschutzstelle to the Finanz- und Wirtschaftsstelle, May 20, 1942, p. 4.

[212] HStAS EA 3/102 no. 29, Der Minister des Kultus und Unterrichts als Höhere Naturschutzbehörde to the Finanz- und Wirtschaftsminister, June 19, 1942.

[213] See GLAK Abt. 235 no. 47677, Schluchseewerk-Aktiengesellschaft to the Ministerium des Kultus und Unterrichts, October 27, 1942, p. 2, and Der Reichsstatthalter in Baden, Planungsbehörde to the Minister für Kultus und Unterricht, October 20, 1942; HStAS EA 3/102 no. 29, Schluchseewerk-Aktiengesellschaft to the Generalinspektor für Wasser und Energie, September 9, 1942.

[214] StAF C 30/1 no. 1268, Der Minister des Innern to the Finanz- und Wirtschaftsminister, December 23, 1942.

"a moderation of the opinion of the state conservation agency."[215] After these efforts had proven futile, the proponents of the project tried to increase pressure: Reich Commissioner Robert Wagner, whose strong distaste for conservation issues had already become clear in the Hohenstoffeln conflict, raged in a letter to the German Forest Service that the conservation officials "do not sufficiently take the delicate situation of our electric power supply into account in their statements."[216] However, Schurhammer was unimpressed and reiterated his position in a memorandum of November 1942.[217] In fact, the conservationists' cause even found a number of supporters in spite of the difficult overall situation. In September 1942, Georg Wagner, a professor of geology at Tübingen University, voiced concerns over a reduction of the waterflow within the Wutach Gorge, and the natural science department of Freiburg University followed suit in December with an essay on the valley's significance for research and teaching. Within the conservation division of the Forest Service, Hans Schwenkel voiced his support for an unharmed Wutach Gorge, and Lutz Heck was also reported to oppose any change to the existing nature reserve.[218] Even Alwin Seifert eventually came out in support of Schurhammer in January 1943, though he had written a report that favored the Schluchseewerk's point of view only 4 months earlier.[219]

This was a small band of conservationists, but it did not fail to impress the Schluchseewerk. And so it came about that while the Sixth Army was dying at Stalingrad, the Schluchseewerk moved to revise its plans in the conservationists' favor. Whereas the original plans left some 17 percent of the original water to the Wutach Gorge, the revised proposal foresaw

[215] StAF C 30/1 no. 1268, handwritten note of July 3, 1942, on Der Minister des Kultus und Unterrichts als Höhere Naturschutzbehörde to the Finanz- und Wirtschaftsminister, June 19, 1942.

[216] HStAS EA 3/102 no. 29, Der Reichsstatthalter in Baden to Generalforstmeister Alpers, Reichsforstamt, December 23, 1942, p. 2

[217] See GLAK Abt. 235 no. 48295, Hermann Schurhammer, Das Wutachtal als Naturschutzgebiet und das Schluchseewerk. Gutachten der Landesnaturschutzstelle Baden, Kolmar, November 30, 1942.

[218] GLAK Abt. 235 no. 47677, letter of Georg Wagner, September 9, 1942; BArch B 245/6 pp. 38–40, 197; HStAS EA 3/102 no. 29, memorandum of Der Reichsstatthalter in Baden, Planungsbehörde, October 9, 1942, p. 2.

[219] GLAK Abt. 235 no. 47677, Reichslandschaftsanwalt Alwin Seifert to the Generalinspektor für Wasser und Energie, January 9, 1943. See also GLAK Abt. 237 no. 50599, Reichslandschaftsanwalt Alwin Seifert to the Generalinspektor für Wasser und Energie, September 7, 1942.

about 35.3 percent remaining in the riverbed.[220] With authorities in Baden locked in conflict, the issue finally moved to Berlin for a decision, and the German Forest Service called all parties to a meeting on March 3, 1943. It would be a euphemism to speak of an unfavorable time for the conservationists' cause: 4 weeks earlier, the Sixth Army had surrendered at Stalingrad, and 2 weeks earlier, Joseph Goebbels had declared "total war" in his infamous *Sportpalast* speech. Still, the conservationists were steadfast in their opposition, whereas the proponents of the Schluchseewerk project stressed the need to use the Wutach's water as well as the generous concessions they had made to the conservationists' demands.[221] Six days later, the German Forest Service finally gave its consent on behalf of the conservation administration to the Wutach's diversion, citing the Schluchseewerk's revised plans as an important reason for its decision.[222] Karl Asal, who had been in charge of conservation within the ministry of education since 1936, later spoke of the meeting and the ensuing decision as an hour of proof where "the true defenders of nature protection" stood firm whereas Lutz Heck of the German Forest Service "surrendered the conservationists' cause," but it is clear in retrospect that the conservationists were approaching the limits of their power.[223] On the day before the meeting with the Forest Service, the project's proponents had met with the Inspector General for Water and Energy to discuss their strategy. Under Todt's leadership, the Inspector General had entertained some sympathy for the conservationists' cause, and Schurhammer was eager to quote the Inspector General's guidelines in early 1942.[224] But after Todt's death in February 1942, Albert Speer oversaw a radical intensification of the war economy, and according to Robert Wagner, Speer was determined to intervene personally if the Forest Service had taken a different decision. His plan was to compel Göring to take the matter into his hands, and

---

[220] GLAK Abt. 235 no. 47677, Schluchseewerk-Aktiengesellschaft to the Ministerium des Kultus und Unterrichts, October 27, 1942, p. 6; HStAS EA 3/102 no. 29, Schluchseewerk AG, Die Wutach im Rahmen der Ausnützung der Wasserkräfte des Schluchseewerks, Freiburg, February 12, 1943.
[221] See GLAK Abt. 235 no. 47677, memorandum of the Badisches Ministerium des Kultus und Unterrichts, April 12, 1943, and HStAS EA 3/102 no. 29, memorandum of the Badisches Finanz- und Wirtschaftsministerium, March 1943. See also HStAS EA 3/102 no. 29, Professor Asal to the Regierungspräsidium Südbaden, April 11, 1956.
[222] StAF C 30/1 no. 1268, Der Reichsforstmeister als Oberste Naturschutzbehörde to the Generalinspektor für Wasser und Energie, March 9, 1943.
[223] BArch B 245/6 p. 169. See also Bärbel Häcker, *50 Jahre Naturschutzgeschichte in Baden-Württemberg. Zeitzeugen berichten* (Stuttgart, 2004), 16.
[224] See HStAS EA 3/102 no. 29, Badische Naturschutzstelle to the Finanz- und Wirtschaftsminister, January 26, 1942.

there can be little doubt that Göring would have swiftly dismissed the conservationists' worries.[225]

The Schluchseewerk had won, but its proponents were anything but jubilant. After all, the project had been stalled for almost a year, and the utility had to cede more precious water to the conservationists' interests than it originally planned. The only advantage from the planners' point of view was that they were now free from the conservationists' petty objections, or at least thought that way until they learned of Schurhammer's lecture at Freiburg University on July 11, 1944. On this occasion, Schurhammer talked about the threat that the diversion of the Wutach's water for hydroelectric purposes constituted to the nature reserve. Moreover, Schurhammer failed to mention that a decision on the matter had already been taken. "The lecture was free for everyone to attend and therefore needs to be seen as an appeal to the general public to forestall the use of the Wutach for energy production," the Schluchseewerk said, expressing its disconcertment in a letter to the ministry of education.[226]

One wonders what the utility would have said if it had known of the actual events at that time. Behind the scenes, the conservationists were working to revoke the decree of the Forest Service, and with the usual administrative procedures exhausted, the conservationists were trying to pull some strings. The Hohenstoffeln conflict provided the precedent: did it not show that a seemingly final decision, like the 1935 decree of the Forest Service that protected only the upper part of the Hohenstoffeln, could be modified later on with the help of powerful agents? And did Ludwig Finckh not enjoy that close connection to Heinrich Himmler that had proven so useful for the Hohenstoffeln's rescue? The conservation officials quickly approached Finckh, who had not been involved in the Wutach case so far, and Finckh began to reanimate his backchannel to the *Reichsführer-SS*.[227] "If there is any path towards success, it goes via the SS," Hans Klose declared in a letter to Finckh.[228] Of course, secrecy was paramount for the attempt to succeed, and Finckh spoke mysteriously

[225] See GLAK Abt. 235 no. 47677, Der Reichsstatthalter in Baden to the Minister des Kultus und Unterrichts, March 6, 1943, and HStAS EA 3/102 no. 29, memorandum of the Badisches Finanz- und Wirtschaftsministerium, March 1943.

[226] GLAK Abt. 235 no. 47677, Schluchseewerk Aktiengesellschaft to the Ministerium des Kultus und Unterrichts, July 22, 1944. For an article in a similar spirit, see Hans Klose, "Große Gedanken der Schöpfung," *Naturschutz* 24 (1943): 77n.

[227] BArch B 245/6 p. 179.

[228] BArch B 245/6 p. 182r.

of "special steps" in his letters.[229] Enthused by the power play behind the scenes, Klose already dreamed of a personal decision of the Führer on the Wutach's fate.[230]

The conservationists' hopes were dampened when Himmler declined to take up the cause. In a letter of August 1943, SS general Hoffmann, the chief of police with the Reich Commissioner for Württemberg and Baden, informed Finckh that Himmler had refrained from personally dealing with the issue because he was, in Hoffmann's discomforting formulation, "currently mastering extremely important and urgent tasks."[231] Furthermore, the *Reichsführer-SS* was hesitant to clash with Reich Commissioner Robert Wagner over the issue; unlike the Hohenstoffeln, the Wutach Gorge was also devoid of ruins that could inspire Himmler's Germanic fantasies. However, Hoffmann himself discovered his love for the Wutach Gorge and vowed to fight for the nature reserve "in the place of the *Reichsführer*."[232] Hoffmann became active for the conservationists' cause, and one of the conspirators reported in January 1944 that Hoffmann's connections were "bearing fruits."[233] "It seems that the last word on the Wutach is not yet spoken," Schurhammer declared in his report to the ministry of education justifying his speech at Freiburg University. Mentioning the involvement of the *Reichsführer-SS*, "as previously in the Hohenstoffeln case," Schurhammer found that "the entire question is still 'in a state of flux.'"[234]

With the entire proceedings shrouded in secrecy, it is difficult to judge the participants' true feelings. Even if they did not know of Himmler's role in the "final solution" of the Jewish question, the conservationists must have known that they were dealing with the leader of a network of terror. Did they have no doubts about the wisdom of meddling with such a figure? After all, it was not a homogeneous group of fanatical Nazis that was pulling the strings in 1943: Finckh certainly qualified as a dedicated Nazi, but Klose and Schurhammer kept a low profile in ideological terms,

[229] GLAK Abt. 235 no. 48295, Ludwig Finckh to Burkhart Schomburg, April 20, 1943.

[230] BArch B 245/6 p. 182r.

[231] GLAK Abt. 235 no. 48275, Der höhere SS- und Polizeiführer bei den Reichsstatthaltern in Württemberg und Baden im Landkreis V und beim Chef der Zivilverwaltung im Elsaß to Ludwig Finckh, August 25, 1943.

[232] *Ibid.*

[233] GLAK Abt. 235 no. 48295, Aus einem Brief des Bürgermeisters der Stadt Waldshut an Dr. Ludwig Finckh, January 18, 1944.

[234] GLAK Abt. 235 no. 47677, Badische Landesnaturschutzstelle to the Minister des Kultus und Unterrichts, September 5, 1944.

and the latter did not join the Nazi Party until 1937.[235] In any case, playing with fire did not produce a positive result: the decree of the Forest Service remained in force until the end of Nazi rule, and the Schluchseewerk even tried to invoke its authorization in the 1950s. However, a protest movement for the preservation of the Wutach Gorge was gathering at that time and finally forced the utility to shelve the plan in 1960.[236] During the Nazi era, the war's progress had prevented harm to the Wutach Gorge: construction on the Schluchseewerk project started in 1942 and ended in early 1944, and work never began on the Wutach Gorge dam. In fact, the planners did not even start exploratory drilling in the area until 1951.[237] Therefore, the Wutach is still the wild river that it used to be today, without dams or diversions. If the metaphor were not so inadequate in this context, it would be tempting to say that the conservationists had lost the battle and won the war.

All in all, the four campaigns suggest a mixed verdict on conservation work during the Nazi era. In the Hohenstoffeln case, Finckh's campaign ultimately met with success, whereas the fight to save the Ems River resulted in almost total defeat. In the case of the Wutach, the conservationists ultimately prevailed, but that was because of fortunate circumstances rather than the Nazi regime's support; in the case of the Schorfheide nature reserve, the accomplishments were not more than an accidental by-product of Göring's penchant for hunting. The case studies show that there was some degree of sympathy for conservation among Nazi leaders, but that by no means assured the actual success of conservation. In the case of the Ems River, the Nazi leaders' emphatic pledges in defense of the scenic river went along with its actual destruction. Although no one was willing to challenge the legitimacy of conservation as a matter of principle, following up with forceful measures was quite a different matter. Conservation had a place on the agenda of the Nazi regime, but when it was at odds with other goals, conservationists fought an uphill battle. Even in the Hohenstoffeln case, the ultimate success looks much less impressive if one takes the previous history of long hesitation

---

[235] NSDAP Membership no. 5146461, from May 1, 1937.
[236] See Chaney, *Visions*, 189–228.
[237] See Schluchseewerk AG, *Ein halbes Jahrhundert mit Wasserkraft dabei. Schluchseewerk AG Freiburg 1928–1978* (Freiburg, 1978), 29; and StAF F 30/6 no. 142, Niederschrift über die Besprechung verschiedener Fragen, die das Schluchseewerk berühren, bei der Baudirektion Freiburg on December 18, 1951, p. 8.

and weak compromises into account. It took sustained protest, a favorable development in the labor market, and Heinrich Himmler's Germanic fantasies to save the scenic mountain. Given that, the positive outcome was clearly not what one could call a promising precedent. Seen among the other stories, the Hohenstoffeln case looks more like a fortunate exception.

Although the degree of success differed from case to case, the conservationists' strategies were remarkably similar. The Nazi regime clearly encouraged administrative activity and negotiations behind closed doors, whereas anything that smacked of public protest was monitored suspiciously. It was fine for the conservationists to be obstinate in an internal meeting, even if that stalled a war economy project for months; it was not acceptable to voice protest in public, as the government's strong reaction to Finckh's Berlin rally in 1934 shows. If conservation was to succeed, or at least make some headway, the path forward was negotiations within the administration. Even in the Hohenstoffeln case, success was ultimately the result of helpful connections behind the scenes, rather than Finckh's public campaigning. Clearly, to understand the inner workings of conservation in Nazi Germany, one needs to talk about bureaucracy.

5

On the Paper Trail: The Everyday Business
of Conservation

Being popular is probably the most natural goal of any social movement. Therefore, it does not look surprising on first glance that German conservationists were investing a significant amount of time and energy into lectures and public education; a recurring slogan declared that "conservation is a matter for the people (*Naturschutz ist Volkssache*)."[1] And yet it is rewarding to take a closer look. If conservationists addressed the general public, it was often not aimed at developing a powerful lobby for the conservationists' cause, at least not in the first place. Rather, the goal was to assure compliance with government regulations. As early as 1929, Schoenichen had published a book on "Dealing with Mother Green" (*Der Umgang mit Mutter Grün*) that gave instructions on the proper behavior in nature, in which his humorous style (or attempt thereat) poorly concealed his arrogant attitude.[2] "The starting point for all conservation efforts is a decent and well-mannered conduct towards plants, animals, and the landscape," Hans Schwenkel declared in 1941, and other conservationists likewise pledged "to educate the people in the preservation and reverent contemplation of our *Heimat* nature."[3] Typically, one regional government published a decree that supplemented the call to win the public for the cause of conservation with a warning that failure to record

---

[1] HStAD NW 60 no. 1603 p. 299; WAA LWL Best. 702 no. 184b vol. 2, Wilhelm Lienenkämper, Das Naturschutz-ABC, p. 16; LASH Abt. 320 Eiderstedt no. 1846, Lamprecht and Wolf, Aufgaben des Natur- und Heimatschutzes im Kreise Husum (undated), p. 5; G. Löhr, "Der gegenwärtige Stand und die Aufgaben des Naturschutzes in der Rheinpfalz," *Blätter für Naturschutz und Naturpflege* 18 (1935): 108.

[2] Walther Schoenichen, *Der Umgang mit Mutter Grün. Ein Sünden- und Sittenbuch für jedermann* (Berlin-Lichterfelde, 1929).

[3] Schwenkel, *Taschenbuch*, 16; Emeis, "Stand," 173.

hitherto unknown natural monuments with the authorities was punishable by law.[4] Clearly, the conservation community saw administrative work as its core activity and popularizing its concern as a mere afterthought.

A strong role for state agencies had always been a hallmark of German conservation, as well as of many other parts of German politics and life. Still, the dominance of state officials during the Nazi era was unprecedented: never before had conservation work been bureaucratic work to such an extent. Once again, the national conservation law defined an important watershed, and administrative files grew notably in volume after 1935.[5] That, however, is almost the only thing that can be said in general about the administration's work during the Nazi era: going through the surviving files, the most striking feature is the enormous diversity of conservation work. The agenda of the national conservation law had ranged from small-scale natural monuments to the landscape in general, and that left a great deal of leeway for local peculiarities and personal preferences. Some used the new option to protect the countryside in general and created large landscape protection reserves (*Landschaftsschutzgebiete*).[6] Others focused on smaller issues like the protection of hedgerows that were important for birdlife and erosion control.[7] Karl Oberkirch, the state conservation advisor for the Ruhr region, chose private animal parks as his enemy of choice, even attacking them as "bird and animal concentration camps"; officials in the Weissenburg district attacked an untidy tavern for marring the "beauty of the landscape."[8] After the German invasion of the Sudetenland in the fall of 1938, the regional government of Franconia ordered the removal of the blue arrows that the military

---

[4] StAW Landratsamt Bad Kissingen no. 1233, Regierung von Unterfranken und Aschaffenburg to the Bezirksämter and Oberbürgermeister der Stadtkreise, March 20, 1937, p. 12.

[5] See WAA LWL Best. 702 no. 192a; HStAD BR 1011 no. 45 vol. 2; HStAD Landratsamt Siegkreis no. 434; StAW Landratsamt Ebern no. 1336; HStADd Best. 10747 no. 2255 and 2256; and StAD G 15 Friedberg B 100.

[6] See HStAD NW 72 no. 531 p. 15; StAB MBV 502, Amtsblatt der Regierung in Minden of September 24, 1938.

[7] See BArch B 245/25 pp. 1–5; HStAD NW 72 no. 531 p. 14; and StAN Rep. 212/19[VII] no. 2923, Staatlich anerkannter Ausschuß für Vogelschutz, Organisations- und Propagandaleiter Garmisch-Partenkirchen, February 7, 1938.

[8] HStAD RW 24 no. 961, Naturdenkmalpflege und Naturschutz im Gebiete des Siedlungsverbandes Ruhrkohlenbezirk. Tätigkeitsbericht des Bezirksbeauftragten für Naturschutz in Essen für die Geschäftsjahre 1935/1936 und 1936/1937, p. 15; StAN Rep. 212/19[VII] no. 2546, Bezirksamt Weissenburg to the Bürgermeister Suffersheim, December 17, 1938.

had painted on walls and buildings to mark the troops' path. In Hesse, conservationists urged hunters to design their shooting blinds so that they were "organically embedded into the landscape."[9] Even Jewish cemeteries could make it onto the conservationists' agenda: in 1938, Hans Stadler, certainly no philo-Semite, ordered his subordinates to screen the region's Jewish cemeteries for natural monuments.[10]

For many conservationists, the national conservation law was an uplifting experience. For example, the conservation advisor for the Husum district on the North Sea outlined an ambitious agenda for action within months after the law's passage. Crediting previous efforts as "worthy preparations," his document promised a "strict organization" aimed at a "properly planned and accurate stock-taking on the basis of the law." The advisor sought to collect information with a flurry of questionnaires, and armed with this information and the "systematic cooperation of a network of co-workers in all parts of the district," he hoped to bring the area's natural treasures "safely under protection (*unter Dach und Fach*)."[11] The penchant for registration and organization was definitely typical: compiling comprehensive inventories was a highly popular activity among conservationists, and advisors routinely asked their co-workers for "a voluminous list of spots worthy of protection."[12] Of course, a certain amount of red tape was an inevitable by-product of the upswing of conservation work, but efforts often moved far beyond administrative necessities. At times, one could get the impression that for contemporary conservationists, only a properly registered natural treasure was a real natural treasure.

The emphasis on registration and organization was all the more surprising because the conservationists were by no means legalist purists who narrow-mindedly focused on a proper execution of the law's provisions. Quite to the contrary, many conservationists were activists in the

---

9 StAN Rep. 212/19[VII] no. 2535, Regierung von Oberfranken und Mittelfranken to the Bezirksverwaltungsbehörden, December 10, 1938; StAD G 38 Eudorf no. 47, Der Reichsstatthalter in Hessen to the Forstämter, July 1, 1937.

10 StAW Landratsamt Obernburg no. 210, Regierung von Unterfranken und Aschaffenburg to the untere Naturschutzbehörden, January 11, 1938.

11 LASH Abt. 320 Eiderstedt no. 1846, Lamprecht and Wolf, Aufgaben des Natur- und Heimatschutzes im Kreise Husum (1935), p. 1n.

12 StAW Landratsamt Ebern no. 1336, Der Regierungs-Beauftragte der NSDAP für Naturschutz in Unterfranken to Hauptlehrer Hoch in Ebern, March 11, 1935. Similarly, WAA LWL Best. 702 no. 184b vol. 2, Gemeinsame Arbeitstagung der westfälischen Naturschutzbeauftragten und der Fachstelle Naturkunde und Naturschutz im Westfälischen Heimatbund on February 12–13, 1938, p. 4.

literal sense of the word. Wilhelm Lienenkämper even resorted to military language in the description of his work ethic: "Our service needs to be a battle: a battle in words and in writing against ignorance and brutality. Quick intervention if *Heimat* treasures are under siege. Our work does not tolerate delays, for even a single day can mean destruction beyond remedy."[13] To be sure, conservationists were generally more pragmatic than Lienenkämper's martial statement might suggest, and conservationists often agreed to reasonable compromises even if they had the legal means at hand for a stricter approach.[14] However, conservationists repeatedly moved even beyond the broad agenda of the national conservation law. For example, Lienenkämper often dealt with conservation issues that fell under the hunting law, and his lack of formal competence did not bother him at all. "If Mother Nature is threatened, the true friend of nature does not care about jurisdictions."[15] Also, conservation officials repeatedly dealt with inner-city parks, even though the national conservation law gave authority over them to the Department of Labor.[16] If a topic caught the conservationists' attention, they were quick to seize the initiative, seeing formal jurisdiction as an issue of secondary relevance. When rumors spread in 1937 that Germany would reclaim the colonies it had lost after World War I, Hans Klose swiftly proposed setting up a committee for the designation of national parks within the future colonial administration.[17]

The national conservation law prompted the conservation community to move beyond the protection of nature reserves and small-scale natural monuments to engage the landscape as a whole.[18] Some conservationists were eager to push ahead in this direction. "It shall be the complete

---

[13] WAA LWL Best. 702 no. 184, Wilhelm Lienenkämper, Der Deutsche und seine Landschaft. Vom gegenwärtigen Stand der Naturschutzbewegung. Easter edition of the conservation supplement of the Lüdenscheider Generalanzeiger, March 31, 1934.

[14] See HStADd Best. 10747 no. 2251, Der Regierungspräsident zu Dresden-Bautzen to the Landesbauernschaft Sachsen, July 4, 1939; StAD G 38 Eudorf no. 47, Forstamt Homberg to Forstamt Eudorf, October 12, 1938; and Kersten, "Naturschutz," 3602.

[15] WAA LWL Best. 702 no. 184b vol. 2, Tätigkeitsbericht des Bezirksbeauftragten für Naturschutz im Regierungsbezirk Arnsberg für die Geschäftsjahre 1936/1937 und 1937/1938, p. 3.

[16] BArch B 245/101 p. 101; StAW Landratsamt Obernburg no. 210, Regierung von Unterfranken und Aschaffenburg to the Bezirksverwaltungsbehörden, February 17, 1936; StAW Landratsamt Ebern no. 1336, Der Gauheimatpfleger und Beauftragte für Naturschutz der NSDAP Mainfranken to the Bürgermeister, November 1, 1937. See also Karsten Runge, *Entwicklungstendenzen der Landschaftsplanung. Vom frühen Naturschutz bis zur ökologisch nachhaltigen Flächennutzung* (Berlin, 1998), 20.

[17] Wettengel, "Staat und Naturschutz," 396.

[18] See Oberkrome, *Deutsche Heimat*, 14.

landscape," a conservationist from the Rhineland emphatically declared, linking the holistic approach of landscape planning to the totalitarian character of the Nazi state.[19] A number of conferences and lectures followed the same line, urging conservationists to adopt a broader approach in their work. For example, the Reich Conservation Agency sponsored a course in landscape planning, led by Hans Schwenkel, near Lake Constance in 1938.[20] In the Rhineland, some 300 invited participants conducted boat trips in 1937 and 1938 to discuss the problems of the landscape along the Rhine.[21] But in spite of these spectacular events, the usual response from the conservationists' rank and file remained somewhat lukewarm: nature reserves and natural monuments, not landscape planning on a grand scale, remained the mainstay of conservation work.[22] After all, landscape planning was very different from the traditional core activity of the conservation community. It is instructive to read how Schoenichen described the differences between the protection of nature and comprehensive landscape preservation. Whereas nature protection sought to preserve certain areas in a primordial state, Schoenichen argued that the task of landscape preservation was to influence the human use of landscapes in a certain way. Thus, the two fields of activity also required two different mindsets. For nature protection, it was imperative "to fend off all competing claims as far as possible in order to achieve the general goal," whereas landscape preservation required "a certain degree of flexibility" and a readiness to compromise. The two fields of activity thus also called for very different personalities: whereas nature protection required the staunch advocate, the crusader for a certain cause, landscape preservation asked for a manager, a flexible negotiator of deals. Most conservationists were advocates rather than managers, and given that, it is not surprising that they willingly conceded the field of landscape planning to Alwin Seifert and Heinrich Wiepking-Jürgensmann.[23]

---

[19] Quoted in Lekan, "It Shall," 73.

[20] HStAD BR 1011 no. 43 p. 181; Konrad Buchwald, "Geschichtliche Entwicklung von Landschaftspflege und Naturschutz in Deutschland während des Industriezeitalters," in Konrad Buchwald and Wolfgang Engelhardt (eds.), *Handbuch für Landschaftspflege und Naturschutz. Schutz, Pflege und Entwicklung unserer Wirtschafts- und Erholungsland-schaften auf ökologischer Grundlage* (Munich, 1968), 107.

[21] Lekan, *Imagining*, 186–8.

[22] Oberkrome, *Deutsche Heimat*, 259. It is revealing to see how Hans Schwenkel struggled to define landscape preservation (*Landschaftspflege*) as a part of nature protection. (Hans Schwenkel, *Grundzüge der Landschaftspflege*. Landschaftsschutz und Landschaftspflege 2 [Neudamm and Berlin, 1938], 9–14. See also Hans Klose, "Von unserer Arbeit während des Krieges und über Nachkriegsaufgaben," *Naturschutz* 25 [1944]: 4.)

[23] Schoenichen, *Naturschutz als völkische und internationale Kulturaufgabe*, 30, 33.

The designation of nature reserves was a limited approach from the point of view of landscape planning, but conservationists focused on this field with enthusiasm and determination. Precise figures are lacking on a national scale, but on the regional level, the boom is clear.[24] For example, Karl Oberkirch doubled the number of nature reserves in the Ruhr region within 2 years of the national conservation law's passage.[25] The figures for Walther Emeis, conservation advisor for the northern province of Schleswig-Holstein, were no less impressive: whereas ten nature reserves had existed within the provincial boundaries before 1935, Emeis reported twelve new reserves by 1938, with half a dozen additional designations under preparation.[26] In the mountainous Sauerland region, Wilhelm Lienenkämper filed the papers for nineteen nature reserves between 1936 and 1938.[27] Outside Prussia, the results were sometimes even more astounding: authorities in Württemberg designated forty-six nature reserves with a total area of 32,111 acres between 1937 and 1943, and Baden created fifty-eight nature reserves totaling 17,653 acres during those years.[28] These figures appear even more dramatic when one compares them with the meager results for the postwar years: between 1945 and 1959, only twenty-five additional nature reserves were created in the combined states of Baden and Württemberg. All in all, the increase of area under protection amounted to 3,152 acres in the 15 years after the end of the war – only 6 percent of the acreage protected during the Nazi era.[29] Never in German history have so many nature reserves been designated within such a brief period of time.

The burgeoning number of nature reserves certainly attests to the boom of conservation work after 1935. However, it also testifies to a second, more ambiguous fact: the designation of dozens of nature reserves within 2 or 3 years would have been impossible without the indemnity clause in paragraph 24 of the national conservation law. As seen above, this paragraph differed markedly from previous regulations, which had provided for some kind of compensation for property owners in prospective

---

[24] See Wettengel, "Staat und Naturschutz," 389; and Klueting, "Regelungen," 100.

[25] HStAD RW 24 no. 961, Naturdenkmalpflege und Naturschutz im Gebiete des Siedlungsverbandes Ruhrkohlenbezirk. Tätigkeitsbericht des Bezirksbeauftragten für Naturschutz in Essen für die Geschäftsjahre 1935/1936 und 1936/1937, p. 5.

[26] Emeis, "Stand," 142–5.

[27] WAA LWL Best. 702 no. 184b vol. 2, Tätigkeitsbericht des Bezirksbeauftragten für Naturschutz im Regierungsbezirk Arnsberg für die Geschäftsjahre 1936/1937 und 1937/1938, p. 4.

[28] Häcker, *50 Jahre*, 28.

[29] *Ibid.*, 58.

nature reserves. The break with previous traditions was not as radical in conservation practice as in legal theory, but the clause was used, and not only in exceptional cases like the Hohenstoffeln. As late as 1948, the government of North Rhine-Westphalia invoked the paragraph to deny damage claims from the owner of a quarry in the vicinity of Warstein.[30] But the paragraph's use went along with an almost complete absence of discussion over its proper role in conservation work and its moral implications. Even after 1945, publications on the national conservation law were notably silent on this issue. Hans Stadler provided a fitting description of the conservationists' dominant ethic (if that is the right term) when he noted in a memorandum of 1938 that "in order to convert unreasonable National Comrades to one's own opinion, there is sometimes no other option but patriarchal coercion (*väterliche Gewalt*)."[31] Paragraph 24 was finally invalidated through article 14 of the West German basic law of 1949, which ruled out confiscation of property without proper compensation.[32]

It is important to realize that the implementation of paragraph 24 was driven mainly by practitioners in the field. Directions from above usually recommended caution. In their commentary on the national conservation law, Walther Schoenichen and Werner Weber called for "a considerate treatment of the individuals concerned" and noted that "the idea of conservation should not triumph on the basis of the destroyed or badly damaged lives of National Comrades." As a result, Schoenichen and Weber proposed "commensurate compensation" wherever the conservationists' decrees were tantamount to the confiscation of property.[33] Similarly, Karl Cornelius noted in his dissertation on the national conservation law that the provisions only pertained to "cases of egoism."[34] At first glance, conservationists seemed to adhere to the traditional custom of amicable negotiations, and the conservation administration continued to pay compensation to property owners.[35] But the normalcy was deceiving: paragraph 24

---

[30] See Frank Uekötter, "Einleitung," in Radkau and Uekötter, *Naturschutz und Nationalsozialismus*, 27–9.

[31] StAW Landratsamt Bad Kissingen no. 1234, Schutz der Bachläufe und ihrer Uferbäume und Gebüsche. Hans Stadler to all Bürgermeister des Gaues Mainfranken, p. 2.

[32] Schubert, "Zur Entwicklung," 522.

[33] Schoenichen and Weber, *Reichsnaturschutzgesetz*, 114. See also Schubert, "Zur Entwicklung," 498.

[34] Cornelius, *Reichsnaturschutzgesetz*, 45.

[35] See BArch B 245/19 p. 18n; BArch B 245/23 pp. 20, 24; StAN Rep. 212/19[VII] no. 2535, Der Gauheimatpfleger der NSDAP im Gaubereich Franken to the Bezirksamt Weißenburg, December 10, 1935; and WAA LWL Best. 702 no. 191.

of the national conservation law was a perfect instrument to pressure property owners into concessions, and indications are strong that conservationists used this option on a regular basis.

The creation of the Westrup Heath nature reserve on the northern fringe of the Ruhr region provides a case in point. The local waterworks had planned to purchase land to deposit sand, settling with a farmer on a price of 60,000 Reichsmarks for 165 acres of farmland. However, the agreement became void when the land was earmarked for conservation.[36] Officials quickly agreed that the farmer had to receive some kind of payment in return, even more so because the farmer was clearly in economic difficulties at that time. However, the officials were also unanimous that there was no need for the amount to be in the vicinity of the waterworks' bid. As a result, they offered 21,000 Reichsmarks – to the great dismay of the farmer, who, at the instigation of his wife, hastily ended the meeting.[37] After two more rounds of negotiations, the parties finally agreed on 32,000 Reichsmarks – little more than half the previously determined market price![38] Characteristically, there was no reference to paragraph 24 in the administration's records, though there can be no doubt that it played a role in the negotiations. In his annual report, Karl Oberkirch simply mentioned the "difficult negotiations" over the Westrup Heath without providing any figures.[39]

The case was probably typical: the state did not simply confiscate the property but rather used the strong position provided by the national conservation law for a favorable settlement. For the conservationists, paragraph 24 was something like a magic wand: it was not used indiscriminately, but it was at hand whenever trouble arose. It is instructive to read a memorandum written by Wilhelm Münker on a prospective nature reserve in the Sauerland region. He clearly preferred an "amicable settlement without damage for the owner," but also saw inviting Hans Klose for a personal visit as an option, noting that "there can be no doubt about his decision" – certainly not an ideal setting for fair negotiations.[40] In 1936, Wilhelm Lienenkämper and Paul Graebner

---

36 WAA LWL Best. 702 no. 185, Landrat Recklinghausen to the Oberpräsident Münster, July 8, 1936.

37 *Ibid.*, Landrat Recklinghausen to the Oberpräsident Münster, December 9, 1936.

38 *Ibid.*, contract of March 6, 1937.

39 HStAD RW 24 no. 961, Naturdenkmalpflege und Naturschutz im Gebiete des Siedlungsverbandes Ruhrkohlenbezirk. Tätigkeitsbericht des Bezirksbeauftragten für Naturschutz in Essen für die Geschäftsjahre 1935/1936 und 1936/1937, p. 8.

40 WAA LWL Best. 702 no. 191, Wilhelm Münker, Heimat- und Naturschutz-Ausschuß des Sauerländischen Gebirgsvereins to Landeshauptmann Kolbow, June 15, 1937.

pressed a mayor in the same region into a significant reduction of the rent for a nature reserve.[41] A conservation advisor in the Bavarian city of Weissenburg proposed invoking paragraph 24 in a case where an owner had refused to sell an unsightly building, and a Saxon official turned down a compensation claim with the laconic comment "that the law does not contain provisions to that effect."[42] When discussing instructions for forest management on private land for the Wutach nature reserve in 1936, the ministry of finance and commerce for the state of Baden noted that one might expect some concessions in the light of paragraph 24.[43] For officials in charge of conservation, life was much easier with paragraph 24, and a new sense of autonomy took the place of the painful negotiations with property owners of previous years: officials could simply turn down awkward demands without much thought or legal risks. The situation might have been even worse if the last word on issues of compensation had not rested with the Administrative Court of Prussia (*Preußisches Oberverwaltungsgericht*), a court with a strong sense of tradition as a counterweight against drastic administrative decisions and a notable record of resistance to Nazification.[44]

The growing number of nature reserves was only one aspect of the general boom of conservation work during the Nazi era. In light of the enduring conflicts between different agencies within the Nazi state, it was imperative for the conservation community to seek friends and partners. Of course, the most important partner for conservation officials was the civic conservation movement, and the close cooperation between civic and state actors remained the rule in Nazi Germany. The network of conservation advisors provided favorable conditions for cooperation: maintaining close contacts with the administration while standing outside its hierarchy, conservation advisors were ideally suited to link state and civic activities.[45] In some regions, the advisors' network blended with conservation associations to such an extent that it became difficult to differentiate between state and societal action.[46]

---

[41] WAA LWL Best. 702 no. 192, memorandum of July 15, 1936.

[42] StAN Rep. 212/19[VII] no. 2535, memorandum of the Geschäftsführer der Naturschutzstelle Weißenburg, January 30, 1936, p. 1; HStADd Best. 10747 no. 2255, Kreishauptmann Dresden to the Amtshauptmann Löbau, June 24, 1938.

[43] GLAK Abt. 237 no. 49495, Badischer Finanz- und Wirtschaftsminister, Forstabteilung to the Finanz- und Wirtschaftsminister, January 28, 1936, p. 2.

[44] Stolleis, *Gemeinwohlformen*, 126. During the Nazi era, the Administrative Court of Prussia had jurisdiction for all of Germany.

[45] See Schoenichen and Weber, *Reichsnaturschutzgesetz*, 44.

[46] See StAD G 15 Gross-Gerau B 66, memorandum of November 3, 1936, p. 2; StAW Landratsamt Bad Kissingen no. 1234, Bayerische Landesstelle für Naturschutz to the

Nor is it to be forgotten that money kept flowing from the state into the associations' coffers: when the Association for Nature Protection Parks (*Verein Naturschutzpark*), one of the major German conservation leagues, applied for a grant of 28,000 Reichsmarks in 1935, the German ministry of finance gave it 30,000 Reichsmarks instead.[47] However, the network soon grew beyond the core constituency of conservation, and it began to include parties that appear in hindsight as unlikely partners.

These partners included capitalists, workers, peasants, and others. The *Berliner Börsenzeitung*, the newspaper of the Berlin stock exchange, reported favorably on the passage of the national conservation law, giving space to an extensive description of the nature reserves in the capital's vicinity.[48] In Saxony, the *Deutsche Arbeitsfront*, the workers' organization in Nazi Germany, joined the protest against a quarry that threatened a mountain in a popular recreation area.[49] Karl Oberkirch praised the authorities in charge of Autobahn construction for their "excellent" cooperation in his district.[50] In the Rhineland, the supreme official in charge of hunting (*Provinzjägermeister*) took issue with the Labor Service over its drainage and land cultivation work.[51] Even the military became active, ordering an inventory of natural treasures on state property in 1938.[52] During the same year, the Bavarian *Gauleiter* Adolf Wagner, one of the more notorious of the regional Nazi leaders because of his despotic reign, became patron of the Bavarian Conservation League.[53] In 1936, the leader of the Westphalian peasantry (*Landesbauernführer*) proposed friendly cooperation between agricultural and conservation interests "in order to identify what is truly worthy of protection and then save as much of it as possible without jeopardizing the overarching goal of a secure food

---

bayerische Naturschutzbehörden and Naturschutzbeauftragten, December 18, 1936; StAN Rep. 212/19[VII] no. 2542; and HStADd Best. 10747 no. 2251.

[47] BArch R 2/4730 pp. 145, 147, 151.

[48] HStADd Best. 10702 no. 1426, *Berliner Börsenzeitung* no. 304 of July 2, 1935.

[49] HStADd Best. 10747 no. 2255, Der Reichsstatthalter in Sachsen, Landesforstverwaltung to the Kreishauptmann zu Dresden-Bautzen, January 14, 1938.

[50] HStAD RW 24 no. 961, Naturdenkmalpflege und Naturschutz im Gebiete des Siedlungsverbandes Ruhrkohlenbezirk. Tätigkeitsbericht des Bezirksbeauftragten für Naturschutz in Essen für die Geschäftsjahre 1935/1936 und 1936/1937, p. 14.

[51] HStAD BR 1005 no. 156, Der Provinzjägermeister für die Rheinprovinz to the Oberpräsident der Rheinprovinz, July 2, 1934.

[52] StAD G 15 Friedberg B 101, decree of the Reichsminister für Wissenschaft, Erziehung und Volksbildung, July 4, 1938.

[53] StAW Landratsamt Bad Kissingen no. 1237, Bund Naturschutz in Bayern to the Gruppenführer and Vertrauensmänner, October 22, 1938.

supply."[54] Of course, none of these gestures implied a total commitment to the cause of conservation, but they showed that the conservation movement had emerged as a significant political player that others sought to coopt, rather than ignore. Remarkably, a decree of the ministry of commerce warned in 1936 that "there must not be any restrictions for areas used for the purposes of industry and commerce," showing that conservation was now a force to be reckoned with.[55] In fact, the conservation administration even dared to raise its voice when Joseph Goebbels sought to build his Waldhof mansion in a protected area north of Berlin in 1939, and it took repeated interventions from Göring to clear the way for the project.[56] To be sure, Hans Schwenkel complained at a conference in 1939 that conservation was still being "ignored" and "ridiculed" in some places, but that attitude was clearly on the decline during the Nazi era.[57]

The conservationists were more hesitant in their outreach toward touristic interests, revealing class anxieties. Tourist associations had supported conservationists in many conflicts, and yet a strong sentiment within the conservation community ran against everything that smacked of mass tourism; typically, a pamphlet of the Bavarian Conservation League on a nature reserve in the Bavarian Alps distinguished between "serious alpinists of good education" and "idealistic friends of nature" on the one hand and "men and women with strange appearance and manners" on the other.[58] The conservation community was wise enough to refrain from a direct confrontation with the Nazis' *Kraft durch Freude* tourist association, one of the most popular Nazi institutions, but the association's promotion of working-class tourism met with enormous reservations in conservation circles, and rumors persisted about unruly behavior and the destruction of plants during *Kraft durch Freude* hiking excursions.[59] "What will become of the German nation when the low

---

[54] WAA LWL Best. 702 no. 191, Landesbauernschaft Westfalen, Der Landesbauernführer to the chair of the Heimat- und Naturschutz-Ausschuss des Sauerländischen Gebirgsvereins, December 17, 1936. Similarly, GLAK Abt. 235 no. 47680, decree of November 20, 1937.

[55] HStAD BR 1011 no. 43, decree of the Reichs- und Preußischer Wirtschaftsminister, May 12, 1936. Similarly, BArch R 22/2119 p. 113.

[56] Stefan Berkholz, *Goebbels' Waldhof am Bogensee. Vom Liebesnest zur DDR-Propagandastätte* (Berlin, 2004), 35–40.

[57] StAD G 15 Friedberg B 101, Niederschrift über die Arbeitsbesprechung und Bereisung am 19. und 20. Juni in Frankfurt a.M. und Umgebung, p. 12.

[58] StAN Rep. 212/19[VII] no. 2547, Bund Naturschutz in Bayern, Das Naturschutzgebiet am Königssee in den Berchtesgadener Alpen (1921), p. 17.

[59] See StAD G 15 Friedberg B 101, Der Beauftragte für Naturschutz im Bereiche des Landes Hessen to the Beauftragte bei den Kreisstellen für Naturschutz, February 24, 1940; Kersten, "Naturschutz"; Oberkrome, *Deutsche Heimat*, 95, 517. See also Wolfhard

mountain ranges (thank god, the Alps are a more difficult case in this regard!) are fully adjusted to the idle drivers of automobiles, to urban luxury and urban habits and when the restaurant owners' interests come to decide on the fate of Germany's recreation areas?" Hans Schwenkel asked in a report of 1938.[60] It is also striking that direct interventions from Nazi leaders on behalf of conservation were rare; Göring's support for the Schorfheide and Himmler's intervention on behalf of the Hohenstoffeln were clearly isolated incidents. After all, there was a risk involved in forceful initiatives, as Adolf Wagner learned in 1937 when he brusquely ordered the cleanup of the town of Pappenheim, a spa halfway between Nuremberg and Augsburg. The order resulted in an uproar among the town's leaders, and a closer investigation revealed that the *Gauleiter* had driven through the village of Rothenstein and confused it with the spa because of a sign at the entrance of the village. The sign had the word Pappenheim along with an instruction for drivers to "turn right in town," and the latter information had obviously escaped the *Gauleiter's* attention. As a result, Wagner cancelled his bold initiative in the name of "cleanliness and beauty in town and countryside" and, in a rare gesture of remorse, promised to visit Pappenheim in the near future.[61]

Of course, conservationists experienced not only gains during the Nazi era but also disappointments. Ironically, one of the more notable failures occurred in a project with a strong ideological flavor. Schoenichen did not succeed in designating the Kyffhäuser mountain range as a nature reserve in honor of the soldiers killed in World War I, as he had proposed in 1932.[62] However, failed initiatives of this kind must not conceal the fact that the Nazi era was a busy time for the conservation community, especially in the 4 years between the passage of the national conservation law and the onset of World War II. The intense activism in

---

Buchholz, *Die Nationalsozialistische Gemeinschaft "Kraft durch Freude." Freizeitgestaltung und Arbeiterschaft im Dritten Reich* (Ph.D. dissertation, University of Munich, 1976); and Hermann Weiß, "Ideologie der Freizeit im Dritten Reich. Die NS-Gemeinschaft 'Kraft durch Freude,'" *Archiv für Sozialgeschichte* 33 (1993): 289–303.

[60] BArch B 245/6 p. 234.

[61] See StAN Rep. 212/19[VII] no. 2535, Staatsministerium des Innern to the Bezirksamt Weißenburg, October 2, 1937, and letters of the Bürgermeister der Stadt Pappenheim of October 15, 1937, and January 6, 1938.

[62] Schoenichen, *Naturschutz als völkische und internationale Kulturaufgabe*, 55. Therefore, one may doubt whether it would be rewarding to analyze Nazi Germany with a view to the "nationalization of nature": see Richard White, "The Nationalization of Nature," *Journal of American History* 86 (1999): 976–86, and Sara B. Pritchard, "Reconstructing the Rhône. The Cultural Politics of Nature and Nation in Contemporary France, 1945–1997," *French Historical Studies* 27 (2004): 765–99.

this time frame is all the more remarkable because the network of conservation advisors looks much less impressive on closer investigation. The job of conservation advisor was usually an honorary, unsalaried post, and as a result, advisors routinely performed their duties alongside their normal occupations. Seeing that this placed an enormous burden on the advisors, the ministry of education issued a decree in February 1934 that allowed a significant reduction of the workload for teachers serving as conservation advisors.[63] The importance of this decree becomes clear when one notes the prominence of teachers among the conservation advisors: in 1936, they represented twenty-seven of the thirty-four regional conservation advisors in Prussia; in Westphalia and the Rhine Province, fifty-six of ninety-five district advisors worked as teachers.[64] However, the decree came about only because the ministry of education was also in charge of conservation at that time, and when responsibility moved to the Forest Service with the passage of the national conservation law, the cooperative attitude of the ministry changed almost immediately. Although the decree was never formally repealed, teachers working as conservation advisors found it increasingly difficult to gain a reduction in their teaching duties.[65] Thus, the conservation advisors' job became clearly less attractive after 1935.

Environmental historians have repeatedly complained that the consultation of conservation authorities pursuant to paragraph 20 of the national conservation law remained incomplete.[66] To be sure, a national decree of 1938 noted that there had been no hearings, or only severely delayed ones, "in a large number of cases."[67] However, the more serious problem seems to have been that the national conservation law implied an enormous increase of the conservation advisors' workload: deadlines loomed, memoranda were waiting to be written, and countless meetings required the presence of the conservation advisor – and all that in addition to a full-time job! As a result, the mandatory hearing on every project with an impact on the landscape implied an enormous burden for a terribly

---

[63] *Nachrichtenblatt für Naturdenkmalpflege* 11 (1934): 65.
[64] HStAD NW 60 no. 623 p. 97r. For information on other areas, see StAW Landratsamt Bad Kissingen no. 1233, Verzeichnis der Mitglieder der höheren Naturschutzstelle bei der Regierung von Unterfranken und Aschaffenburg und der Beauftragten bei den unteren Naturschutzstellen in Unterfranken as of March 20, 1937; Häcker, *50 Jahre*, 22; *Reichsministerialblatt der Forstverwaltung* 1 (1937): 10n.
[65] HStAD NW 60 no. 623 p. 95.
[66] See Wettengel, "Staat und Naturschutz," 390; and Klueting, "Regelungen," 97.
[67] *Reichsministerialblatt der Forstverwaltung* 2 (1938): 43.

overworked group of people, and conservation advisors often struggled to keep up at least a semblance of supervision. One of the more dramatic accounts came from Karl Oberkirch, who once gave the following description of a meeting on a gas pipeline in the highly industrialized Ruhr area: "I arrived at the meeting without information on the plans. During the negotiations, I frantically tried to copy the course of the pipeline, which cuts through some important areas, onto my own map." In the end, Oberkirch refrained from blocking the project in spite of significant doubts, and all that he accomplished was a lukewarm plea to restore hedgerows after construction.[68]

In light of the conservation advisors' dismal situation, it is striking that there was never a comprehensive discussion of enforcement problems during the Nazi era. Wilhelm Lienenkämper called for the creation of full-time positions for conservation advisors in 1937, and Paul Graebner even warned "of overstretching landscape protection" at a meeting in 1938, arguing with some justification that "this would make any proper supervision impossible."[69] However, these were isolated voices without any impact, and the conservation advisors remained unsalaried and overworked until long into the postwar years. Thus, it would have been a clever strategy to admit the limited resources at hand for the conservation community and define certain priorities. However, there are no indications that the Reich Conservation Agency ever thought along those lines, and the same seems to be true for most of the regional conservation advisors. After all, the network of conservation advisors was a source of great pride for many activists, making it difficult to start a sober discussion of its limits. A 1936 statement by the conservation advisor for the state of Hesse gives an impression of the dominant sentiment: "Hesse is now the first state with a comprehensive conservation organization down to the local level."[70] It is frequently hard to avoid the impression that a *complete* network was more imortant to the conservationists than an *effective* one.

As a result, much of the conservationists' limited resources went into unproductive paperwork that served bureaucratic purposes rather than the protection of nature. A prime example was the banding of birds as

[68] BArch B 245/23 p. 29n.
[69] See WAA LWL Best. 702 no. 184b vol. 1, Wilhelm Lienenkämper, Die Arbeit der Naturschutzbeauftragten. Planvolles Schaffen oder Armeleutebetrieb? (ca. 1937); and WAA LWL Best. 702 no. 184b vol. 2, Gemeinsame Arbeitstagung der westfälischen Naturschutzbeauftragten und der Fachstelle Naturkunde und Naturschutz im Westfälischen Heimatbund on February 12–13, 1938, p. 6.
[70] StAD G 15 Gross-Gerau B 66, memorandum of November 3, 1936, p. 2.

pets: large files in many archives provide an impression of the enormous amount of red tape that this work implied for the conservation administration. In some regions, there were even ideas about forming an association for banding birds, a strange idea even for a state with a mania for organization.[71] In fact, the Reich Conservation Agency made matters even worse by sending an endless flow of decrees to the conservation advisors' network, thus constantly increasing the number of tasks for a notoriously overworked community. Even when the issues themselves were worthwhile, the cumulative effect was that the conservation community gradually drowned in a deluge of initiatives and projects. More than once, a bold announcement was simultaneously the first and the last thing that the agency did on a certain issue. When the yearbook of German hunting recorded a decline in the number of ducks, Schoenichen swiftly started an initiative for the protection of breeding areas, but he never followed up on this decree with an inquiry about results, let alone a progress report.[72] In 1937, a decree from the Reich Conservation Agency announced the formation of a "study group on the effect of mouse poison on birdlife" in cooperation with the German Institute for Agricultural Studies (*Biologische Reichsanstalt für Land- und Forstwirtschaft*), of which nothing was ever heard again.[73] Finally, some initiatives cannot help but to appear petty in retrospect. The best example is certainly a decree of 1937 that focused on an endangered species of special charm: leeches. Because nineteenth-century medical practitioners had driven leeches to the brink of extinction, Schoenichen thought that it was now time to take stock. Therefore, he seriously urged the conservation advisors to identify shallow waters with a lot of vegetation, bare their legs, and "slowly wade in the water, lifting their feet every one or two minutes." Schoenichen closed his decree with information on where to mail the catch.[74] Perhaps that was the sacrifice that Lienenkämper was talking about.

All in all, the net effect of the conservationists' network was lagging significantly behind its potential. One need only read Schoenichen's

---

[71] See LWL Best. 717 file "Vogelberingung," esp. Vogelwarte Helgoland to Bernhard Rensch as Direktor des Landesmuseums für Naturkunde, August 16, 1939; StAN Rep. 212/19[VII] no. 2542, Der Bayerische Landessachverständige für Vogelschutz to the Bezirksamt Weissenburg, April 25, 1938; BArch R 22/2119 p. 22; StAB MBV 502, file "Vogelschutz Vogelberingung"; and LASH Abt. 320 Eiderstedt no. 1847.

[72] StAD G 38 Eudorf no. 47, Der Direktor der Reichsstelle für Naturschutz to the Stabsämter der Gaujägermeister, September 10, 1937.

[73] KAW Landratsamt Warendorf C 303, Der Direktor der Reichsstelle für Naturschutz to the Beauftragten für Naturschutz, February 25, 1937.

[74] HStAD BR 1011 no. 43 p. 185.

complaint of 1938 that he sometimes did not get proper information on appointments and that letters were often returned to the Reich Conservation Agency as "undeliverable" to get an impression how much red tape was tying up the resources of the conservation administration.[75] But for all its deficiencies, the conservationists' work of the late 1930s at least meant a significant departure from the sporadic initiatives of the Weimar years. Whereas conservation work had basically been dependent on the idealism of energetic individuals in the 1920s, the national conservation law encouraged conservation sentiments in all parts of the country: under the law's mandate, a region or a province could no longer simply ignore the protection of nature. Moreover, the conservation advisors' network had clearly gained a momentum of its own, as became clear during World War II. Within months of the war's onset, conservationists were stressing that the protection of nature was also of importance in these more difficult times, and conservation work continued with a surprising degree of normalcy during the first years of the war.[76] For example, in a decree of February 1940, the Forest Service stressed the need to consider the impact on the landscape in all forestry measures in spite of the war conditions.[77] The Heimat League of Saxony (*Landesverein Sächsischer Heimatschutz*) took issue with a quarry in a nature reserve in 1941 even though the project was designated as crucial for the war economy, and a meeting on the beautification of earth deposits during the same year spoke of the issue as an "affair of national importance." In April 1941, the Jordsand Association (*Verein Jordsand*), a group that focused on the protection of birds on the German seashore, started a funding drive to secure the northwestern coastline of the island of Norderoog.[78] Even the military was not off-limits to the conservationists' critique: in January 1940, the regional conservation advisor spoke of "defilement" when soldiers cut down trees

---

[75] See GLAK Abt. 235 no. 6550, Der Direktor der Reichsstelle für Naturschutz to the Vorsitzenden der höheren Naturschutzstellen, February 7, 1938.

[76] See Hans Klose, "Der Ruf der Heimat schweigt nie!," *Naturschutz* 21 (1941): 4; Luitpold Rueß, "Naturschutz im Krieg," *Blätter für Naturschutz* 23 (1940): 30n; StAN Rep. 212/19^VII no. 2542, Bund Naturschutz in Bayern to the Gruppenführer and Vertrauensmänner, November 15, 1939; and LASH Abt. 320 Eiderstedt no. 1807, letter of the Verein Jordsand zur Begründung von Vogelfreistätten an den deutschen Küsten, January 14, 1942.

[77] HStAD NW 72 no. 531 p. 118.

[78] HStADd Best. 10747 No. 2251, memorandum of the Regierungspräsident zu Dresden-Bautzen on the meeting on June 26, 1941; BArch B 245/19 p. 40; LASH Abt. 320 Eiderstedt no. 1807, letter of the Verein Jordsand zur Begründung von Vogelfreistätten an den deutschen Küsten, April 1, 1941. See also Ditt, *Raum*, 344–8.

at the confluence of the Rhine and Sieg Rivers. Conversely, the military meticulously requested a proper permit when it built a secret installation in the Kahler Asten nature reserve in September 1941.[79] When the Association for the Swabian Alb (*Schwäbischer Albverein*) decided to set up a conservation watch in April 1940, the result was an impressive documentation of the enduring vibrancy of nature protection during the first year of the war: more than 700 members volunteered for patrol service in scenic areas to prevent unruly or destructive behavior.[80]

Much of the wartime activity, however, was little more than paperwork. For example, there was never a chance for the realization of the 1942 plan for a European-wide direct-current cable network, a plan that was designed to achieve the abolition of unsightly power lines and protection against air raids at the same time.[81] In other cases, officials simply adhered to their prewar projects: in the Weissenburg district in Bavaria, work continued on the designation of a landscape reserve until February 1944.[82] Many wartime activities stood out for their sheer banality: was it really necessary, to give just one example, to consult the ministry of education of the state of Baden in a conflict over a concrete wall on a lot bordering Lake Constance?[83] Evidently, conservation sentiments remained strong until well into the war and sometimes led to sudden outbursts of activity, as a Westphalian farmer learned when he cut down a scenic hedgerow in January 1943. The county commissioner was aghast, and he did not see any reason to hold back his anger, even telling the farmer "that it is high time for him to go to Russia as a soldier, for that is how he would come to recognize the true value of the German *Heimat*." Somewhat on the defensive, the farmer muttered that he had returned from front duty in the east the previous fall.[84]

Going through the wartime files, it is striking that Nazi ideology generally continued to play only a marginal role in everyday conservation

---

[79] BArch B 245/19 p. 233; WAA LWL Best. 702 no. 192, memorandum of the Oberpräsident der Provinz Westfalen, September 25, 1941. See also StAW Landratsamt Bad Kissingen no. 1233, Heeresstandortverwaltung Bad Kissingen to the Landrat Bad Kissingen, November 26, 1940.

[80] Georg Fahrbach, "Zum Geleit," in Hans Schwenkel, *Taschenbuch des Naturschutzes* (Salach/Württemberg, 1941), 6.

[81] See Maier, "Unter Wasser," 164.

[82] See proceedings in StAN Rep. 212/19[VII] no. 2539.

[83] See GLAK Abt. 235 no. 16203, Der Minister des Kultus und Unterrichts to Ursel Küppers, December 22, 1941.

[84] WAA LWL Best. 702 no. 184, Landrat Sümmermann to the Oberpräsident der Provinz Westfalen, January 25, 1943.

work. In 1942, the Bavarian Conservation League sent out Christmas greetings that stressed conservation as a counterweight to "the materialist thinking of the Bolsheviks and the plutocrats," but declarations of this kind were rather rare.[85] It is interesting to note that Schurhammer's memorandum on the Wutach of November 1942 was completely devoid of Nazi ideology, even though any lever must have been welcome to him at that time. Of course, it is difficult, in this case as in many others, to determine the motives behind this ideological restraint, but it is remarkable that it was by no means exceptional.[86] At the same time, there are no signs that the war undermined the conservationists' general confidence in the Nazi regime. No one remembered Vietinghoff-Riesch's proposal of 1936 "to acknowledge war as a destructive force for the landscape."[87] Practical work, not ideological imperatives, continued to provide the crucial glue for the alliance between conservation and National Socialism. However, practical work began to serve a double purpose during the war: it sought not only to help the cause of conservation but also to demonstrate the urgent need for manpower, thus giving the impression to military authorities that it was unwise, if not irresponsible, to recruit conservation officials as soldiers. Of course, one should not reduce all wartime activities to this selfish motive: the tireless Wilhelm Münker continued his work for the Committee for the Rescue of Deciduous Forest through the war though he was too old even for the *Volkssturm* units that the Nazis recruited in the final days of the war.[88] However, when conservationists were busily shuffling papers during the war, this often reflected not only their dedication to the protection of nature but also their desire to stay away from the front lines. To be sure, conservationists were not generally exempted from conscription, and more and more conservationists were drafted as the war progressed, but it is interesting to note that this process occurred at a rather leisurely pace.

Perhaps no other agency faced stronger pressure to demonstrate its indispensability than the Reich Conservation Agency. Even if one saw conservation as a legitimate endeavor in times of war, the role of Klose's agency as a coordinator and moderator was clearly not necessary for the

---

[85] StAW Landratsamt Bad Kissingen no. 1237, Bund Naturschutz in Bayern to the Obleute unserer Kreisgruppen, Christmas 1942.

[86] GLAK Abt. 235 no. 48295, Hermann Schurhammer, Das Wutachtal als Naturschutzgebiet und das Schluchseewerk. Gutachten der Landesnaturschutzstelle Baden, Kolmar, November 30, 1942. See also BArch B 245/11 p. 47n.

[87] Vietinghoff-Riesch, *Naturschutz*, 37.

[88] Münker received the last grant for his committee work in January 1945. (HStAD NW 60 no. 1603 p. 2.)

persistence of conservation work. It is no coincidence that lieutenant general Walter von Unruh, who was in charge of identifying redundant officials starting in the summer of 1942, proposed in March 1943 the closing of the Reich Conservation Agency for the duration of the war.[89] It thus becomes understandable that the Reich Conservation Agency began to focus on a new field of activity: the occupied territory in Eastern Europe. As early as February 1940, Hans Klose reported on the Ludwigshöhe national park near the formerly Polish town of Posen: Klose proposed downgrading the area to a simple landscape protection reserve "because the park does not match our ideas of a national park."[90] However, Klose soon learned that his power base did not allow forceful initiatives in the occupied territories: although records show that plans existed from early 1940 to put the national conservation law into force in the occupied area, the law's actual introduction was delayed until March 11, 1941.[91] The Reich Conservation Agency diligently compiled a list of nature reserves and natural treasures in occupied Poland, but it never managed to move beyond simple inventories toward concrete measures.[92] In a letter of February 1943, Klose lashed out against the administration in Eastern Europe issuing decrees on conservation issues without any authority to do so, but the complaint showed Klose's lack of power as much as his anger over this "incredible" act.[93]

In retrospect, it seems that Klose was probably fortunate that his excursions into Eastern European affairs turned out to be so hapless. After all, this saved Klose from implication in the most infamous chapter of conservation work during the Nazi era: the involvement of members of the conservation community in the development of plans that were essentially blueprints for genocide. The wars against Poland and the Soviet Union set the stage for activities that were unprecedented in the history of modern warfare. The issue at stake in Eastern Europe was *Lebensraum*, one that had already played a major role in *Mein Kampf*. "The acquisition of new soil for the settlement of the excess population possesses an infinite number of advantages, particularly if we turn from the present to the future," Hitler wrote.[94] Historians have stressed that *Lebensraum* was not simply a blueprint for expansion. It is striking that the intentions laid

---

[89] BArch RW 42/36 p. 244. On Unruh's work, see Rebentisch, *Führerstaat*, 470–9.
[90] BArch B 245/137 p. 150.
[91] BArch B 245/88 p. 235; B 245/137 pp. 8, 160; R 22/2119 p. 239.
[92] BArch B 245/88. See also B 245/137 pp. 23, 29.
[93] BArch B 245/137 p. 14.
[94] Hitler, *Mein Kampf*, 138. On the quest for Lebensraum as a key pillar of Hitler's Weltanschauung, see Jäckel, *Hitlers Weltanschauung*.

out in *Mein Kampf* aimed at the Soviet Union, a country that Germany did not share a border with until 1939, and Hitler never provided a clear idea before the war of what should happen to Poland, even though some kind of dominance over or conquest of Poland was obviously necessary for the realization of his fantasies of eastward expansion. Pointing out this strange vagueness, Martin Broszat described the quest for *Lebensraum* as a "metaphor and utopian circumscription of a continual quest for ever greater power and freedom of action."[95] But although the notion of *Lebensraum* ultimately remained an elusive, indistinct concept, the territorial gains of Nazi Germany between 1939 and 1942 spurred ideas about the future use of the land. "The Volga shall become our Mississippi," Hitler declared in one of his usual monologues over dinner. On another occasion, he dreamed of an Autobahn making "the beauty of the Crimea" accessible from the German heartland.[96] However, there were also more elaborate plans for Soviet territory, set up with the help of eminent researchers. Some of these experts belonged to the conservation community.[97]

The best-known blueprint was the General Plan East (*Generalplan Ost*), which evolved under the direction of Konrad Meyer within the Reich Commissariat for the Strengthening of German Nationality (*Reichskommissariat für die Festigung des deutschen Volkstums*). To be sure, there were also planners working for Alfred Rosenberg as the official Minister for the Occupied Eastern Territories and for Hans Frank as Governor General of occupied Poland, but the Reich Commissariat, led by Heinrich Himmler and a part of the SS empire since 1941, ultimately prevailed over its rivals.[98] Born in 1901, Konrad Meyer was a typical representative of what Ulrich Herbert described as the "generation of matter-of-factness (*Generation der Sachlichkeit*)": like many members of his generation, he combined a faith in technocratic planning with a readiness to use radical and repressive means and a racist and antidemocratic

[95] Martin Broszat, "Soziale Motivation und Führer-Bindung des Nationalsozialismus," *Vierteljahreshefte für Zeitgeschichte* 18 (1970): 407.

[96] Kershaw, *Hitler 1889–1936*, 526, 584.

[97] The Reich Commissariat for the Strengthening of German Nationality generally sought to enlist experts from a wide array of backgrounds. See Hartenstein, *Neue Dorflandschaften*, for a more comprehensive discussion of the Nazis' planning efforts.

[98] Mechtild Rössler and Sabine Schleiermacher, "Der 'Generalplan Ost' und die 'Modernität' der Großraumordnung. Eine Einführung," Rössler and Schleiermacher (eds.), *Der "Generalplan Ost." Hauptlinien der nationalsozialistischen Planungs- und Vernichtungspolitik* (Berlin, 1993), 9; Marcel Herzberg, *Raumordnung im nationalsozialistischen Deutschland* (Dortmund, 1997), 108–11.

mindset.[99] In spite of his youth, Meyer came to occupy a number of influential positions: he was professor of agriculture in Berlin, member of the Prussian Academy of Sciences, and the Reich Commissariat's chief of planning as head of the Staff High Commission for Planning and Land-Use (*Stabshauptamt für Planung und Boden*).[100] It is a matter of debate whether Meyer was a member of the conservation community, but there could be no doubt about Heinrich Wiepking-Jürgensmann, the longtime rival of Alwin Seifert for supremacy in the German landscape planning profession. It is noteworthy that in choosing Wiepking-Jürgensmann over Seifert, the Reich Commissariat hired the person with a lower ideological profile; unlike Seifert, Wiepking-Jürgensmann never joined the Nazi Party – in contrast to Meyer, who was a high-ranking SS officer[101] – and he was actually denounced as a friend of Jews by a colleague during the first years of Nazi rule.[102] However, it only adds to the horror of the General Plan East that it was not simply the product of a group of political radicals, and Wiepking-Jürgensmann's attitude was by no means exceptional among the experts involved.[103] For Wiepking-Jürgensmann, the key attraction of work within the Reich Commissariat was what Konrad Meyer called the "complete freedom of planning (*volle Planungsfreiheit*)": the unique chance to plan on a grand scale, without any need to take the petty demands of the local population into account.[104] Before the war, an airport or the Autobahn qualified as a big landscaping

[99] See Ulrich Herbert, "'Generation der Sachlichkeit.' Die völkische Studentenbewegung der frühen zwanziger Jahre," in Ulrich Herbert, *Arbeit, Volkstum, Weltanschauung. Über Fremde und Deutsche im 20. Jahrhundert* (Frankfurt, 1995), 31–58. For a stimulating application of the generational approach, see Michael Wildt, *Generation des Unbedingten. Das Führungskorps des Reichssicherheitshauptamtes* (Hamburg, 2002).

[100] Rössler and Schleiermacher, "Generalplan Ost," 8.

[101] Ute Deichmann, *Biologists under Hitler* (Cambridge, Mass., and London, 1996), 123.

[102] See Zeller, "Ich habe"; and Gröning and Wolschke-Bulmahn, *Grüne Biographien*, 18. On Wiepking-Jürgensmann's position in the Reich Commissariat's hierarchy, see Mechthild Rössler, "*Wissenschaft und Lebensraum.*" *Geographische Ostforschung im Nationalsozialismus. Ein Beitrag zur Disziplingeschichte der Geographie.* Hamburger Beiträge zur Wissenschaftsgeschichte 8 (Berlin and Hamburg, 1990), 167.

[103] See Ingo Haar, "Der 'Generalplan Ost' als Forschungsproblem. Wissenslücken und Perspektiven," in Rüdiger vom Bruch and Brigitte Kaderas (eds.), *Wissenschaften und Wissenschaftspolitik. Bestandsaufnahmen zu Formationen, Brüchen und Kontinuitäten im Deutschland des 20. Jahrhunderts* (Stuttgart, 2002), 363; Robert L. Koehl, *RKFDV. German Resettlement and Population Policy 1939–1945. A History of the Reich Commission for the Strengthening of Germandom* (Cambridge, 1957), 71; Hartenstein, *Neue Dorflandschaften*, 454; and Raphael, "Radikales Ordnungsdenken," 15.

[104] Czesław Madajczyk, "Einleitung," to Czesław Madajczyk (ed.), *Vom Generalplan Ost zum Generalsiedlungsplan. Dokumente* (Munich, 1994), xvii. See also Hartenstein, *Neue Dorflandschaften*, 78–81.

project.[105] Now, the planners' team could command a playing field the size of a country: the 1943 version of the General Plan East dealt with some 270,000 square miles of land. By way of comparison, in 1938, Germany comprised only 225,000 square miles.[106]

The most important result of Wiepking-Jürgensmann's activity, the famous "general decree No. 20/VI/42," showed that from a strictly technical point of view, the planners' work was state of the art. The decree dealt with the conservation of water and soil, called for the planting of hedgerows and a comprehensive clean air policy, and so forth.[107] What made the decree ghastly was its general context. In January 1941, some 5 months before the German invasion of the Soviet Union, Heinrich Himmler told a meeting of SS officials "that the destruction of thirty million Slavs was a prerequisite for German planning in the east, implying that the 'inevitable war with Bolshevism' must be utilized for this purpose."[108] Following up on this line of reasoning, the overarching goal of the landscape planners' work was to make the land suit a purported German national character, "so that Germanic-German man (*der germanisch-deutsche Mensch*) feels at home, settles down, falls in love with his new *Heimat* and becomes ready to defend it."[109] In its original form, the plan proposed transferring thirty-one million of the area's forty-five million residents to western Siberia over 30 years. The figures and details later changed somewhat, but became no less disturbing.[110] In fact, it is precisely the project's cool, neutral language that makes it such a shocking document: it was not an isolated product of fascist mania, but a carefully prepared product of technical expertise.[111]

There was never a systematic attempt to implement the General Plan East, and a first "test run" conducted in the Lublin district remained incomplete though it claimed thousands of lives.[112] In fact, the Nazis'

105 Schoenichen, "Wie lässt sich," 277.
106 Madajczyk, "Einleitung," xi.
107 See BArch B 245/88 pp. 4–8; and Oberkrome, *Deutsche Heimat*, 1–14. Michael Hartenstein pointed out that where plans reached a concrete stage, the results were remarkably free of "blood-and-soil" romanticism or a mystic glorification of the eternal peasant. (Hartenstein, *Neue Dorflandschaften*, 460.)
108 Koehl, *RKFDV*, 146n.
109 BArch B 245/88 p. 4.
110 Madajczyk, "Einleitung," vii.
111 Rössler and Schleiermacher, "Generalplan Ost," 7.
112 See Götz Aly and Susanne Heim, *Vordenker der Vernichtung. Auschwitz und die deutschen Pläne für eine neue europäische Ordnung* (Hamburg, 1991), 432–8; and Bruno Wasser, "Die 'Germanisierung' im Distrikt Lublin als Generalprobe und erste Realisierungsphase des 'Generalplans Ost,'" in Rössler and Schleiermacher, *Generalplan Ost*, 271–93. See also his *Himmlers Raumplanung im Osten* and Isabel Heinemann,

administration in the occupied territories soon evolved into an ineffective, labyrinthine set of institutions, and the East essentially became a dumping ground for unqualified or otherwise unloved officials. Unable to decide between the goals of extermination and exploitation, occupation policy sought to achieve both at the same time, resulting in administrative chaos and endless turf wars.[113] There was no direct connection between the General Plan East and the infamous "final solution of the Jewish question," but it is easy to see that the murder of the European Jews would have been a prelude to a giant project of "ethnic cleansing" in Eastern Europe if the Nazis had won the war. After all, the plan's genocidal implications are obvious in retrospect. As Czesław Madajczyk has argued, the General Plan East would have been "the final solution of the problem of Central Europe."[114] Therefore, the lack of implementation does by no means reduce the activities of these experts to mere paperwork: the experts were readily fulfilling an important wish of Nazi leaders who found that scientific expertise was indispensable for their murderous plans. As Lutz Raphael wrote, "it was not the least the work of the SS staff and their experts that bestowed murdering and robbing on a giant scale with the aura of scientifically legitimated programs."[115]

The Reich Commissariat's planners were never held accountable for their inhumane work. Heinrich Wiepking-Jürgensmann became professor at the University of Hanover, and even Konrad Meyer found a job there in 1955.[116] This situation is all the more remarkable because it did not take an insider to know about the true nature of their wartime work. It was sufficient to read the article that Lutz Heck published in Naturschutz,

"Wissenschaft und Homogenisierungsplanungen für Osteuropa. Konrad Meyer, der "Generalplan Ost" und die Deutsche Forschungsgemeinschaft," Isabel Heinemann and Patrick Wagner (eds.), Wissenschaft – Planung – Vertreibung. Neuordnungskonzepte und Umsiedlungspolitik im 20. Jahrhundert (Stuttgart, 2006), 52. Der Generalplan Ost in Polen 1940–1944 (Basel, 1993). Meyer later used this lack of implementation for his defense at one of the follow-up trials to the Nuremberg International Military Tribunal, convincing the court that his work simply aimed at a peacetime plan unrelated to the genocide in Eastern Europe – a grave error that put the experts' work beyond the historic purview for decades. (Isabel Heinemann, "Rasse, Siedlung, deutsches Blut." Das Rasse- und Siedlungshauptamt der SS und die rassenpolitische Neuordnung Europas [Göttingen, 2003], 574.)

[113] See Rebentisch, Führerstaat, 310, 317, 325.

[114] Madajczyk, "Einleitung," xvi. See also Aly and Heim, Vordenker, 439n.

[115] Raphael, "Radikales Ordnungsdenken," 38. See also Ulrich Herbert, "Vernichtungspolitik. Neue Antworten und Fragen zur Geschichte des 'Holocaust,'" in Herbert, Nationalsozialistische Vernichtungspolitik 1939–1945. Neue Forschungen und Kontroversen (Frankfurt, 1998), 24n.

[116] See Kellner, Wiepking, 280–7, and Gert Gröning and Joachim Wolschke-Bulmahn, "'Ganz Deutschland ein großer Garten.' Landespflege und Stadtplanung im Nationalsozialismus," Kursbuch 112 (1993): 31.

the leading journal of the conservation community, in 1942. Describing "the government's landscaping work in the East," Heck described how the Reich Commissariat "has not only given thought to the creation of German towns and villages but also to the creation of a landscape that shall become a new *Heimat* for many Germans." In what followed, Heck published the May 1942 agreement between the German Forest Service and the Reich Commissar for the Strengthening of German Nationality that made Wiepking-Jürgensmann a member of both institutions. And as if to make the general intention clear to even the most superficial reader, Heck closed with remarks of brutal clarity: "Being the area of settlement that Germany so desperately seeks, the wide space of the East needs to be conquered a second time by means of a complete transformation. The supreme goal must be to change a deserted, foreign landscape into a German one. For the first time in history, a nation is undertaking the modeling of a landscape in a conscious way."[117] After all, there was no need for secrecy: a project of colonization required settlers willing to move eastward, and that made publicity almost indispensable. As if to augment the project's inherent lunacy even further, the Nazis sought to attract settlers from Denmark and the Netherlands as well to compensate for a lack of skilled farmers in Germany.[118]

The war's progress led to a successive curtailment of the landscape planners' work. Himmler lost interest in the General Plan East after the German defeat in Stalingrad, and work essentially stopped in mid-1944, though the project was never officially abandoned.[119] The battle of Stalingrad was also a turning point for the Reich Conservation Agency, which in early 1943 comprised five expert officials, all of them male, and a support staff of eight female employees.[120] Unruh failed in his proposal to close the agency entirely, but several decrees reduced the agency's responsibilities, and it was little consolation that one of these decrees, after ordering the reduction of work "to the extent indispensable for the war," encouraged the conservationists to voice their concerns "with vigor" in wartime planning projects.[121] After air raids in early 1944 inflicted significant damage, the Reich Conservation Agency moved out of Berlin to the town of Bellinchen on the Oder River, only to flee again westward when

[117] Heck, "Behördliche Landschaftsgestaltung," 61n. See also Birgit Karrasch, "Die 'Gartenkunst' im Dritten Reich," *Garten und Landschaft* 100, 6 (1990): 54.
[118] See Koos Bosma, "Verbindungen zwischen Ost- und Westkolonisation," in Rössler and Schleiermacher, *Generalplan Ost*, 201.
[119] Madajczyk, "Einleitung," xi; Koehl, *RKFDV*, 159.
[120] BArch RW 42/36 pp. 166–8.
[121] *Reichsministerialblatt der Forstverwaltung* 7 (1943): 151. See also Wettengel, "Staat und Naturschutz," 390n; and Klose, "Von unserer Arbeit," 3.

the Red Army approached in early 1945. In March 1945, the Reich Conservation Agency finally took an impromptu seat in Egestorf, a village in the Lüneburg Heath, where Klose and his co-workers spent the last months of the war.[122] The situation of the Bavarian Conservation Agency was even more dismal. Bombs destroyed the agency's records in February 1944, and the Bavarian ministry of the interior closed it toward the end of the year. The Bavarian Conservation League, which had claimed to be "the largest conservation organization of Europe" in 1939, effectively suspended its work in 1943.[123] Some action remained: on June 5, 1944, Wilhelm Münker assembled a meeting on the expansion of the Kahler Asten nature reserve, and Karl Friedrich Kolbow even sent cordial greetings "for the project's success" as head of the provincial administration, but the episode cannot help but appear strange in retrospect, and the Allied invasion of Normandy the following day certainly did not improve the prospects of the endeavor.[124] Sporadic efforts of this kind finally gave way to the complete collapse of conservation work in the final months of the war.

Needless to say, the exigencies of the war were a depressing experience for the conservation community. However, the peacetime years after the passage of the national conservation law appeared in a different light in retrospect. In an influential speech in 1948, Hans Klose spoke of a "high time for German conservation" between 1936 and 1939.[125] Was that an adequate label for the peacetime work of the conservation community? The conservationists certainly made some significant strides within a brief period of time, but as the following chapter will show, these gains were more than offset by comprehensive land reclamation projects and the hasty buildup of a war economy. Conservation work in Nazi Germany always looked far better on paper than in reality. At times, one cannot avoid the impression that the endless deluge of decrees and reports was also an escape from the more dire realities outdoors. Characteristically, there was never an open discussion of the state of conservation work, let alone an attempt to examine the

---

[122] BArch R 2/4731 p. 59r; Wettengel, "Staat und Naturschutz," 396.

[123] StAW Landratsamt Obernburg no. 210, letter of the Bayerische Landesstelle für Naturschutz of February 18, 1944, and Der Landesbeauftragte für Naturschutz in Bayern to the höhere und untere Naturschutzbehörden, November 8, 1944; StAN Rep. 212/19[VII] no. 2542, Bund Naturschutz in Bayern to the Gruppenführer and Vertrauensmänner, January 10, 1939; StAW Landratsamt Bad Kissingen no. 1237.

[124] WAA LWL Best. 702 no. 191, Wilhelm Münker, Reisebericht, Erweiterung des Naturschutzgebietes am Asten, negotiations on June 5, 1944.

[125] Klose, "Weg," 43. See also Klose, "Von unserer Arbeit," 2.

enforcement issue in a comprehensive way. Conservationists may have sensed that there was a wide gap between the bureaucratic dreams and the actual state of the environment, but they refrained from any deeper reflection on this issue. And still, Klose's statement is a remarkable one, for it provides a good impression not of the actual quality of nature protection in the late 1930s but of the spirit that was driving conservation work at that time. It was a period of vibrancy, of enthusiastic work, of cooperation with a multitude of agents, a time when conservation had the ear of the powerful – in short, a time of euphoria and hope. For a group of people who had cultivated a sense of marginality to the point where it was a source of identity, this was a seminal experience.[126] The late 1930s were probably not a "high time" for conservation, but this was a time when conservationists were "high" – and it took decades for some of the protagonists to become clean.[127]

Of course, the conservationists of the Nazi era could not help but acknowledge at times that certain trends of contemporary society ran counter to their own interests. But statements of this kind usually retained an optimistic cast; jeremiads of cultural despair, a fixture in conservation rhetoric since the times of Rudorff and Riehl, became notably rare during the Nazi era. The Jordsand association mentioned the deleterious ecological impact of the cultivation of wasteland in 1936 but swiftly added that it was "an inevitable necessity."[128] The Bavarian Conservation League noted in 1936 that "the concerns of conservation often have to yield to the demands of the economy nowadays" – and continued with a call for enhanced public relations efforts.[129] In a 1937 report, Karl Oberkirch laconically declared that conservation "was fulfilling its difficult duties within the confines of economic feasibility."[130] In Bavaria, Hans Kobler dismissed worries over the Four Year Plan's environmental toll with an emphatic pledge of allegiance to Hermann Göring: "the same man who is in charge of the Four Year Plan also time and again requests more attention

[126] See Wolfgang Erz, "Naturschutz und Landschaftspflege im Rückblick auf ein Vierteljahrhundert Deutscher Naturschutztage und heute," *Jahrbuch für Naturschutz und Landschaftspflege* 33 (1983): 19.

[127] See Hans Klose, "Fünf Jahre Reichsnaturschutzgesetz," *Naturschutz* 21 (1940): 85.

[128] LASH Abt. 320 Eiderstedt no. 1806, advertising leaflet of the Verein Jordsand, sent to the Kreisverwaltung des Kreises Eiderstedt on October 29, 1936.

[129] StAW Landratsamt Bad Kissingen no. 1237, Bund Naturschutz in Bayern to the Gruppenführer and Vertrauensmänner, April 28, 1937.

[130] HStAD RW 24 no. 961, Naturdenkmalpflege und Naturschutz im Gebiete des Siedlungsverbandes Ruhrkohlenbezirk. Tätigkeitsbericht des Bezirksbeauftragten für Naturschutz in Essen für die Geschäftsjahre 1935/1936 und 1936/1937, p. 15.

to the protection of nature with supreme vigor."[131] In his influential book on the protection of the landscape, Hans Schwenkel even expressed his confidence that "the age of a purely materialist design of the landscape," of "regulated brooks and rivers," was gone, a truly surprising statement in light of the contemporary work on the Ems River.[132] Vietinghoff-Riesch once took solace in the idea "that even the authoritarian government of National Socialism can only gradually come to exorcise the demon that finds its expression in the mistreatment of the landscape."[133]

It clearly did not take a dedicated Nazi like Erich Gritzbach, who touted "National Socialism as a true nature-protection movement" in his servile biography of Göring, to see the relationship between the conservation community and the Nazis in a positive light.[134] Of course, the countless difficulties of everyday conservation work did not vanish during the Nazi era, but the conservationists took these exigencies more lightly after 1935 – a remarkable development for a movement that had originally stemmed from a deep sense of loss. But with the prolonged experience of war, the conservation community's enthusiasm for Nazism gradually came to appear somewhat fragile. Whereas peacetime publications often reflected the impression that with the Nazi regime, the conservationists had finally found a political system that took their concerns seriously, statements during the war, and especially after the German invasion of the Soviet Union in June 1941, displayed a more sober perspective. A certain sense of disaffection began to appear in the conservationists' writing: it is revealing that although a book by Schoenichen called conservation a "völkisch" issue in its title in 1942, the book itself was clearly less fraught with ideology than earlier publications and actually could be read as a blueprint for international cooperation on conservation issues after the war.[135] Although open resistance was still out of the question, one cannot help but notice a gradual disillusionment among at least some conservationists. Of course, it is difficult to assess the sentiment's extent in the absence of an open discussion, but it did at times find an expression in writing. Perhaps the most impressive document of this trend came from Wilhelm Lienenkämper.

---

[131] StAW Landratsamt Bad Kissingen no. 1237, Hans Kobler, Vortrag, gehalten bei der Bezirksversammlung der Gendarmerie in Garmisch-Partenkirchen on November 7, 1938, p. 6n.
[132] Schwenkel, *Grundzüge*, 195.
[133] Vietinghoff-Riesch, *Naturschutz*, 5.
[134] Gritzbach, *Hermann Göring*, 95.
[135] See Schoenichen, *Naturschutz als völkische und internationale Kulturaufgabe*.

Lienenkämper has already been mentioned on numerous occasions in this book, and there is no need to add much by way of introduction. What makes Lienenkämper so interesting is that he represents a merger of the two dominant strands of behavior during the Nazi era: he was both a devoted Nazi, who delved far into the depths of Nazi rhetoric, and a politically savvy conservation advisor in the Sauerland region – Schoenichen and Klose rolled into one. Thus, it is highly instructive that the sense of disillusionment had reached even one of the most energetic and committed conservationists of the Nazi era. His document was not straightforward but rather took the form of a poem, a playful style that allowed allusions and criticisms without running the risk of making incriminatory statements. In fact, Lienenkämper did not write the poem himself: the document listed the northern German writer Rudolf Kinau as the author, but Lienenkämper's sympathy becomes clear from the fact that in September 1942, he forwarded the poem to Karl Friedrich Kolbow, head of the provincial administration and chairman of the Heimat League of Westphalia, obviously seeing him as a kindred spirit.[136] A brief thank you note showed that this belief was not mistaken.[137]

The poem dealt with a small, unnamed river that had so far escaped the attention of the Labor Service. It was thus still a scenic brook, with many twists and turns and an abundant plant and animal life along its banks. But the poem depicted this idyllic spot as under threat, and secrecy was paramount to its preservation. Any information on the place, the poem's narrator warned a female friend, could spell the end of the marvelous scenery:

Du, Anneliese, sag mal, kannst du wirklich schweigen?	Tell me, Anneliese, can you truly keep a secret?
Sagst du es ganz gewiß auch keinem Menschen nach?	Can you do so absolutely, and let no one know at all?
Ich kann dir etwas Feines, Märchenhaftes zeigen –	I can show you something fine, something that's a wonder:
Ich weiß hier in der Nähe einen kleinen Bach.	A little brook I know of, quite close by.

The poem dwelt at length on the river's beauty, but the description was not an end in itself. It was the backdrop for the poem's central point:

---

136 WAA LWL Best. 702 no. 184, Landschaftsstelle für Naturschutz Altena-Lüdenscheid to Landeshauptmann Kolbow, September 27, 1942.

137 *Ibid.*, response of September 29, 1942. For what follows, see the attachment to Lienenkämper's letter.

a scathing indictment of the Labor Service's mania for river regulation, along with mockery of the Nazi obsession with secrecy. But there was more to this poem: it evoked doubts whether the conservationists' alliance with the Nazis had really paid off. After all, how could one be jubilant about the Nazi experience if a scenic spot demanded painstaking secrecy? The poem's river, depicted as a human being, was leading a tragic life; and chances are that Lienenkämper's personal feelings were not much different:

Nur hin und wieder bleibt ihm fast der Atem stehen:	From time to time, he almost holds his breath,
Von jedem blanken Spaten fühlt er sich bedroht,	In every shining spade he feels a menace lurk,
Und hört und sieht er zwei in festem Gleichschritt gehen,	And if he sees or hears two men in cadence marching,
Hält er sofort die Strömung an und stellt sich tot.	He halts his stream at once and plays the corpse.
Er fängt erst wieder an zu plätschern und zu fließen	He only dares once more to ripple and to babble
Wenn alle Uniformen lange außer Sicht.	When he sees uniforms all passed far out of view.
So kann er oft erst seinen Frieden nachts genießen,	So is it that the night is oft his only respite:
Bei Tage kann er es vor Angst und Sorge nicht.	By day, for care and fear, he knows no peace.
Komm etwas näher noch! Wir können's ruhig wagen.	Come slightly closer still! We can chance it,
Du darfst nur nicht mit mir in gleichem Schritt –	Just do not let yourself fall into step.
Und darfst mich nicht nach seinem Namen fragen –	And never dare to ask me for its name –
Um Gottes willen nicht! Der Arbeitsdienst hört mit!	Lest, God forbid, the Labor Service hear!

It is difficult to decide how many conservationists subscribed to the sentiment that this poem mirrored so eloquently. Sentiments are always hard to determine for a historian, and especially so in totalitarian regimes. However, it seems reasonable to assume that after the first wave of enthusiasm over the national conservation law was over, and especially when the enduring war threatened to push conservation ever farther down on the political agenda, a good part of the German conservation community, and probably a majority, became familiar with sentiments of this kind, even though they probably did not embrace them from the bottom of their hearts. After all, it did not take an oppositional attitude to harbor doubts about the community's proximity to the Nazi regime. Historians have long recognized that the cadre of fanatical Nazis has always been notably small and that attitudes in many parts of German society diverged notably from the Nazis' ideals. It is no coincidence that the Nazi regime monitored public opinion much more nervously than contemporary Japan or the Italian fascists.[138] However, it is equally striking that these doubts never led to any more general critique of the Nazi regime even when the fortunes of war clearly turned against the Germans. As far as we know, there was no contribution, however minimal, from the conservation movement to the German resistance. Obviously, the credentials that the Nazi regime had earned through the passage of the national conservation law did not wear off completely until the Nazis' total defeat.

The general dilemma of the conservation community was familiar to many Germans of the Nazi era: how far do you go in terms of concessions and compromises toward a totalitarian regime? However, few groups underwent, or at least displayed, such a radical change of heart as the conservationists. Before 1933, they had been a group of nature lovers who cared little about politics and never dreamed of affiliating themselves with a political movement – after the Nazis' seizure of power, and especially after the national conservation law of 1935, most members of the conservation community touted nature protection as a quintessential goal of Hermann Göring and Adolf Hitler. It was, in a way, an almost Faustian bargain that conservationists entered in their rapprochement to the Nazis. And a poem like the one above could not help to reveal a suspicion that this bargain had not paid off.

---

[138] Cf. Wolfgang Schieder, "Kriegsregime des 20. Jahrhunderts. Deutschland, Italien und Japan im Vergleich," in Christoph Cornelißen, Lutz Klinkhammer, and Wolfgang Schwentker (eds.), *Erinnerungskulturen. Deutschland, Italien und Japan seit 1945* (Frankfurt, 2003), 34.

6

Changes in the Land

When radio announcers in Bavaria broadcast the current traffic situation, chances are good that you will hear a reference to Irschenberg Mountain. Located on the Autobahn between Munich and Salzburg, the Irschenberg creates a steep incline for drivers heading for Munich, and when vacationers head back in droves from the Alps or Italy, congestion on the Irschenberg is almost inevitable. Of course, the drivers' reactions differ widely depending on individual tempers, driving time, and the other people in the car. However, few realize that their frustration is, at least in part, a result of arbitrary decisions in the Nazi era. It was the personal wish of Fritz Todt to follow the difficult route over the Irschenberg Mountain, for only such a path would offer a panoramic view of the Alps and the scenic Chiemgau.[1] After Todt's death in 1942, Hitler even thought of building a mausoleum for Todt on the Irschenberg as a special tribute to the supreme engineer of the Nazi era. Construction was to start after the victorious conclusion of World War II.[2]

The example of Irschenberg Mountain shows that an environmental history of the Nazi era will remain incomplete if it deals only with laws, institutions, and people. The Nazi regime also had an impact on the German landscape, and this impact was the result of both intentional design, like the Irschenberg detour, and the unintended consequences of other Nazi projects. However, it is quite difficult to provide an evaluation of this impact that moves beyond anecdotal evidence. A number of tricky problems demand caution in any investigation of the environmental

[1] Zeller, *Straße, Bahn, Panorama*, 159n.
[2] Franz W. Seidler, *Fritz Todt. Baumeister des Dritten Reiches* (Munich, 1986), 392.

impact of the Nazi era. Perhaps the greatest obstacle is the dearth of previous research: the question of the impact on the land has ranked low among the band of environmental historians working on the Nazi era, and off-hand remarks like Gröning's and Wolschke-Bulmahn's flat statement that conservation was ineffective during the Nazi era have clearly more to do with the authors' disdain for the Nazis than with careful analysis.[3] A few years ago, David Blackbourn bemoaned the general lack of attention to the physical environment in German historiography. His argument aimed at fostering "a sense of place" among German historians: "what about *real* geographies – if you will pardon that provocative adjective?"[4] As far as the Nazi era is concerned, the question is still mostly unanswered.

A second problem lies in the great geographical diversity of Germany. Changes in the land can mean something very different depending on the location between the lowlands bordering the North Sea and the Bavarian Alps; the German rivers include the Rhine, whose run between Mainz and Bonn has been celebrated countless times for its scenic beauty, and the Emscher, one of the world's most heavily polluted rivers, which runs through the highly industrialized Ruhr region. Even more, the identification of general trends meets with difficulties because the precise meaning of changes in the land depends strongly on local conditions: a quarry can mean the destruction of a scenic mountain, as in the case of the Hohenstoffeln, but it can also be inconspicuous from a conservation standpoint or even advantageous: a guidebook of 1939 noted that an abandoned quarry can be "a gem of a hill" and "a part of pristine nature" if it gives home to wild plants and animals.[5] Therefore, a truly comprehensive estimate of the environmental impact of the Nazi era would need to assemble a jigsawlike combination of countless local stories into a general narrative picture – an extremely difficult endeavor given the current state of research, and certainly one that goes beyond the scope of this study.

The need to go into tiny details is because of a third problem of a proper evaluation of the environmental impact of the Nazis: the absence

[3] Gröning and Wolschke-Bulmahn, *Liebe zur Landschaft Teil 1*, 196. Similarly, Thomas Adam, "Die Verteidigung des Vertrauten. Zur Geschichte der Natur- und Umweltschutzbewegung in Deutschland seit dem Ende des 19. Jahrhunderts," *Zeitschrift für Politik* 45 (1998): 25.
[4] Blackbourn, *Sense of Place*, 15n. Emphasis in the original.
[5] Rolf Dircksen, *Landschaftsführer des Westfälischen Heimatbundes*. vol. 2: *Weser- und Wiehengebirge* (Münster, 1939), 27. See also Werner Konold, "Nutzungsgeschichte und Identifikation mit der Kulturlandschaft," in Ulrich Hampicke, Birgit Litterski, and Wendelin Wichtmann (eds.), *Ackerlandschaften. Nachhaltigkeit und Naturschutz auf ertragsschwachen Standorten* (Berlin, 2005), 14.

FIGURE 6.1. The Autobahn between Munich and Salzberg, 75 years into the future. A 1934 painting by Fritz Bayerlein. Picture from Alwin Seifert, *Im Zeitalter des Lebendigen* (Planegg, 1942), p. 22.

of enduring and truly revolutionary changes in land use. Many of the important developments were building on previously existing trends. The Nazis introduced a new feature into the German landscape with the construction of the Autobahn – but the 2,050 miles of Autobahn that had been built by 1939 pale in comparison with the boom of road construction in the early nineteenth century, when the German road network grew from 9,180 to 32,920 miles between 1820 and 1850.[6] The Nazis sponsored the buildup of industry in preparation for war – but the industrialization of Germany goes back to the nineteenth century. In fact, the Nazis' rearmament policy did not even require a fundamental redirection of the path of German industrialization: heavy industry and the chemical industry had always been two of the key pillars of the German industrial economy. Even the increased cultivation of unused land in the quest for autarky was no peculiar feature of the Nazi era: as early as 1922, Hans Klose complained that the treaty of Versailles forced Germans to put large

---

[6] Hans-Ulrich Wehler, *Deutsche Gesellschaftsgeschichte vol. 2. Von der Reformära bis zur industriellen und politischen "Deutschen Doppelrevolution" 1815–1845/49* (Munich, 1989), 120.

tracts of wasteland, precious from a conservation standpoint, into agricultural use.[7] To be sure, the situation looked different in Eastern Europe, where warfare inflicted massive damage because of the Nazis' scorched-earth policy. In his monograph on Russian conservation, Douglas Weiner pointed out that the Nazi war of extermination pertained not only to the local population but also to Russia's nature: "wherever the Germans came across *zapovedniki* [nature reserves], they inflicted sadistic carnage."[8] Of course, World War II had also a deleterious impact on the land within the German borders, but it was clearly more limited than the damage in Eastern Europe. Most of the fighting in World War II took place beyond the German borders, and not until the last months of the war did the land war finally come to the country that had started the war. To be sure, Allied air raids had made Germany into a battlefield long before the invasion, but the damage that bombing inflicted on Germany's nature clearly pales in comparison with the destruction in many German cities. The only exception were places with traffic links of strategic importance, where the Allied goal to disrupt the German transportation network and the notorious inaccuracy of bomb attacks often added up to a particular toll. For example, a bridge near the town of Schildesche, to the north of Bielefeld, which carried a crucial railroad link between the Ruhr region and Berlin, became the target of a prolonged bombing campaign during the final months of the war that turned the surrounding area into a landscape of utter destruction.[9]

A fourth problem that augments the difficulties of a proper balance even further is the short duration of the Nazis' reign. Twelve years are a short period by natural history standards, and it is revealing that the four case studies discussed in Chapter 4 all extend beyond the Nazi era. The conflict over the Hohenstoffeln quarry started shortly before World War I and finally reached its conclusion when the owners refrained from resuming mining operations after 1945. In the case of the Schorfheide, the time span is even longer: Göring's regime was only one chapter in the Schorfheide's long dual history as a hunting and nature reserve. The regulation of the Ems River during the Nazi era went back to a plan of 1928, and the struggle over the Wutach Gorge nature reserve began with Schurhammer's initiative of 1926 and finally reached its happy conclusion

[7] Hans Klose, "Über die Lage der Naturdenkmalpflege bei Conwentz' Tod," *Beiträge zur Naturdenkmalpflege* 9 (1922): 466.

[8] Weiner, *Little Corner*, 58.

[9] Jürgen Büschenfeld, Wolfgang Klee, and Rüdiger Uffmann, *Bahnen in Bielefeld* (Nordhorn, 1997), 29.

in 1960 when the Schluchseewerk power plant withdrew its plans for a diversion of the Wutach's water. Of course, the Nazi regime played a prominent role in all of these conflicts. But at the same time, it would be misleading to depict the outcomes as a sole result of Nazi policy.

When Germans think of the Nazis' impact on the land, two projects usually stand out: Autobahn construction and the hydrological projects of the Labor Service. However, the actual situation is more complex in both cases than collective memory would have it. Contrary to a popular myth, the builders of the Autobahn usually showed little interest in the Landscape Advocates' advice. In his detailed examination of the Autobahn project, Zeller estimates that expenses for landscape purposes amounted to only 0.1 percent of the total costs of Autobahn construction.[10] The Labor Service did bring about enormous changes in the German landscape, as the figures in a 1941 book demonstrate: since the Nazis' seizure of power, some 657,000 acres of farmland had been protected from flooding thanks to the Service's river regulation work, whereas the draining of arable land had improved the productivity of some 1,811,000 acres.[11] In some cases, the result is still visible in the cityscape today. In cities like Münster and Hanover, the work of the Labor Service led to the creation of lakes within the city limits, the Aasee and the Maschsee respectively, and many residents of Münster and Hanover saw these lakes as conducive to the quality of living. And yet it is imperative to take a closer look: the Nazis valued the Labor Service in the first place for its contribution to a spiritual national awakening, rather than for its material achievements, and the Labor Service was much less effective than possible as a result.[12] Furthermore, even when work was done during the Nazi era, it is a matter of debate whether the projects actually left a distinctive Nazi imprint on the German landscape.

The regulation of the Ems River provides a case in point. The work during the Nazi era certainly changed the face of the scenic river significantly. But the work actually progressed according to the plan of 1928, and the guiding idea behind this plan was a classic hydrological paradigm that had nothing to do with Nazism: the goal was to siphon away redundant

---

[10] Zeller, *Straße, Bahn, Panorama*, 198; and Thomas Zeller, "'The Landscape's Crown.' Landscape, Perceptions, and Modernizing Effects of the German Autobahn System, 1934 to 1941," in David E. Nye (ed.), *Technologies of Landscape. From Reaping to Recycling* (Amherst, Mass., 1999), 230. See also pp. 79–80.

[11] Will Decker, *Der deutsche Arbeitsdienst. Ziele, Leistungen und Organisation des Reichsarbeitsdienstes*, 3rd edition (Berlin, 1941), 16.

[12] See Patel, *Soldaten*, 408.

water as quickly as possible to prevent flooding. It is even more striking that work continued along the same lines in the postwar years.[13] A more general rethinking of the project's wisdom did not start until the 1970s, and it was because of the growing environmental sentiment in the West German population; in the town of Telgte, some 2,000 citizens signed an appeal to "keep hands off the Ems" in 1974. The planners gradually came to revise their plans for the Ems, though traditional thinking remained a factor to be reckoned with. When two schoolboys interviewed a hydrologist in charge of the Ems in the mid-1980s, he tried to soothe them with the information that on a recently regulated stretch, the river was running in curvatures for fully 57 percent of its length, whereas it followed a straight course for only 43 percent of its run. Obviously, it had not yet occurred to this official that thinking in terms of straight and curvaceous lines might be part of the problem.[14]

Thus, it would be wrong to speak of the Ems regulation as a quintessential Nazi project. A more appropriate perspective sees the work during the Nazi era as one chapter in a much longer history of river regulation: after all, the guiding ideas of the Ems regulation project were quite similar to the notions underlying the famous regulation of the Rhine begun by Johann Gottfried Tulla in the early nineteenth century.[15] From a hydrological perspective, the rise of environmentalism in the 1970s was the most important turning point, while the Nazi era was a time of continuity. While conservationists had been calling for a nature reserve along the banks of the Ems River as early as 1933, the wish has only been fulfilled in recent years with the backing of the European Union's Habitats Directive of 1992.[16] In fact, one could argue that the Nazis obstructed a general rethinking of the project: when the memorandum of 1934 indicated that the conservationists were moving beyond petty details to demand a voice in the project's overall design, the Nazi intervention made any further discussion impossible.

A similar argument can be made regarding the Nazi regime's impact on the pollution of the atmosphere. As with the hydrological project,

---

[13] See Kaiser, *Geschichte*, 116–21.
[14] Kaatz and Schulze-Dieckhoff, *Wenn die Ems*, 104, 112.
[15] See Mark Cioc, *The Rhine. An Eco-Biography, 1815–2000* (Seattle and London, 2002), Chapter 3.
[16] WAA LWL Best. 305 no. 54, Freie Künstlergemeinschaft Schanze to Landeshauptmann Kolbow, November 27, 1933. See also Bianca Knoche, "Ich hab' die Mutter Ems in ihrem Bett geseh'n . . . Veränderungen des Flusses," in Alfred Hendricks (ed.), *Alles im Fluss? Die Ems – Lebensader für Mensch und Natur* (Münster, 2004), 118, 120.

the crucial turning point lay in the postwar years, when growing protest from the public at large gradually pushed authorities into action.[17] It is almost certain that air pollution grew from 1933, but that was an inevitable by-product of the general trend of the economy. With the Great Depression hitting its low point in the winter of 1932/1933, air pollution from industrial production was also at a minimum. A more adequate comparison weighs the pollution situation of the late 1930s against that of a decade earlier, and no one reported a significant difference in this regard. A wartime remark that "the air is barely better in the centers of industry than a generation ago" indicates that continuity was strong.[18] Of course, the war economy meant an additional burden in terms of pollution, though officials tried to keep the damage within limits: in 1934, the Nazis introduced a special secret licensing procedure for war production plants, and the decree admonished the officials to check these plans as thoroughly as plans from a civil project to forestall "a disadvantage to the workers, the neighbors, and the public at large."[19] But that was legal theory: in practice, the chance to intervene forcefully against a war production plant was rather slight, especially during the war. When the Nazi Party's district organization for Leipzig (*NSDAP-Kreisleitung*) filed a protest against a foundry in the spring of 1940, even though the installation was one of only three in Germany and indispensable for the war, the soot and stench must have been truly intolerable.[20]

In the light of the boom of conservation work during the Nazi era, it is important to ask whether this affected the overall environmental balance in a significant way. As we have seen, the total number of nature reserves grew significantly after the passage of the national conservation law. By 1940, Hans Klose was reporting more than 800 protected areas.[21] Unfortunately, the Reich Conservation Agency lost its inventory of nature reserves during the war, making precise figures on the acreage under protection difficult to come by, but it is safe to assume that the area in question was only a small fraction of the land affected by the Labor Service

---

[17] See Uekötter, *Rauchplage*, Chapters 16–18.
[18] BArch R 154/39, Reichsanstalt für Wasser- und Luftgüte to H. B. Rüder, January 14, 1944.
[19] HStAD Regierung Aachen no. 12974, Der Reichswirtschaftsminister und Preussische Minister für Wirtschaft und Arbeit to the Regierungspräsidenten, October 30, 1934. For further information on this topic, see Uekoetter, "Polycentrism."
[20] StAL Stadtgesundheitsamt no. 234 p. 57.
[21] Wettengel, "Staat und Naturschutz," 389.

projects. The increase in protected land was certainly impressive in terms of percentage points, but compared with the area worthy of protection, it was still meager; in 1960, an article reported that only 0.13 percent of the heaths in the northern province of Schleswig-Holstein and only 0.2 percent of the moorland were designated as nature reserves.[22] Furthermore, it is important to realize that designation as a nature reserve provided a weak protection, if any, in the chaotic situation toward the end of the war. With the supply of coal increasingly unreliable, people resorted to the use of wood and began pillaging local forests, and nature reserves were not spared in the process. "In most cases, the war and post-war years have left a mark on the nature reserves," a decree of the North Rhine-Westphalian ministry of education noted in 1949.[23] The results of the Nazis' forest expansion policy were equally disappointing. The goal had been to add some six million acres to the twenty-five million acres of forest land that existed in 1933. However, the foresters widely missed this ambitious goal: between 1933 and 1945, the annual average increase in forest land was only 3,700 acres.[24] The balance becomes even more dismal if one considers the Nazis' systematic overuse of forest reserves because of the demands of rearmament and autarky, which thinned out the German forests: estimates put the decline of the wood reserves in Germany's forests at 14 percent between 1936 and 1945. For the territory of the Federal Republic, the decline was 27 percent between 1936 and 1950.[25] Although trees were still standing, the forests were more empty and often provided a dismal picture, and it frequently took years, if not decades, until they recovered.

However, it is important to move beyond the constrained perspective of the conservationists of the Nazi era. As mentioned above, contemporary conservationists were so dedicated to an administrative mindset that compiling inventories and registering natural treasures became the mainstay of conservation work, gradually concealing the simple idea that an area's value in terms on conservation was independent of its administrative status. Moreover, it seems that the traditional mindset of German conservation sometimes led the community to ignore natural treasures in unusual places. For example, discussions about a sewage farm on the northern outskirts of Münster routinely depicted the area as a trouble

---

[22] Ernst-Wilhelm Raabe, "Zur Problematik des Naturschutzes in Schleswig-Holstein," *Die Heimat* 67 (1960): 105. Similarly, Siekmann, *Eigenartige Senne*, 351.

[23] *Amtsblatt des Kultusministeriums, Land Nordrhein-Westfalen* 2, 1 (October 1, 1949): 9.

[24] Imort, "Eternal Forest," 60.

[25] Steinsiek and Rozsnyay, *Grundzüge*, 278.

spot for conservation during the interwar years.[26] It would take a different generation of conservationists to realize that the area also implied an
enormous potential for the protection of nature: with wetlands becoming increasingly scarce in the region, the sewage farm began to attract
a large number of birds, which were indifferent to the artificial origin
of the area. In fact, conservationists rallied in the defense of this highly
unnatural setting in the 1970s when plans emerged to build a nuclear
power plant on the site. The plan was finally abandoned, and the area
continues to attract bird lovers to this day.[27] To be sure, stories of this
kind do not transform the generally negative environmental balance of
the Nazi era into a more neutral or even a positive one, but they serve
as a reminder that one should meet the conservationists' retrospective
indictments of the environmental toll of the Nazi era with a good deal of
skepticism.[28]

All in all, it seems that a general assessment of the Nazi era's environmental balance is surprisingly difficult – and that is already an interesting
finding in itself. After all, few regimes have better chances to mold the
environment to their liking than totalitarian regimes in time of war, and
the Nazi regime waged war for almost half of its life span. For example, the environmental record of communist China is so bleak that Judith
Shapiro wrote of "Mao's war against nature," whereas no historian has
so far spoken of "Hitler's war against nature."[29] Similarly, it would have
been highly uncharacteristic for Hitler to sign a decree similar to Stalin's
order of August 29, 1951, justly called "one of the darkest days for nature
protection in Soviet history" by Douglas Weiner, which slashed the system of *zapovedniki* to a tenth of its former size.[30] As totalitarian regimes
go, the Nazis' environmental impact was clearly a moderate one – not as a
result of a systematic environmental policy, to be sure, but rather because
of the existence of incoherent, and often conflicting, policies within the
Nazi state. During the Nazi era, it was possible to ignore or suppress the

---

[26] See proceedings in BArch B 245/23.
[27] See Michael Harengerd and Christoph Sudfeldt, "Rieselfelder Münster," *LÖBF-Mitteilungen* 20.2 (1995): 74–6.
[28] See Klose, "Weg," 38.
[29] See Judith Shapiro, *Mao's War Against Nature. Politics and the Environment in Revolutionary China* (Cambridge, 2001).
[30] Weiner, *Little Corner*, 129. Paul Josephson and Thomas Zeller reach a similar conclusion in their comparison of the transformation of nature under Hitler and Stalin: "In Nazi Germany private ownership of industry, and a public-private mix of resource ownership limited the size of nature transformation projects to those where the regime could build consensus." (Josephson and Zeller, "Transformation," 125.)

demands of conservation and to pursue projects in spite of doubts in the conservation community; the conflicts over the Ems River and the Wutach Gorge may serve as prime examples. However, it was not possible to argue that the protection of nature was irrelevant as a matter of principle. Of course, that was a meager accomplishment: what it could mean in practice became clear in the Ems regulation project, where a strong rhetorical commitment to the cause of conservation went hand in hand with the actual destruction of the scenic river to serve farming and employment interests. Hitler did call for the cultivation of unused land in the quest for autarky, but that notion never gained a status in Nazi rhetoric similar to notions of "conquest" and "mastery of nature" in communist ideology.[31] It is striking that whereas it is possible to trace Hitler's gigantomanic plans for the redesign of Berlin as the capital of a greater Germany in all their brutal details, there was no similar blueprint for the transformation of the German environment. There was, of course, the General Plan East for the transformation of the East European environment, but it is important to realize that, although conservation experts took part in the planning process, the main thrust of the General Plan East was not ecological in the current sense of the word: the goal was to Germanize the land and to transform it into a food-producing colony. In sum, the Nazis' official commitment to the cause of conservation seems to have made something of a difference, if only to prevent a truly devastating environmental toll. The Nazi era was a time of change also from an environmental perspective, but it was not a crucial turning point.

The call for a differentiated perspective is all the more important because environmental historians have repeatedly stressed the developments that occurred *after* the Nazi era: the economic boom of the postwar years and its impact on the environment. Historians like Christian Pfister and Arne Andersen have argued that the 1950s constitute a crucial watershed in environmental history.[32] Energy use increased enormously, driven by a decline of relative costs that was mainly the result of a growing supply

---

[31] See Bolotova, "Colonization," 109–15.
[32] See Christian Pfister (ed.), *Das 1950er Syndrom. Der Weg in die Konsumgesellschaft* (Bern, 1995); Arne Andersen, *Der Traum vom guten Leben. Alltags- und Konsumgeschichte vom Wirtschaftswunder bis heute* (Frankfurt and New York, 1997); Arne Andersen, "Das 50er-Jahre-Syndrom – Umweltfragen in der Demokratisierung des Technikkonsums," *Technikgeschichte* 65 (1998): 329–44; and Jörn Sieglerschmidt (ed.), *Der Aufbruch ins Schlaraffenland. Stellen die Fünfziger Jahre eine Epochenschwelle im Mensch-Umwelt-Verhältnis dar?* Environmental History Newsletter Special Issue 2 (Mannheim, 1995).

of cheap oil. Road traffic increased dramatically, with controversial discussions on the motorization of Germany following in the 1950s.[33] With growing car use, urbanites increasingly sought a home outside the city, making suburbanization an important trend of postwar environmental history. In the field of agriculture, the gradual shift from traditional to industrialized agriculture over the course of the twentieth century culminated in a rapid transformation of farming practicies in the 1960s.[34] All in all, it seems that the environmental toll of the age of mass consumption was clearly greater than that of the Nazi era.

But what if one compares the Nazi era not with the following epoch but with the preceding one, the 1920s? This question is even more difficult to answer than the other ones in this chapters, for few decades of German history give a more confusing picture from an environmental perspective than the years of the Weimar Republic. Ambiguities abound: some states passed conservation laws – but the failure of the Prussian conservation law was seen as a major defeat. Agriculture changed considerably because of the growing use of mineral fertilizer and the introduction of tractors – and yet it is only in hindsight that these changes appear as the first steps toward industrialized agriculture. In the late 1920s, the consumer society appeared on the horizon – but these beginnings were soon thwarted by the Great Depression. The automobile began to change the urban environment and residential patterns – but compared with the United States, automobile use was lagging significantly. The shortage of coal during World War I inspired feverish efforts to improve fuel combustion – but when rationalization led to an oversupply of coal since the mid-1920s, fuel efficiency lost much of its thrust. Clearly, if one may speak at all of the 1920s as a distinct era from an environmental history perspective, it is as an era of ambivalence.

With few exceptions, the environmental impact of the Nazi era has not found a place in Germany's collective memory. In fact, it seems that the exigencies of the immediate postwar years are remembered much more clearly nowadays than the environmental problems of the Nazi era, especially when the party at fault was an occupying power: people in southwest Germany still vividly recall the clear-cutting of forests directed by Allied authorities, even coining the word *Franzosenhiebe* ("French cuts")

---

[33] See Dietmar Klenke, *Bundesdeutsche Verkehrspolitik und Motorisierung. Konfliktträchtige Weichenstellungen in den Jahren des Wiederaufstiegs* (Stuttgart, 1993).
[34] See Kluge, *Agrarwirtschaft*; and Daniela Münkel (ed.), *Der lange Abschied vom Agrarland. Agrarpolitik, Landwirtschaft und ländliche Gesellschaft zwischen Weimar und Bonn* (Göttingen, 2000).

to pinpoint the blame. In contrast, the serious overuse of the forest reserves during the Nazi era mostly fell into oblivion.[35] Fewer still remember that it was the Nazi regime that allowed the introduction of leaded gasoline in Germany. Whereas tetraethyl lead was introduced as a fuel additive in the United States in 1923, scientists and government officials in Germany monitored this trend with a great deal of skepticism. In 1928, the German Department of Transportation even spoke, without a trace of irony, of a "large-scale experiment currently under way in the United States," stressing the need to diligently monitor deleterious effects on the other side of the Atlantic.[36] The government refrained from a formal ban out of trade considerations, but tetraethyl lead did not come into use in Germany during the Weimar years. With German gasoline containing large amounts of knock-resistant benzole, the need for an antiknock fuel additive was smaller in Germany than in the United States. In the 1930s, the IG Farben chemical giant built two plants for the production of tetraethyl lead, but the plants' output was originally used only in aviation. It was not until 1939 that permission was granted for the use of tetraethyl lead in German automobile traffic when the low quality of Austrian gasoline called for an effective fuel additive.[37] Some biologists may remember the peculiar "rubble vegetation" (*Trümmervegetation*) that grew in destroyed cities after the war, but that chapter ended to no one's regret with the rebuilding of Germany's urban areas.[38]

It is only in recent years that the Nazis' impact on the landscape has received major attention from the general public. Many Germans were stunned in 1992 when an aerial survey of forest reserves in Brandenburg revealed a swastika-shaped patch of larch trees in a pine forest in Zernikow, some sixty miles north of Berlin. An unknown forester had planted the sylvan swastika with a diameter of almost 200 feet in 1938, with the design visible only from the air, and only during the fall and winter when the larch tree's needles turn brown. It had survived not only

[35] See Küster, *Geschichte des Waldes*, 220n, and Zundel and Schwartz, *50 Jahre Forstpolitik*, 34n. See also Erich Hornsmann, "Von unseren Anfängen," *Unser Wald. Zeitschrift der Schutzgemeinschaft Deutscher Wald* no. 3 (June, 1997): 71.

[36] BArch R 86 no. 2368 vol. 1, Reichsverkehrsminister to the Reichsminister des Innern, July 23, 1928.

[37] For a more extensive discussion of this story, see Frank Uekoetter, "The Merits of the Precautionary Principle. Controlling Automobile Exhausts in Germany and the United States before 1945," in E. Melanie DuPuis (ed.), *Smoke and Mirrors: The Politics and Culture of Air Pollution* (New York and London, 2004), 119–53.

[38] Hansjörg Küster, *Geschichte der Landschaft in Mitteleuropa. Von der Eiszeit bis zur Gegenwart* (Munich, 1995), 344.

the defeat of the Nazi regime but also four decades of communist rule. The majority of the 100 larch trees were felled in 1995 and 2000, and the swastika was generally seen as the curious, but ultimately meaningless, act of an unknown fanatic.[39] However, dealing with the Nazis' impact on the German landscape usually requires more than a chainsaw and a few hours of time. Residents of the Bavarian town of Berchtesgaden are only too familiar with this problem because they have to live with a veritable historic minefield within their town limits: Hitler's cherished mountain resort on the Obersalzberg.

Hitler came to the Obersalzberg for the first time in the spring of 1923, on a clandestine visit to Dietrich Eckart, a fellow National Socialist and important figure in Hitler's rise to prominence, who was hiding on the Obersalzberg to escape a court order. Hitler immediately fell in love with the scenic area and came back on a regular basis. When he was released from prison after his putsch of 1923, he withdrew to Berchtesgaden to dictate the second volume of *Mein Kampf*. In the late 1920s, Hitler rented a house on the Obersalzberg that he later bought and expanded into an imposing residence, the so-called Berghof, which served as the de facto seat of government when he was present. For Hitler, the Obersalzberg was a retreat from the demands of the ministerial bureaucracy, a place without self-important bureaucrats who constantly disturbed his bohemian lifestyle. In addition to Hitler's residence, numerous buildings were built to provide for the Führer's comfort and security, whereas the local population was forced to leave, often without proper compensation. Hermann Göring, Albert Speer, and Martin Bormann also built personal homes in close proximity to the dictator. Martin Bormann was the driving force behind construction on the Obersalzberg, and his fervor soon moved far beyond mere necessities. As a trained farmer, Bormann set up a farm on the Obersalzberg that was intended as a model for the prospective colonization of Eastern Europe. However, the enterprise was a blatant failure, and the farm ran up a huge deficit because of the harsh environmental conditions. The most costly project was the construction of a lodge on the Kehlstein Mountain above the Obersalzberg at an altitude of 6,100 feet, a spectacular house that Bormann envisioned as the Nazi party's gift for Hitler's fiftieth birthday on April 20, 1939. It turned out to be an exemplary case of the Nazis' wastefulness: Hitler rarely visited the

[39] See *Berliner Zeitung* of December 5, 2000, p. 27. A picture of the swastika can be seen on the cover of Brüggemeier, Cioc, and Zeller, *How Green*. See also the information *ibid.*, p. iv.

FIGURE 6.2. Adolf Hitler and Martin Bormann during a walk on the Obersalzberg in the summer of 1940. The driving force behind the transformation of the scenic mountain, Bormann had a personal residence close to Hitler's Berghof. Photo from Ullstein Bild.

Kehlsteinhaus because of his vertigo, and the building served no military purposes, in spite of Allied suspicion to the contrary.[40] Major political acts took place on the Obersalzberg: in February 1938, the Austrian chancellor Kurt Schuschnigg came to the Berghof residence in a vain attempt to fend off the annexation of his country; half a year later, the British prime minister Neville Chamberlain visited Hitler's mountain resort for negotiations that led to the Munich agreement of September 1938, the culmination of Chamberlain's ill-fated appeasement policy. It was on the Obersalzberg

---

[40] To this day, English-language publications are available in the Berchtesgaden region which promise an account of "Hitler's alleged mountain fortress."

that Hitler drafted instructions to the German *Wehrmacht* for the invasion of Poland; on June 6, 1944, Hitler slept on the Obersalzberg while Allied forces were landing in Normandy. Hitler left the Berghof for the last time on July 14, 1944.[41]

On April 25, 1945, an air raid leveled the Nazi installations on the Obersalzberg, and what was left of Hitler's Berghof was blown up in 1952. The American military opened a hotel, "General Walker," on the Obersalzberg, Bormann's farm was transformed into a golf course, and though the goal to provide for the recreation of soldiers was paramount, the American presence on the Obersalzberg gave the German government a convenient excuse for not dealing with the area's heritage. In fact, the American military did little in the way of exorcising the demons of the place, and even rebaptized the Kehlsteinhaus the "Eagle's Nest," a problematic title given the fact that the eagle has traditionally served as a symbol of imperial power. However, facing up to the place's history became crucial when the American military announced its withdrawal from the Obersalzberg in 1995, and the Bavarian government realized that the place called for sensitivity: simply replacing the military use with a civilian one was out of the question. It asked the renowned Institute of Contemporary History in Munich to set up a museum to provide an account of both the place's history and Nazi rule in general. Opened in October 1999, the *Dokumentation Obersalzberg* drew some 110,000 visitors in its first year alone, a testimony to the enduring public interest in the history of Nazi Germany. However, the ghosts of the past continue to haunt the place: when the Intercontinental hotel group opened a mountain resort on the Obersalzberg in 2005, it became one of the most publicized hotel openings in German history and certainly the most controversial: more than 5,000 articles, from London's *Telegraph* to the *New Strait Times* of Singapore, commented on the project. This is all the more remarkable because Intercontinental had conceived the hotel with sensitivity and painstaking diligence. The hotel's design avoided any allusion to Nazi monumentalism or völkisch splendor, and the management mandated a two-day training course for its employees so that they could answer the guests' questions in a decent and proper way. Contracts provide for the instant discharge of employees involved in neo-Nazi activities, and house rules reserve a

---

[41] This discussion of the Obersalzberg is based on Chaussy, *Nachbar Hitler*; Hilmar Schmundt, "Am Berghof, Obersalzberg," in Porombka and Schmundt, *Böse Orte*, 30–57; Florian M. Beierl, *Hitlers Berg. Geschichte des Obersalzbergs und seiner geheimen Bunkeranlagen* (Berchtesgaden, 2004); and Ernst Hanisch, *Der Obersalzberg. Das Kehlsteinhaus und Adolf Hitler* (Berchtesgaden, 1995).

similar right with respect to guests. Still, the thoughtful preparations did not quell doubts about the project's wisdom. Few observers offered an outright condemnation of the project, but many wondered whether the Obersalzberg was really the right spot for a cozy hotel.[42]

After all, places are not only physical space but also a seat for myths and legends, as Werner Konold, chair of the institute of landscape management at the University of Freiburg, pointed out in a recent article.[43] Hitler sensed that already, and he had his favorite stories about the Obersalzberg. The main windows of his Berghof residence offered a panoramic view of the Untersberg, a mountain right on the border between Germany and Austria. Thus, the mountain symbolized the unification of the countries that Hitler achieved with the *Anschluss* of 1938, and in one of his wartime monologues, Hitler referred to this view as illustrative of his longing for the Austrian *Heimat*. But there was a second story that was even more troubling. A local legend had it that the Untersberg was the seat of the dormant Charlemagne, who was waiting, together with his heroic army, for a time of awakening. When the right time had come, Charlemagne would emerge from the Untersberg and reunite the German nation. With fantasies about a German awakening ripe after the defeat in World War I, it is not difficult to imagine the associations that the story evoked in the interwar years, and it is little wonder that Hitler liked the tale. Living across from the Untersberg Mountain, he saw fulfilling Charlemagne's mystic mission as his personal goal.[44]

But there was a third local legend about the place. If Hitler looked left while standing on his porch, he would see the Watzmann, a mountain range that was even more imposing than the Untersberg. The legend about the Watzmann took place in an age of giants, when king Watzmann, a cruel ruler and enemy of peasants and herdsmen, went hunting with his family. His chase brought him to a family that was peacefully watching its gazing animals. The king's dogs attacked and killed the family and the herd, while the ruler watched the murderous scene with boisterous pleasure.

[42] For an overview of press coverage, see *Süddeutsche Zeitung* no. 45 (February 24, 2005), p. 15, and no. 57 (March 10, 2005), p. 38; *Der Spiegel* no. 51 (2004): 144–6; and *Die Zeit* no. 10 (March 3, 2005), p. 73, no. 18 (April 28, 2005), p. 51.

[43] See Werner Konold, "Stein und Wasser im Bild der Heimat," *Schriftenreihe des Deutschen Rates für Landespflege* 77 (2005): 33–7.

[44] On this and the following tale, see Hanisch, *Obersalzberg*, 8n. See also Yvonne Weber-Fleischer, "Die Überlieferung von den Herrschern im Berg – Dargestellt am Beispiel der Untersbergsage," Ulrike Kammerhof-Aggermann (ed.), *Sagenhafter Untersberg. Die Untersbergsage in Entwicklung und Rezeption* (Salzburg, 1991/1992), esp. pp. 72n, 86n.

But then thunder arose, and the dogs, thirsty for blood, turned against king Watzmann and tore him and his family apart. Their bodies turned into stone and became what is today the Watzmann mountain range.[45] The tale clearly mirrored the perpetual conflicts between the nobility and the peasantry over the former's hunting privileges in the premodern era, but it is also open to a more current interpretation. After all, the story implies a clear-cut indictment of tyranny, along with the promise that a tyrannical ruler would ultimately face a just revenge. It might be a good idea, for the citizens of Berchtesgaden, to tell this story more often.

---

[45] Manfred von Ribbentrop, *Um den Untersberg. Sagen aus Adolf Hitlers Wahlheimat* (Frankfurt, 1937), 6–8. Höfler and Zembsch, *Watzmann*, 17n, provide an abridged and slightly different account.

7

Continuity and Silence: Conservation after 1945

Uncertainty was the dominant sentiment in the German population in the summer of 1945. Of course, people were glad that they had survived the war, but the exigencies of everyday life made it difficult to rejoice. Six years of war had taken its toll practically everywhere, and living conditions were always difficult and often disastrous. In many cases, city dwellers were hit particularly hard: the war had destroyed more than half of all urban housing, and the remaining population was mostly starving. The food supply was meager at best: in the summer of 1945, the average urbanite received only 1,300 calories a day in Munich, 1,000 in Stuttgart, and 700 to 800 in the Ruhr region.[1] This dismal situation was made worse by a total lack of political power: after the unconditional surrender of the Nazi regime on May 8, 1945, there was no longer a national authority, neither institutionally nor in spirit, that could voice the concerns of the German population. Instead, Allied soldiers stood in all parts of Germany, and everybody knew that these soldiers were under the impression of a kind of warfare that the world had never seen. Therefore, it should come as no surprise that few Germans showed much interest in politics in 1945; whereas the German defeat in World War I had led to a political radicalization, most Germans were now tired of anything that smacked of ideology. If Germans turned their eyes toward the future at all, it was often in a timid mood. What would the occupying powers do with Germany, now that the fate of the country lay in the hands of the former enemies? However, at least one man knew what to do. In June 1945, Hans Klose sent

---

[1] Manfred Görtemaker, *Geschichte der Bundesrepublik Deutschland. Von der Gründung bis zur Gegenwart* (Munich, 1999), 28n.

out a circular to the conservation community that was nothing short of a call to arms: "conservationists to the front" was his rallying cry. After an overview on the range of challenges that conservation had to meet now that the war was over, Klose asked for "the utmost activation of the conservation administration" and even urged those conservation advisors who felt unable to fulfill their duties with the right determination to resign their posts. "Nowadays, we can only tolerate those people within our ranks who are fanatically willing to fight for the cherished nature of our *Heimat*, nowadays more under threat than ever, to the greatest extent possible." For Klose, this was the hour of proof for the conservation community: "time will show whether it is up to the challenge." [2]

This passionate call to arms is even more remarkable if one realizes the dismal situation of Klose's Reich Conservation Agency. On its flight from Berlin to the town of Egestorf, some 20 miles south of Hamburg, the agency had lost the greater part of its administrative archives and all of its maps, and only 5 percent of the former office library made it to the Lüneburg Heath. In particular, the agency had lost its inventory of nature reserves, a document that the Nazis called, with a distinctly nationalist touch, the "national book of conservation" (*Reichsnaturschutzbuch*).[3] Just as important, the conservationists' network of the Nazi era had suffered badly during the war, and a good part of the agency's energies went into reestablishing contacts with conservation advisors and finding replacements for dead or missing people. Klose managed to become the center of a large network of communication within a brief period of time, but the feedback often struck a tone that differed markedly from Klose's energetic appeal. For example, a conservation advisor from the northern town of Stade reported that he was "in decent health again" and that he had given "a presentation with color pictures for hospitalized soldiers" two days earlier.[4]

Even where conservation advisors had survived the war, their continued membership in the conservation network was under threat because of

[2] WAA Best. 717 file "Reichsstelle (Bundesstelle) für Naturschutz (und Landschaftspflege)," Der Direktor der Reichsstelle für Naturschutz, Denkblätter der Reichsstelle für Naturschutz über die künftige Wahrnehmung von Naturschutz und Landschaftspflege. Teil D: Ueber die Dringlichkeit stärksten Naturschutzeinsatzes, June 26, 1945, p. 4n.

[3] *Ibid.*, Der Direktor der Reichsstelle für Naturschutz to the Beauftragte bei den besonderen und höheren Stellen für Naturschutz, July 1945, p. 3. On the nationalist implications of the *Reichsnaturschutzbuch* project, see BArch R 2/4730 p. 77.

[4] WAA Best. 717 file "Reichsstelle (Bundesstelle) für Naturschutz (und Landschaftspflege)," Der Direktor der Reichsstelle für Naturschutz to the Beauftragte bei den besonderen und höheren Stellen für Naturschutz, July 1945, p. 6.

the Allied denazification efforts. The goal of denazification was to subject all functionaries and members of the Nazi Party to a screening procedure and subsequent judgment by special denazification boards (*Spruchkammern*), with punishments ranging from imprisonment and confiscation of property to the deprivation of the right to vote. Historians generally agree that denazification failed to reach its desired goal: many culpable party members escaped judgment or achieved favorable rulings, whereas verdicts focused overwhelmingly on party members who were only guilty of minor misdemeanors.[5] Nonetheless, denazification procedures meant a significant hurdle that conservation advisors had to cross before they could resume their former work, and many conservationists strove to find a rationale for their membership in the Nazi Party that did not preclude a continuation of activism. "Colleagues who are relieved from their full-time jobs or are otherwise incriminated (*belastet*) will need to resign from their posts as conservation advisors," Hans Klose declared in a circular of August 1945. However, Klose's line of reasoning became clear when he added that "we may expect only a few resignations because we conservationists have, with few exceptions, refrained from political activity."[6] In the following months, Klose used his authority as a person who never joined the Nazi Party to write reports and affidavits that conservation advisors could present to denazification boards to win the desired clearances.[7] Even in difficult cases, conservationists could be confident that some colleague would be willing to attest to an inner distance to the Nazi regime. In one of the more notorious cases, Karl Oberkirch wrote a favorable report for Hans Schwenkel that described him as an apolitical person, asserting that he spoke critically of Hitler when they met in May 1943.[8] Schwenkel complemented this whitewashing with tacit revisions in his writing: when he published the second edition of his "pocketbook

[5] See Lutz Niethammer, *Die Mitläuferfabrik. Die Entnazifizierung am Beispiel Bayerns* (Berlin and Bonn, 1982), and Clemens Vollnhals (ed.), *Entnazifizierung. Politische Säuberung und Rehabilitierung in den vier Besatzungszonen 1945–1949* (Munich, 1991).

[6] WAA Best. 717 file "Reichsstelle (Bundesstelle) für Naturschutz (und Landschaftspflege)," Der Direktor der Reichsstelle für Naturschutz to the Beauftragten bei den besonderen und höheren Stellen für Naturschutz, early August, 1945.

[7] See BArch B 245/11 p. 39; B 245/57 pp. 217–17r; B 245/94 p. 61; B 245/249 pp. 104–5, 354; B 245/251 pp. 167–67r, 448–48r; B 245/253 pp. 14–14r, 140–40r; 355–55r; B 245/255 pp. 433, 438–38r; and WAA Best. 717 file "Oberste Naturschutzbeh. Land NRW Kultusministerium," Ministerialrat Dr. Josef Busley to Museumsdirektor Reichling, January 17, 1947. In a letter to Busley, Klose even spoke of "that strange part of our judicial system, the so-called denazification." (BArch B 245/249 p. 218.)

[8] HStAD NW 60 No. 622 pp. 137–8.

for conservation" in 1950, he provided a pleasant citation from Goethe where the 1941 edition had quoted Hermann Löns celebrating the Germanic love of nature.[9] When a Festschrift for Hans Schwenkel included a comprehensive list of his publications in 1956, his ugly anti-Semitic essay of 1938 had strangely escaped the compiler's attention.[10]

Denazification was more difficult where conservation advisors had been discharged for political reasons during the Nazi era. Cases of this kind were rare but tricky, as can be seen in the case of Westphalia, where Hermann Reichling had been forced to resign from his posts as director of Münster's natural history museum and provincial conservation advisor.[11] The case was delicate because a number of conservationists had been involved in the intrigues against Reichling, including Wilhelm Lienenkämper, who had declared in 1935 that he was unwilling "to cooperate with a provincial conservation advisor of this class."[12] Thus, the conservation administration was faced with a thorny situation when Hans Klose strongly urged reappointing Lienenkämper as conservation advisor for the Sauerland region in 1947.[13] It was clearly unwise to ignore Klose's advice, and Lienenkämper was certainly an energetic conservationist, but at the same time, nobody wanted to offend a person who had suffered from the Nazi regime. However, Reichling indicated that he was willing to move beyond these events when he proposed a private meeting with Lienenkämper to talk things over. Arranged by Josef Busley, the supreme conservation official in the state of North Rhine-Westphalia, the exchange settled the matter.[14] The conservationists' community spirit, along with a masculine ethos that a "talk between men" could solve even

---

[9] Schwenkel, *Taschenbuch*, 9; Hans Schwenkel, *Taschenbuch des Naturschutzes. Ein Ratgeber für Wanderer und Naturfreunde*, 2nd edition (Salach/Württemberg, 1950), 9. See also the revisions in Chapter 2, where Schwenkel stressed the breadth of conservation ideas in 1950 where in 1941 he had focused on the proximity of conservation and National Socialism: Schwenkel, *Taschenbuch (1941)*, 9–16 and Schwenkel, *Taschenbuch (1950)*, 12–23.

[10] Konrad Buchwald, Oswald Rathfelder, and Walter Zimmermann (eds.), *Festschrift für Hans Schwenkel zum 70. Geburtstag*, Veröffentlichungen der Landesstelle für Naturschutz und Landschaftspflege Baden-Württemberg und der württembergischen Bezirksstelle in Stuttgart und Tübingen 24 (Ludwigsburg, 1956), 52–5. Compare Schwenkel, "Vom Wesen."

[11] On Reichling's discharge, see Ditt, *Raum*, 327–9.

[12] WAA LWL Best. 702 no. 184b vol. 1, Sauerländischer Gebirgsverein, Heimat- und Naturschutzausschuss to the Oberpräsident Münster, May 22, 1935.

[13] HStAD NW 60 no. 712 p. 3.

[14] WAA Best. 717 file "Oberste Naturschutzbeh. Land NRW Kultusministerium," Hermann Reichling to Ministerialrat Josef Busley, January 28, 1947; HStAD NW 60 no. 712 pp. 13, 15. Remarkably, the precise nature of the exchange never became public.

the most difficult problems, was obviously stronger than the wounds of the past.

Reichling's behavior mirrored the dominant sentiment in conservation circles, as well as most parts of German society, after the Nazi era: it was not good to talk too much about the past. It is striking that decrees of the postwar years usually focused on the here and now, shrouding the Nazi experience in graceful silence.[15] And yet the past kept coming back to haunt the conservationists, in spite of all wishes to the contrary. The most important battle centered on the national conservation law of 1935: during the first months after the war, assuring the law's continued validity was paramount to the conservation community. With the national conservation law largely devoid of Nazi rhetoric, chances were good for a positive judgment from the Allied authorities, and Josef Busley noted as early as October 1945 "that there is no reason to fear that the national conservation law may no longer remain in force."[16] Nonetheless, nervousness was widespread among the conservationists, for too much was at stake. Not only would the decision of the Allied authorities determine the fate of an excellent law, but a negative decision also would have opened the door for a more thorough investigation of the conservation community's Nazi past. Therefore, conservationists were grateful for more than one reason when one state after another reported that the military authorities had cleared the national conservation law. In April 1946, Klose declared in one of his circulars that the battle for the law had been won.[17] Some people continued to challenge the validity of the national conservation law, but that was usually because of personal interests and failed to attract major attention.[18]

Whereas the fight for the national conservation law was waged in a defensive mode, the conservationists were more active, if not enthusiastic,

---

[15] E.g., StAW Landratsamt Bad Kissingen no. 1233, Regierungspräsident Würzburg to the untere Naturschutzbehörden, October 22, 1945, and Bund Naturschutz in Bayern to the Leiter der Orts- und Kreisgruppen, October 24, 1945.

[16] HStAD NW 72 no. 528 p. 3. Similarly, Burkhardt Riechers, *Naturschutzgedanke und Naturschutzpolitik im Nationalsozialismus* (M.A. thesis, Berlin Free University, 1993), 88.

[17] LASH Abt. 320 Eiderstedt no. 1845, Der Oberpräsident der Provinz Schleswig-Holstein to the Landräte and Oberbürgermeister, December 11, 1945; HStADd Best. 12513 no. 360, Der Präsident der Deutschen Verwaltung der Land- und Forstwirtschaft in der sowjetischen Besatzungszone to the Präsidenten der Provinzial- und Landesverwaltungen in Potsdam, Schwerin, Halle, Dresden und Weimar, August, 9, 1946; HStAD NW 60 no. 633 p. 7; NW 60 no. 623 p. 140.

[18] E.g., HStAD NW 60 no. 694 p. 37. See also the legal brief in Albert Lorz, *Naturschutz-, Tierschutz- und Jagdrecht*, 2nd edition (Munich, 1967), 4.

in a second conflict over the Nazi era's heritage: the issue of ministerial responsibility. As soon as the war was over, many conservationists vigorously urged transferring authority over conservation issues back to the state ministries of education, thus restoring the state of affairs in many German states prior to 1935.[19] The demands clearly mirrored the marginal role that conservation had played in the Forest Service, and yet it is impossible to understand the vigor of the debate if one fails to realize the unique chance that it offered in dealing with an uncomfortable past. After all, the transfer of authority had been solely the result of the personal interest of Hermann Göring, and the topic thus provided an ideal opportunity to depict conservation as the helpless victim of arbitrary decisions of Nazi leaders. Characteristically, Karl Oberkirch spoke of an "act of violence" in 1946.[20] The drive turned out to be a double success: ministries of education became responsible for the protection of nature in many states, and the debate certainly helped to dispel uncomfortable thoughts about the conservation community's decade-long flirtation with Nazism.

The most difficult battle pertained to the Reich Conservation Agency, and it took a full 7 years to assure its continued existence. Technically, the Reich Conservation Agency was an anachronism because a German Reich no longer existed after the German defeat: the Allied powers dissolved all German-wide institutions and instead sponsored the creation of new authorities on the local, regional, and state level. In fact, Klose could have received a job in the Rhineland in the fall of 1945, but he chose to stay in Egestorf and fight for the survival of his agency.[21] Ever the skillful manager, Klose managed to secure funding from the provincial administration in Hanover, and the Reich Conservation Agency began to serve simultaneously as the provincial conservation advisor for Hanover, a province that would soon be transformed into the West German state of Lower Saxony.[22] With all that, the agency was seriously overworked, and the difficult traffic situation made it hard to maintain close contacts with conservationists in all parts of Germany, but Klose managed to retain his

---

[19] WAA Best. 717 file "Reichsstelle (Bundesstelle) für Naturschutz (und Landschafts-pflege)," Der Direktor der Reichsstelle für Naturschutz to the Beauftragten bei den besonderen und höheren Stellen für Naturschutz, July 1945, p. 2; BArch B 245/166 p. 107.

[20] HStAD NW 60 no. 623 p. 95. Similarly, *ibid.* p. 171; B 245/166 pp. 106, 108.

[21] See HStAD NW 72 no. 528 p. 4.

[22] WAA Best. 717 file "Reichsstelle (Bundesstelle) für Naturschutz (und Landschafts-pflege)," Der Direktor der Reichsstelle für Naturschutz to the Beauftragten bei den besonderen und höheren Stellen für Naturschutz, July 1945, p. 2n.

pivotal position at least in the West German conservation community. In October 1948, the second conference of German conservation advisors passed a resolution in support of Klose's agency.[23] That was all the more necessary because funding from the state of Lower Saxony had expired earlier that year. After April 1, 1948, funding shifted from state to state every 3 months, a scheme that implied an enormous amount of stressful negotiation and was clearly only a makeshift to secure the agency's immediate survival.[24] Thus, Klose was relieved when the West German Economic Council (*Wirtschaftsrat*) decided to support his agency beginning April 1, 1949, even more so because the Economic Council's budget was scheduled to become that of the Federal Republic of Germany. "The legacy of Hugo Conwentz will be preserved," a jubilant Hans Klose declared in a circular of May 1949.[25] His position came under threat once more when the State Council (*Bundesrat*), one of the two chambers of the West German parliament, decided to abolish Klose's agency in 1951, but that decision was reversed the following year.[26] Relocated from Egestorf to Bonn and renamed "Federal Agency for Nature Protection and Landscape Preservation" (*Bundesanstalt für Naturschutz und Landschaftspflege*) in 1953, the agency maintains its position as the supreme conservation authority in the country to the present day.[27] Since 1993, it has borne the name Federal Agency for Nature Conservation (*Bundesamt für Naturschutz*).

It is important to realize that the conflicts over Klose's agency had nothing to do with the cause of conservation per se. Neither industry nor other vested interests tried to use the opportunity to weaken the conservation movement, and if Allied authorities showed any interest in the matter, it was in a positive vein. In July 1947, for example, a British officer offered his help in rebuilding the Bird Protection League, saying that "there are a number of Englishmen in the British Occupation Zone who would like to take part in bird protection work."[28] The issue at stake in the conflict over Klose's agency was states' rights: a strong federal agency

---

[23] See HStAD NW 60 no. 623 p. 140; and Klose, Ecke, *Verhandlungen*, 9.

[24] Klose, Ecke, *Verhandlungen*, 8.

[25] WAA Best. 717 file "Reichsstelle (Bundesstelle) für Naturschutz (und Landschaftspflege)," Zentralstelle für Naturschutz und Landschaftspflege, Rundschreiben B 41, May 13, 1949.

[26] Engels, "Hohe Zeit," 378; Hans Klose, *Fünfzig Jahre Staatlicher Naturschutz. Ein Rückblick auf den Weg der deutschen Naturschutzbewegung* (Giessen, 1957), 45–7.

[27] Klose, *Fünfzig Jahre*, 47, 55.

[28] WAA Best. 717 file "Reichsstelle (Bundesstelle) für Naturschutz (und Landschaftspflege)," letter of the Reichsstelle für Naturschutz of July 18, 1947.

threatened to dominate conservation authorities in the individual states. The state of Bavaria, traditionally the staunchest defender of states' rights in Germany, even issued a decree in 1947 prohibiting Bavarian conservation officials from having any contact with Klose's agency. "There is no imminent need for a centralized regulation of conservation issues, so different and dependent on the specific region," the Bavarian ministry of the interior reasoned.[29] However, Klose had a powerful ally in the traditional preference of the German conservation community for nationwide legislation. As mentioned above, the National Conservation Law of 1935 was cherished in part because it was the first law that established common rules for all of Germany, and conservationists were struggling to maintain this status quo. Many members of the German conservation community saw maintaining uniform rules and regulations as a good in itself, and it was only natural that the conference of conservation advisors warned of a fragmentation of conservation work in 1948.[30] However, the goal of preserving identical legal provisions in all parts of Germany proved elusive even before the East German government replaced the national conservation law of 1935 with a "law for the preservation and care of *Heimat* nature" (*Gesetz zur Erhaltung und Pflege der heimatlichen Natur*) in 1954.[31] As early as 1951, the state of Baden passed amendments to the national conservation law.[32]

All these conflicts forced the German conservationists to confront the Nazi legacy, and conservationists were clearly struggling to find some kind of rationale for dealing with the Nazi regime. In the months immediately following the German collapse, some conservationists felt that it was time to rethink the approach to conservation in the light of the war experience and the Nazis' horrendous crimes. Perhaps the most touching documentation of this sentiment came from Edith Ebers, a Bavarian conservationist who wrote an emphatic pledge for peace and international understanding that became the first postwar publication of the Bavarian Conservation League. "The disastrous collapse of our community indicates that something was wrong in our relationship towards nature," Ebers wrote,

---

[29] StAN Rep. 212/17^{IV} no. 101, Regierung von Ober- und Mittelfranken als Höhere Naturschutzbehörde to the Stadträte der kreisfreien Städte and the Landratsämter, November 11, 1947.

[30] Klose, Ecke, *Verhandlungen*, 9, 14n. See also Schoenichen, *Natur als Volksgut*, 39.

[31] Hugo Weinitschke, *Naturschutz gestern, heute, morgen* (Leipzig, 1980), 44; Runge, *Entwicklungstendenzen*, 63; and Oberkrome, *Deutsche Heimat*, 284.

[32] Häcker, *50 Jahre*, 16.

arguing that an intimate connection to pristine nature would be an anti-
dote against the "aberrations of mass psychology."[33] However, the call
to develop conservation into a driving force for peace and reconciliation
failed to gain momentum, and a more complacent view began to gain
ground in the conservation community: there was no need to rethink the
ethos of conservation because there had been no noteworthy connection
between conservation and the Nazi regime.[34] A key proponent of this
perspective was Hans Klose: "if there has ever been an apolitical part of
German society, averse to party strife, it was the *Heimat* community, the
associations of conservationists, hikers, mountaineers, and historians,"
Klose declared in 1946.[35] It is easy to show that Klose's assertion was false:
claiming that the fight for the Hohenstoffeln was "solely about the love of
nature and the *Heimat*" was an outright lie, and Klose knew that. In a letter of the same year, he wrote that Finckh had stood "quite amicably by the
former regime."[36] Nonetheless, Klose repeated his argument in a speech at
the second conservation advisors' conference, and his description of "the
path of German conservation" became a canonical text that government
decrees quoted to dispel uncomfortable thoughts about the Nazi era.[37]
From now on, the ruling doctrine was that there was no need to discuss
the relationship between conservation and National Socialism because
there had been no significant connection between the two movements.

In short, restoration was the dominant trend in conservation circles
during the postwar years. Resuming the earlier work, which the war
unfortunately had interrupted, was the overarching goal, and the flirt
with Nazism was seen, if at all, as an insignificant accident of history.
But continuity and normalcy were deceiving: the conservation community did change as a result of the Nazi experience, though this change

---

[33] Edith Ebers, *Neue Aufgaben der Naturschutzbewegung*. Naturschutz-Hefte 1 (Munich, 1947), 3.

[34] Some environmental historians, most notably Arne Andersen, have nonetheless argued that conservation was discredited in postwar society because of its proximity to the Nazis, but this argument was already contradicted by Burkhardt Riechers in 1996: compare Arne Andersen, "Heimatschutz. Die bürgerliche Naturschutzbewegung," in Franz-Josef Brüggemeier and Thomas Rommelspacher (eds.), *Besiegte Natur. Geschichte der Umwelt im 19. und 20. Jahrhundert*, 2nd edition (Munich, 1989), 157; and Burkhardt Riechers, "Nature Protection during National Socialism," *Historical Social Research* 29, 3 (1996): 52. See also Thomas Adam, "Parallele Wege. Geschichtsvereine und Naturschutzbewe-gung in Deutschland," *Geschichte in Wissenschaft und Unterricht* 48 (1997): 425.

[35] BArch B 245/3 p. 54.

[36] BArch B 245/3 p. 54, B 245/7 p. 60.

[37] Klose, "Weg." See also *Amtsblatt des Kultusministeriums, Land Nordrhein-Westfalen* 2, 1 (October 1, 1949): 6; and Lienenkämper, *Schützt*, 4.

took place without lengthy discussions. Whereas the conservationists were quick to reestablish lines of communication within their own camp, the outreach toward the broader society was hesitant at best. It is important to remember that the Nazi era had been a departure from the conservation community's tradition of political disengagement. For the first time, conservationists had affiliated closely with a political movement – and that movement then set off a war that claimed tens of millions of lives and plotted a genocide that had no parallel in world history. Seen from this perspective, it becomes clear why the Nazi era was a traumatic experience for the conservationists, and many drew the conclusion that it was unwise to move close to any political movement, no matter how innocuous it might seem. It is striking that conservationists of the 1950s took pride in the nonpartisan character of conservation work.[38] Many conservationists went even further, stressing the need to close ranks and concentrate on the handful of people who had shown themselves to be good, trustworthy conservationists. Once again, Hans Klose pointed the way, and his presentation on "the path of German conservation" depicted the conservation community as a small band of like-minded spirits who had formed "an integrated and incorruptible whole for a long time."[39] Conservationists maintained a close cooperation among themselves and a strong corporate identity, but they were highly distrustful of society at large. The conservation community knew that it had burned its fingers.

This distrust of society, and especially of politics, went hand in hand with a proximity to state authorities. The German conservation movement continued its étatist tradition of close ties to the government and in fact stressed the need for forceful state interventions even more vigorously than before. It is striking that it never occurred to the conservation community that one could read the situation of the postwar years as a call for a more liberal interpretation of rules and regulations. In a famous sermon on New Year's Eve 1946, Cologne's Cardinal Josef Frings gave his consent to the theft of coal if there was no other way to stay warm, a move that made *fringsen* the household word for stealing out of necessity.[40] The conservationists' reaction was precisely the opposite: with everyone oblivious of the cause of conservation, the times called for staunch defenders

---

[38] See Jens Ivo Engels, *Ideenwelt und politische Verhaltensstile von Naturschutz und Umweltbewegung in der Bundesrepublik 1950–1980* (Habilitationsschrift, Freiburg University, 2004), 39.

[39] Klose, "Weg," 30.

[40] Gerhard Brunn, Jürgen Reulecke, *Kleine Geschichte von Nordrhein-Westfalen 1946–1996* (Cologne, 1996), 25.

of nature who would take a firm stand against that trend. Pointing to
the "negligent implementation" of conservation regulations since 1945,
the *Rhönklub*, a regional conservation league in northern Bavaria and
eastern Hesse, called in 1952 for "the strict enforcement of the provisions in force."[41] In his annual report for 1948, Wilhelm Lienenkämper
even bemoaned "the weak backbone" of many conservationists and officials, chastising "a growing fear of being unpopular in the general population."[42] Lienenkämper was probably extreme in his view, but when
conservationists thought of popularity as a problem rather than an asset,
this mirrored the extent to which some conservation advisors relied on
the state for help.

As a result, few conservationists gave much thought to the fact that
government had changed since the demise of Nazi rule. What mattered
to the conservationists was the authority of the state, and whether this
authority found its legitimation in the charisma of the Führer or in parliamentary elections was ultimately an issue of secondary relevance. The
tactical nature of the conservationists' rapprochement to the state became
clear in 1947 when Hans Klose criticized contemporary plans to replace
the national conservation law with individual state laws in a private letter.
Remarkably, Klose's attack not only focused on the abhorred "atomiza-
tion" of conservation work but also pertained to "the democracy, whose
manifestations so far have not been very convincing."[43] Klose's view was
clear: from a conservation standpoint, democracy was worthy only if it
helped the conservationists' cause. In the postwar years, many conservationists accepted democracy not because of fundamental convictions but
simply because it happened to be the political system at that time. Essentially, conservationists embraced democracy for the same reason that they
had embraced the Nazis: to do something for nature, one had to cooperate
with the powers-that-be.

Some conservationists continued to come up with proposals that
depicted the protection of nature as conducive to peace and democracy,

[41] StAW Landratsamt Bad Kissingen no. 1233, letter of the Rhönklub e.V. Fulda, April
1952, p. 1. Similarly, WAA Best. 717 file "Reichsstelle (Bundesstelle) für Naturschutz
(und Landschaftspflege)," Der Direktor der Reichsstelle für Naturschutz, Denkblätter
der Reichsstelle für Naturschutz über die künftige Wahrnehmung von Naturschutz und
Landschaftspflege. Teil F: Zur Frage der zeitgebotenen Propaganda, July 22, 1945, p. 3;
LASH Abt. 320 Eiderstedt no. 1807, circular no. 2/46 of Verein Jordsand zur Begründung
von Vogelfreistätten an den deutschen Küsten, August 18, 1946; and Runge, *Entwicklungstendenzen*, 53.
[42] HStAD NW 60 no. 711 p. 35r.
[43] BArch B 245/11 p. 34r.

but those attempts never lost their air of artificiality.[44] When conservationists sought to legitimate their activity, the dominant point of reference was *Heimat*, the love of the regional nature.[45] In theory, the *Heimat* sentiment provided a bridge toward the general population because the *Heimat* idea grew increasingly popular in postwar society – more popular, in fact, than it had ever been during the Nazi era.[46] For example, about one-fifth of German film production between 1947 and 1960 drew on *Heimat* sentiments.[47] Nonetheless, the conservation community refused to think of the general population as a potential ally, and conservationists routinely bemoaned the "dwindling respect for nature" and the growing "estrangement between man and the natural environment" in postwar society.[48] To be sure, the environmental toll of the postwar years was significant, but it might have been a good idea for the conservation community to think not only about the estrangement between man and nature but also about the estrangement between themselves and the rest of society. At a conference of conservation advisors in Schleswig-Holstein in 1951, one speaker bluntly declared, "essentially, modern man is a mystery to us."[49]

Historians have long recognized that many careers of the Nazi era found a continuation in the Federal Republic, and the conservationists were no exception.[50] All in all, the conservation community of the early 1950s looked remarkably similar to that of the late 1930s. In retrospect, it is sobering to see what conservationists could get away with. For example,

[44] See Engels, "Hohe Zeit," 367–74.
[45] See Klose and Ecke, *Verhandlungen*, 27; and WAA Best. 717 file "Oberste Naturschutzbeh. Land NRW Kultusministerium," Der Provinzialbeauftragte für Naturschutz und Landschaftspflege to the Kultusministerium des Landes Nordrhein-Westfalen, October 3, 1950.
[46] See Alon Confino, "'This lovely country you will never forget.' Kriegserinnerungen und Heimatkonzepte in der westdeutschen Nachkriegszeit," in Habbo Knoch (ed.), *Das Erbe der Provinz. Heimatkultur und Geschichtspolitik nach 1945* (Göttingen, 2001), 235–51; Oberkrome, *Deutsche Heimat*, 34, 437n; and Applegate, *Nation*, 242.
[47] See Willi Höfig, *Der deutsche Heimatfilm 1947–1960* (Stuttgart, 1973); Margit Szöllösi-Janze, "'Aussuchen und abschließen' – der Heimatfilm der fünfziger Jahre als historische Quelle," *Geschichte in Wissenschaft und Unterricht* 44 (1993): 308–21; and Elizabeth Boa and Rachel Palfreyman, *Heimat. A German Dream. Regional Loyalties and National Identity in German Culture 1890–1990* (Oxford, 2000), 10.
[48] WAA LWL Best. 702 no. 184b vol. 2, Tätigkeitsbericht des Bezirksbeauftragten für Naturschutz und Landschaftspflege im Reg.Bez. Arnsberg und des Landschaftsbeauftragten für Naturschutz in den Kreisen Altena und Lüdenscheid für das Jahr 1948/49, p. 3; Raabe, "Problematik," 175.
[49] BArch B 245/64 p. 383r.
[50] See Norbert Frei, *Karrieren im Zwielicht. Hitlers Eliten nach 1945* (Frankfurt and New York, 2001).

SS member Günther Niethammer published an article on the bird population in Auschwitz in 1942 in which he expressed his gratitude to the commander of the Auschwitz Concentration Camp Rudolf Höss, and yet he could become director of the zoological Museum Alexander König in Bonn in 1950 and president of the German Society of Ornithologists (*Deutsche Ornithologen-Gesellschaft*) in 1967.[51] The careers of Heinrich Wiepking-Jürgensmann and Konrad Meyer have already been mentioned above: both found jobs at the University of Hanover, even though they had worked for Heinrich Himmler's Reich Commissariat for the Strengthening of German Nationality.[52] It is shameful that people of this kind were allowed to teach the next generation of German conservationists, but one should be careful with assumptions that Wiepking-Jürgensmann and Meyer simply imbued their students with racist or inhuman ideas. Günther Grzimek, who designed the park for the 1972 Olympic Games in Munich, a park that is heralded to this day as a showcase of democratic landscape planning, was a student of Wiepking-Jürgensmann's between 1937 and 1941.[53]

The situation in the German Democratic Republic (GDR) differed from that in the western part of Germany, though the difference was smaller than one would expect.[54] Georg Bela Pniower and Reinhard Lingner, two landscape planners who had experienced prosecution during the Nazi era, rose to prominence in the GDR.[55] Lingner had been close to the Communist Party before 1933, whereas Pniower had been a member of the Social Democratic Party during the Weimar years and after 1933 was ineligible for freelance work as a landscape architect as a "half-Jew" (*Halbjude*). For the socialist rulers, they were attractive not only because of their expertise but also because of their loyalty in political terms, as became clear in 1951 when Pniower turned down an offer from West Berlin's Charlottenburg University of Technology and accepted a chair at Humboldt University in East Berlin. However, the GDR also hired a number of landscape

---

[51] Günther Niethammer, "Beobachtungen über die Vogelwelt von Auschwitz (Ost-Oberschlesien)," *Annalen des Naturhistorischen Museums in Wien* 52 (1942): 164–99. Information on Niethammer's career from Ernst Klee, *Das Personenlexikon zum Dritten Reich. Wer war was vor und nach 1945* (Frankfurt, 2003), 436.

[52] See p. 159.

[53] Mader, *Gartenkunst*, 158.

[54] Oberkrome, *Deutsche Heimat*, 314.

[55] It is noteworthy that Pniower was also exceptional in that he published a scathing critique of Seifert's preference for native species in 1952: see Charlotte Reitsam, *Das Konzept der "bodenständigen Gartenkunst" Alwin Seiferts. Fachliche Hintergründe und Rezeption bis in die Nachkriegszeit* (Frankfurt, 2001), 222n.

architects who had been members of the Nazi Party and had worked for Nazi projects. Werner Bauch, Hermann Göritz, Hinrich Meyer-Jungclaussen, Otto Rindt, and Rudolf Ungewitter had been Landscape Advocates in the Autobahn project under the guidance of Alwin Seifert and nonetheless pursued careers in East Germany; only Ungewitter later fled from the GDR. After all, it did not require a shift of paradigms to work as a landscape architect in both Nazi Germany and the socialist GDR: in both cases, the guiding idea was to remedy the damage done by a free-wheeling liberalist economy.[56]

In contrast to the "don't ask, don't tell" approach in West Germany, the East German government put pressure on the conservation community to confront its Nazi past, though the reason was mainly of a tactical nature. From a socialist perspective, conservation associations were simply remnants of bourgeois society, and relating them to fascism was a convenient way to spur their demise.[57] Under pressure from state authorities, the Heimat League of Saxony compiled a comprehensive inventory of all articles and quotations in the league's journal between 1933 and 1941 that smacked of Nazi rhetoric, something that associations in West Germany never bothered to do.[58] The socialist rulers also attacked the league because they suspected military implications when the league spoke of *Heimat* protection (*Heimatschutz*). Desperate to find some proof for the true meaning of the term, the Heimat League of Saxony sent a letter to Ernst Rudorff's daughter asking "for a brief explanation what your cherished father thought of when choosing this word."[59] However, these measures did not initiate any soul-searching among the Saxon conservationists. Quite the opposite: the league began to claim antifascist credentials, if only out of necessity, and it played the innocent victim. "What have we done? Every criminal knows why he is convicted. But we do not know anything," the league's director complained in 1948.[60] The league was

---

[56] See Andreas Dix, "Nach dem Ende der 'Tausend Jahre.' Landschaftsplanung in der Sowjetischen Besatzungszone und frühen DDR," in Radkau and Uekötter, *Naturschutz und Nationalsozialismus*, 343–50; and Hermann Behrens, *Von der Landesplanung zur Territorialplanung.* Umweltgeschichte und Umweltzukunft 5 (Marburg, 1997), 44n, 148. See also Andreas Dix, *"Freies Land." Siedlungsplanung im ländlichen Raum der SBZ und frühen DDR 1945–1955* (Cologne, 2002); and Oberkrome, *Deutsche Heimat*, 398–400.

[57] See Oberkrome, *Deutsche Heimat*, 281.

[58] HStADd Best. 12513 no. 68, Verzeichnis der in den Heimatschutzmitteilungen enthaltenen nicht tragbaren Aufsätze und Redewendungen (undated).

[59] HStADd Best. 12513 no. 77, Sächsischer Heimatschutz to Elisabeth Rudorff, April 21, 1947.

[60] HStADd Best. 12513 no. 360, Sächsischer Heimatschutz to Paul Bernhardt, June 10, 1948.

disbanded soon thereafter, and communication with the more traditional conservation leagues on the other side of the iron curtain was minimal, but some remnants of conservation traditions survived even under socialist rule.[61]

Of course, the extent of traditionalism in East Germany paled in comparison with that in the West, where the conservation movement of the 1950s looked conspicuously similar to that of the early twentieth century. It is fitting that Schoenichen published a volume on the history of the German conservation movement in 1954 that provided an extensive discussion of the intentions of the movement's founding fathers – Schoenichen called on his readers "to contemplate the work of these founders of conservation with reverence" – whereas everything that happened after Ernst Rudorff and Hugo Conwentz was shrouded in graceful silence.[62] The glorification of the movement's pre-1933 roots was clearly an attempt to legitimate the conservation movement after the traumatic Nazi experience, not the least for Schoenichen himself, who was certainly mindful of his former attempts to depict conservation as a quintessential Nazi concern. At the same time, it is equally clear that a strongly traditionalist movement was ill suited for the dynamism of postwar West German society. As a result, the rapid transformation of West German society stood in stark contrast to the general standstill of the conservation movement. When a growing interest in the protection of nature emerged in the general population in the early 1960s, a phenomenon that was instrumental for the rise of a modern environmental movement in West Germany a few years later, the conservation community mostly ignored this trend and stuck to its own circles, favoring administrative work behind the scenes over spearheading a people's movement.[63] It would take a different generation of conservationists to recognize the opportunities that a strong popular sentiment harbored for the environmental cause.

However, it would be misleading to depict the rise of environmentalism as a definite watershed that totally transformed the German conservation movement in all its parts; after all, continuity was far too strong in terms of personnel, institutions, and ideas. That was especially true when it

---

[61] See Oberkrome, *Deutsche Heimat*, 526; Willi Oberkrome, "Suffert und Koch. Zum Tätigkeitsprofil deutscher Naturschutzbeauftragter im politischen Systemwechsel der 1920er bis 1950er Jahre," *Westfälische Forschungen* 51 (2001): 446; and Hermann Behrens, "Naturschutz und Landeskultur in der Sowjetischen Besatzungszone und in der DDR. Ein historischer Überblick," in Bayerl and Meyer, *Veränderung*, 221.

[62] Cf. Schoenichen, *Naturschutz, Heimatschutz*. Quotation p. ix.

[63] For an extensive discussion of this argument, see Uekötter, *Naturschutz im Aufbruch*.

came to dealing with the Nazi past: the popular notion that there were no significant links between conservation and National Socialism persisted in conservation circles long after the conservationists of the Nazi era had left the scene. It seems reasonable to assume that this phenomenon had a lot to do with the peculiar development of environmentalism in West Germany. More than in other countries, the German environmental movement grew out of a convergence of divergent traditions and ideas. Input came from the political left as well as the right; even the Green Party, which has established itself as a distinctly leftist party, was founded in the late 1970s with major imput from conservatives like Herbert Gruhl.[64] Whereas environmentalism became closely affiliated with the political left in the United States, it remained more of a middle-of-the-road topic in Germany. More than once, key political initiatives came from people who cannot qualify by any measure as leftists. For example, the first wave of environmental legislation in the early 1970s was the result of the initiative of the German minister of the interior Hans-Dietrich Genscher, a member of the FDP, the party of economic liberalism, who embraced the issue in part because it gave his party a distinct profile in the governing coalition with the Social Democrats.[65] Genscher's initiative is even more remarkable because civic activism on environmental issues was still in its infancy in Germany at that time, whereas the contemporary move by the American president Richard Nixon to embrace environmentalism was clearly a response to a popular sentiment that had found its best-known expression in the legendary Earth Day celebration on April 22, 1970.[66] Klaus Töpfer, who was the German minister for the environment from 1987 to 1994 and later moved to become Executive Director of the United Nations Environment Programme in 1998, was a prominent member of the conservative Christian Democrats.

The merger of different political strands into one movement inevitably created tensions, and a significant amount of disputes and infighting has been a hallmark of German environmentalism in the last 35 years. For example, internal conflicts in the Bird Protection League in the 1980s

---

[64] Cf. Markus Klein and Jürgen W. Falter, *Der lange Weg der Grünen. Eine Partei zwischen Protest und Regierung* (Munich, 2003), and E. Gene Frankland, "Germany: The Rise, Fall and Recovery of *Die Grünen*," in Dick Richardson and Chris Rootes (eds.), *The Green Challenge: The Development of Green Parties in Europe* (London and New York, 1995), 23–44.

[65] Cf. Kai F. Hünemörder, *Die Frühgeschichte der globalen Umweltkrise und die Formierung der deutschen Umweltpolitik (1950–1973)* (Stuttgart, 2004), 154n.

[66] Cf. J. Brooks Flippen, *Nixon and the Environment* (Albuquerque, 2000).

were quite similar to the conflicts within the Sierra Club in the 1960s, with the difference being that whereas David Brower finally left the Sierra Club in 1969 after prolonged disputes with a more traditional rank and file, Jochen Flasbarth, the leader of the internal rebellion as head of the Bird Protection League's youth branch, later served as president for more than 10 years and transformed the league, which changed its name to NABU (*Naturschutzbund Deutschland*) after reunification, into one of the major environmental advocacy groups in Germany.[67] However, the difficult merger of disperse groups also seems to have discouraged discussions about the movement's history, and specifically the Nazi past. Not only did the constant disputes consume a good part of the movement's intellectual energies, but environmentalists also realized that any discussion of the past would run an enormous risk of being overtly divisive. It is striking that references to the Nazi era were notably rare in the ongoing internal debates. Perhaps lack of knowledge was partly to blame: the notion of an "environmental revolution" nourished a widespread impression that the environmental movement had no history worth talking about. However, environmentalists may also have refrained from meddling with the past because raising the Nazi issue was the discursive equivalent of the "nuclear option": arguing that somebody was standing in line with the Nazis is clearly the ultimate insult in Germany politics, and usually the end of all discussions. Although many leftists were at odds with more conservative members of the environmental movement, they did not hate them sufficiently as to put them in line with Nazism. A common sense of identity clearly discouraged invoking Nazism in the ongoing debates.

In short, if environmentalists recognized their own history at all, they usually saw it as a burden that one had better not talk about. Thus, the Nazi past became something like an awkward shadow, a theme that was simultaneously in the air and impossible to talk about. However, it would be wrong to fault the conservation community alone: the tradition of silence would have been impossible if the general public had shown a significant interest in the conservationists' past. However, the public debate on National Socialism centered on different issues, and not without reason: even a dedicated environmental historian has to admit that the continuity of personnel in the judiciary was more worrisome than the continuity within the conservation community. As a result, few people called on the conservationists to confront their Nazi past, and even

---

[67] Cf. Michael P. Cohen, *The History of the Sierra Club 1892–1970* (San Francisco, 1988), and May, *NABU*.

authors whose opposition to Nazism was beyond doubt saw little reason to take a closer look. In his 1947 essay on *The Revolt of Nature*, Max Horkheimer spoke of the general "modern insensitivity to nature," with Nazism making no difference for better or worse. "National Socialism, it is true, boasted of its protection of animals, but only in order to humiliate more deeply those 'inferior races' whom they treated as mere nature."[68] If even Max Horkheimer, a key member of the Frankfurt School of Social Research, did not find this issue worth studying, it becomes understandable why the pressure on the conservation community to discuss their involvement in the Nazi regime remained low. Although many institutions and companies started to look into their Nazi past in the 1980s and 1990s, the environmentalists acted as if dealing with the Nazi legacy was not one of their concerns.

The tradition of forgetfulness finally ended in 2002, when the German minister for the environment Jürgen Trittin opened the Berlin conference on conservation in Nazi Germany. The present author having been personally involved in the organization of this conference, he is certainly not in a position to evaluate its merits. However, it seems legitimate to stress that the mere existence of a conference under the auspices of the German minister for the environment marked a watershed in the discussion on the Nazis and the environment. Academic research on the topic dates back to the 1970s, but its status in the context of current environmental politics remained somewhat unclear: were historic inquiries a welcome contribution to ongoing debates – or a burden, a vicious effort to throw dirt on a worthy cause? With a leading Green Party member opening a conference on the topic, the question finally found the answer that it deserved: it is essential to face up to one's history, even if it is painful to do. Many results of the conference, Jürgen Trittin declared, "will be uncomfortable for a friend of nature protection – but they are the historic truth."[69] For the environmental movement, there will be no way back from this statement.

---

[68] Max Horkheimer, *Eclipse of Reason* (New York, 1947), 104, 105.
[69] Jürgen Trittin, "Naturschutz und Nationalsozialismus – Erblast für den Naturschutz im demokratischen Rechtsstaat?," in Radkau and Uekötter, *Naturschutz und National-sozialismus*, 38.

8

Lessons

When environmental historians recount a chapter from the history of nature protection, they often do so in a sympathetic mode. However, the situation is different if that chapter happens to be the history of conservation in Nazi Germany: few will read this book with much sympathy for the conservation community of the Nazi era. The reasons do not call for explanation: the cruelty of the Nazis' rule, and the immense human toll that it claimed, make Hitler's regime a disturbing topic even more than 60 years after his death. Seeing a cause dear to one's heart aligned with such a regime is painful, and many readers will have read this book with a sentiment of "never again." But understandable as this sentiment may be, it is also clear that it calls for specification: what precisely has to be done to prevent a repetition of this story? What are the lessons that the current environmental movement, or other social movements, for that matter, should learn from the Nazi experience?

Of course, this question is anything but new, and a number of authors have put forward answers to it. Anna Bramwell was the first to connect historical and political discussions when she argued that there was a "green party" in Nazi Germany, with Richard Walther Darré, the Nazis' minister of agriculture and Reich Peasant Leader (*Reichsbauernführer*), at its center.[1] However, her argument quickly drew massive criticism from other researchers. "To extract a conservationist message from Darré, one would have had to ignore the bulk of his writing," Raymond Dominick

---

[1] Anna Bramwell, *Blood and Soil: Walther Darré and Hitler's Green Party* (Abbotsbrook, 1985).

wrote in 1987.[2] Bramwell nonetheless reiterated her argument in a second book 4 years later, where she argued that Darré was part of a "Steiner Connection." However, this argument was even more devoid of credible evidence and actually contradicted her original thesis: whereas she had discussed the conflicts between Darré and Seifert extensively in her earlier book, she now played down disagreements and instead stressed the common reference to anthroposophy.[3] This book also stood out for gross errors, falsely asserting that "Nazi Germany was the first country in Europe to form nature reserves."[4] More thorough research showed that Darré was not involved to any significant extent in nature or landscape protection work and that Darré's interest in organic farming did not become prominent until 1945: it was part of his defense at the Nuremberg Trial.[5] Bramwell's argument hinged on a loose parallelism, and even this parallelism was based on a highly dubious empirical basis.[6] Finally, her argument is also wrong in its general approach: there was never a coherent "green faction" in Nazi Germany but rather a set of different groups and actors characterized by an enormous amount of infighting. All the while, Nazi leaders showed at best sporadic interest in conservation issues. Bramwell's argument continues to have some currency in right-wing circles, where it can serve to smear current environmentalists, but that says less about environmentalism than about the superficial reading of these authors.[7]

A second proposal for lessons from the Nazi experience dealt with the topic of nonnative species. In a much-quoted essay, Gert Gröning and Joachim Wolschke-Bulmahn argued that the current criticism of nonnative

[2] Dominick, "Nazis," 522.

[3] Anna Bramwell, *Ecology in the 20th Century: A History* (New Haven and London, 1989), 198. For a thorough criticism of this book, see Piers H. G. Stephens, "Blood, Not Soil: Anna Bramwell and the Myth of 'Hitler's Green Party,'" *Organization & Environment* 14 (2001): 173–87.

[4] Bramwell, *Ecology*, 199.

[5] See Gerhard, "Richard Walther Darré." See also *Neue Politische Literatur* 31 (1986): 501–4, for a critical assessment of Bramwell's first book.

[6] Robert Pois put forward a similiar argument that hinged on nothing more than a loose parallelism: see Robert A. Pois, *National Socialism and the Religion of Nature* (London and Sydney, 1986), esp. pp. 3, 38, 58.

[7] E.g., Thomas R. DeGregori, *Agriculture and Modern Technology: A Defense* (Ames, Iowa, 2001), Chapter 7. For some reason, the legend that Darré was a proponent of organic farming can also be found in leftist publications, e.g., Peter Staudenmaier, "Fascist Ideology: The 'Green Wing' of the Nazi Party and Its Historical Antecedents," in Janet Biehl and Peter Staudenmaier (eds.), *Ecofascism. Lessons from the German Experience* (Edinburgh, 1995), 13.

plants continued themes and perspectives that also played a role during the Nazi era: "In parts of Germany, hostility against certain groups of foreigners is increasing. Perhaps the mania for so-called native plants is just another side of this construction of nature philosophy," Gröning and Wolschke-Bulmahn reasoned.[8] In a later publication, they even argued that a stance against nonnative species "became part of the state doctrine during National Socialism."[9] However, other publications take a much more balanced approach to the issue, and for good reasons.[10] The subject clearly calls for a multidisciplinary approach; issues of ideology certainly have a place in these discussions, but so do biological and agricultural perspectives. But even as a historical argument, the article betrays little more than the authors' selective reading. For example, Alwin Seifert, who is quoted at length in the article, had not always been a staunch critic of nonnative plants: as Thomas Zeller found out, he initially offered two drafts of a landscaping concept for the Autobahn to Fritz Todt, with only one of them emphasizing native species.[11] Furthermore, the preference for native plants was never mandatory in Nazi Germany, and most conservationists favored a pragmatic approach. In 1937, the Reich Conservation Agency gave its consent to a nature reserve that comprised mostly trees of foreign origin and even approved a subsidy for the project.[12] In 1938, a meeting of conservationists in Münster discussed whether "exotic trees" could deserve a nature protection decree, and the concluding advice "to always look at historic importance" clearly showed that the issue had been discussed without the dogmatism that one would expect in an ideologically charged field.[13] Even Hans Schwenkel could speak of nonnative species in a positive way at times: in the brochure following up on Hitler's decree on the preservation of hedgerows, Schwenkel noted that the species that made up the German hedgerows were "in part southerly children."[14]

---

[8] Gert Groening and Joachim Wolschke-Bulmahn, "Some Notes on the Mania for Native Plants in Germany," *Landscape Journal* 11 (1992): 125.

[9] Gert Gröning and Joachim Wolschke-Bulmahn, "The Native Plant Enthusiasm: Ecological Panacea or Xenophobia," Landscape Research 28 (2003): 79.

[10] See most prominently Uta Eser, *Der Naturschutz und das Fremde. Ökologische und normative Grundlagen der Umweltethik* (Frankfurt and New York, 1999).

[11] Zeller, "Ganz Deutschland," 276. See also p. 78n.

[12] BArch B 245/101 p. 101. Compare Schoenichen and Weber, *Reichsnaturschutzgesetz*, 10.

[13] WAA LWL Best 702 no. 184b vol. 2, Gemeinsame Arbeitstagung der Westfälischen Naturschutzbeauftragten und der Fachstelle Naturkunde und Naturschutz im Westfälischen Heimabund on February 12–13, 1938, p. 9.

[14] GLAK Abt. 235 no. 47680, Der Führer hält seine schützende Hand über unsere Hecken. Hans Schwenkel, Reichsbund für Vogelschutz, p. 3. Compare Schwenkel, *Grundzüge*, 95.

In fact, one author delivered nothing short of a full-scale assault on the supposed "mania for native plants in Germany" as late as 1941: banning all plants deemed "foreign" would mean "that we are stuck with a few old wildflowers."[15]

Another set of authors has argued that the Nazi experience calls for a reconsideration of the regionalist concept of *Heimat*. Briefly, the argument is that the term *Heimat* was, and continues to be, so deeply imbued with the ideology of National Socialism that the use of the term is risky at best.[16] The argument clearly echoes Victor Klemperer's famous indictment of the language of the Third Reich: "one should lay many words of the Nazi language into a mass grave for a long time, and some forever."[17] But again, a sober look at the historical record provides a far more balanced picture. The Nazis never made *Heimat* a prominent part of their propaganda, and for a reason: it was clearly at odds with both the Nazi state's centralism and the regime's expansionist goals.[18] It is no coincidence that the *Heimat* concept was so much in vogue in the postwar years. People sensed that this was not only a concept that long predated the Nazi era but also one of the few relatively uncorrupted words that allowed an expression of collective identifications as Germans. In many cases, Germans spoke of *Heimat* after 1945 where they had previously said "nation." Remarkably, American authors like Celia Applegate have discounted the importance of *Heimat* in Nazi Germany or even, like William Rollins, written a eulogy of the *Heimatschutz* movement.[19] Furthermore, this approach, favored most recently by a group of authors including Reinhard Piechocki and Stefan Körner, is also dubious as a matter of principle. After all, the argument aims at a total ban on a word, rather than a redefinition that takes

---

[15] Karl Foerster, "Bodenständige Pflanzen. Schlichtende Gedanken zu diesem Begriff," *Die Gartenschönheit* 22, 6 (1941): 128.

[16] See Reinhard Piechocki et al., "Vilmer Thesen zu 'Heimat' und Naturschutz," *Natur und Landschaft* 78 (2003): 241–4; and Stefan Körner, "Naturschutz und Heimat im Dritten Reich," *Natur und Landschaft* 78 (2003): 394–400. For further authors assuming a "contamination" of the term, see Michael Neumeyer, *Heimat. Zu Geschichte und Begriff eines Phänomens* (Kiel, 1992), 123; Wolfgang Lipp, "Heimatbewegung, Regionalismus. Pfade aus der Moderne?," *Kölner Zeitschrift für Soziologie und Sozialpsychologie* Sonderheft 27 (1986): 336. For a more extensive critique, see Frank Uekötter, "Heimat, Heimat, ohne alles? Warum die Vilmer Thesen zu kurz greifen," *Heimat Thüringen* 11, 4 (2004): 8–11.

[17] Klemperer, *LTI*, 27.

[18] See 37–8.

[19] See Applegate, *Nation*; and Rollins, *Greener Vision*. See also the nuanced interpretations in Boa and Palfreyman, *Heimat*, and Peter Blickle, *Heimat. A Critical Theory of the German Idea of Homeland* (Rochester and Suffolk, 2002).

the historic use of the term into account. Even ignoring questions about the implementation of such a ban, it is doubtful whether *Heimat* really deserves such a ban. After all, the Nazis were masters of the use of words and concepts that were foreign to their core ideas but useful in making their regime more popular. Should we cease to talk of soil in German because the word was part of the infamous Nazi slogan "blood and soil"? In fact, if one bans every word that ever played even a fleeting role in Nazi rhetoric, one quickly ends up with a ban on most words in Germany's political dictionary.

It is revealing to note that all three approaches are based on a strangely monolithic picture of Nazi rule: the sheer presence of certain ideas in the Nazi era is deemed sufficient for an indictment. Remarkably, there is no discussion in any of the publications quoted on the extent of the commitment to National Socialism, of the importance of the link or its general character, or even of countervailing tendencies. In essence, the articles follow an exceedingly simple, three-step approach: There was a certain trend in the Nazi era; there is a similar trend nowadays; consequently, the latter is tainted by the former. With a bit of polemic, one might call this the contagionist school of conservation history: anything present in today's conservation work that bears any resemblance to ideas or practices of the Nazi era is suspect as a matter of principle, and in danger of spreading a deadly virus. However, the folly of such an approach becomes obvious when one thinks of further correlations that a contagionist approach would need to condemn. If Himmler saved the Hohenstoffeln Mountain, should we destroy it? If the Nazis encouraged the consumption of wholemeal bread, should we get back to classic white bread?[20] The Nazis built four-lane limited access highways; should this innovation be banned? It was in Nazi Germany that researchers first discovered the link between smoking and lung cancer, and the regime launched an ambitious antismoking campaign that included bans on certain forms of advertising and restrictions on smoking in many public spaces.[21] A cigarette, anyone?

The historiographic pitfall of such an approach is obvious: identifying parallelisms between the past and the present cannot be anything more than a first step at best. But there is also a moral pitfall that gives reason for doubt. The contagionist approach treats all contacts as uniformly

---

[20] Uwe Siekermann, "Vollkornbrot in Deutschland. Regionalisierende und nationalisierende Deutungen und Praktiken während der NS-Zeit," *Comparativ* 11, 1 (2001): 27–50, and Jörg Melzer, *Vollwerternährung. Diätetik, Naturheilkunde, Nationalsozialismus, sozialer Anspruch* (Stuttgart, 2003), 206.

[21] Robert N. Proctor, *The Nazi War on Cancer* (Princeton, 2000), 174n.

evil: it condemns the issue under discussion – be it nonnative species, or environmentalism, or the notion of *Heimat* – as part of the most infamous regime of world history. With that, the discussion ends at a point where it ought to start. Who would want to defend nonnative species if that makes him a bedfellow of Adolf Hitler? However, it is easy to see that the need for nuance in moral judgments is imperative *precisely because* of the monstrosity of the Nazis' crimes. After all, a uniform indictment ends up putting very different types of behavior on a par. Of course, the conservationists who adopted Nazi rhetoric deserve a staunch and unambiguous critique, but it has to be a different one than that of Wiepking-Jürgensmann's work in the Reich Commissariat for the Strengthening of German Nationality. It is disheartening to see Hans Klose hoping for a favorable intervention from Heinrich Himmler in 1943, and yet there should be a difference, and a marked one, between one's evaluation of Klose's behavior and that of the murderers of Auschwitz.

Of course, one should not overlook the obvious in the quest for lessons: the Nazi experience shows that environmental ideas could coexist with racist and anti-Semitic clichés, thus demonstrating the importance of clarity in the discussion of the ethical motives of conservation. After all, it was this clarity that was lacking in discussions of the Weimar years. If racist and antidemocratic ideas won a place in conservation rhetoric during the 1920s, this was not because of the fact that all conservationists agreed on these points but rather because few people took issue with them. The general line of reasoning discouraged a controversial discussion of these rightist sentiments, seeing debates on these ideologically charged issues as detrimental to the overarching goal of conservation. The fallacy of this argument is obvious in retrospect, and the apathy of the conservation community in the late Weimar years was a direct result of this dominant mindset. Of course, it is naïve to think that the conservationists alone could have saved the Weimar Republic, but if one takes into account that the dearth of a democratic ethos was typical of so many parts of German society it becomes clear that the conservationists' stance was part of a more general problem. Defending democracy and human rights is a task for all members of society, and not just of politicians, jurists, and members of political parties.

And yet it would be short-sighted to focus on ideological issues only. As Chapter 2 has shown, the ideological rapproachement of the conservation community toward Nazi ideology remained incomplete. Conservationists often came to adopt Nazi rhetoric, but a seamless merger of both sets of ideas never materialized. Moreover, the ideological commitment of members of the conservation community remained highly uneven: there were ideologists like Walther Schoenichen and Hans Schwenkel and fanatics like Ludwig Finckh, but also more sober figures like Hans Klose and Hermann Schurhammer. Some historians have neglected the latter group because it did not fit the stereotype of the dedicated Nazi that they sought to paint. However, it is important to realize that the conservation community of the Nazi era continued to include people who were lukewarm about the Nazis because that leads to what is arguably the most important lesson of this story: one did not have to be an ideological fanatic to cooperate with the Nazis. In fact, one did not even have to adopt racist rhetoric or anti-Semitic clichés at all to entertain a close relationship with the Nazis. The case of Hans Klose, who became the supreme conservation advisor of Germany without ever joining the Nazi Party, provides a fitting illustration. All that it took to join the conservation community during the Nazi era was a willingness to cooperate with Nazi authorities – and, of course, a readiness to be silent about any points of disagreement. As it turned out, the vast majority of the German conservationists were willing to pay this price.

It is in the light of this tactical rapprochement that the true importance of the Nazi experience emerges. It is important to examine the ideological underpinnings of conservation, not least because extreme right-wing parties have made some attempts in Germany to enter the political mainstream in recent years through claiming ecological credentials.[22] But at the same time, it would be difficult to see a truly burning need in this regard. After all, the tactical nature of that approach has been only too apparent, and few people have taken notice, let alone converted to Nazism for ecological reasons; a recent publication called right-wing environmental groups in Germany "more annoying than dangerous."[23] However, remembering the tactical alliance of conservation and National Socialism will be important to everyone working on international conservation issues, for authoritarian regimes continue to be an unfortunate presence on the global scene. It would be wrong to simply refrain from conservation work in authoritarian states, but it would be equally wrong to behave like

---

[22] See Oliver Geden, *Rechte Ökologie. Umweltschutz zwischen Emanzipation und Faschismus* (Berlin, 1999); Thomas Jahn and Peter Wehling, *Ökologie von rechts. Nationalismus und Umweltschutz bei der Neuen Rechten und den "Republikanern"* (Frankfurt and New York, 1991); and Jonathan Olsen, *Nature and Nationalism: Right-Wing Ecology and the Politics of Identity in Contemporary Germany* (Houndmills and London, 1999).

[23] Franz-Josef Brüggemeier, Mark Cioc, and Thomas Zeller, "Introduction," in Brüggemeier, Cioc, and Zeller, *How Green*, 1.

the conservation community during the Nazi era: to simply take advantage of the opportunities that authoritarian regimes offer and not care about the rest. The history of conservation in Nazi Germany provides an important reminder that naïve cooperation with the powers-that-be may turn out to be a terrible mistake.

In 1937, Schoenichen planned an international conference on the protection of nature, together with an international conservation exposition, in Berlin for September 1939.[24] The conference never happened because of the worsening of international relations that preceded the onset of World War II, but it is rewarding to speculate about what conservationists from other countries would have said about the accomplishments of Nazi Germany. Chances are that many of them would have been deeply impressed by the National Conservation Law, the comprehensive network of conservation advisors, and the general boom of conservation work since 1935; after all, Germany was probably the only European country that experienced such a boom in the 1930s. It is even more rewarding to ask oneself, What would *I* have said? Would I have inquired about the forces behind the passage of the National Conservation Law? Would I have wondered how it had been possible to designate dozens of nature reserves in some regions within 2 or 3 years? Would I have found out about paragraph 24 of the National Conservation Law, the option to confiscate property of environmental merit, and the blatant violation of property rights that it had led to in everyday conservation work? Chances are that a number of environmentalists, and in any case too many of them, would have behaved just as thoughtlessly as did so many German conservationists: that their guiding thought would have been that the protection of nature required the use of every lever that one could seize and that one should take quick advantage of one's opportunities. Learning from the Nazi experience may be more difficult, and more painful, than many conservationists have thought.

---

[24] WAA LWL Best. 702 no. 195, Der Direktor der Reichsstelle für Naturschutz to the Vorsitzende der Naturschutzstellen der Länder, der preußischen Provinzen und des Ruhrsiedlungsbezirks, December 27, 1937; BArch B 245/196 pp. 382–3, 392–3.

Appendix

Some Remarks on the Literature and Sources

The history of conservation during the Nazi era is one of the better-researched topics in German environmental history, and some 25 years of scholarly activity have produced a considerable number of important books and a multitude of essays on a wide range of topics.[1] It is not the intention of the following remarks to give a complete account of the range of publications or to provide in-depth descriptions of the major works: a comprehensive overview that the author wrote in 2002 filled thirty-five pages.[2] The goal of this appendix is more modest in that it seeks to provide a rough overview on the most important books and articles as a guide to everyone who would like to read more. At the same time, it will give a more precise idea of the general direction in which this book seeks to push conservation history.[3]

It is not surprising that the majority of publications have appeared in German, but a number of important contributions are in English. The most recent monograph is Thomas Lekan's *Imagining the Nation in Nature*, a book that draws strongly on Lekan's research on conservation work in the Rhineland from the late 1800s to 1945. The books of Alon Confino and Celia Applegate provide important insights into different aspects of German regionalism, whereas Raymond Dominick discussed the Nazi era extensively in his account of the German environmental

---

[1] The publications mentioned in the following are listed in alphabetic order in the "selected bibliography" at the end of this appendix.

[2] See Frank Uekötter, "Natur- und Landschaftsschutz im Dritten Reich. Ein Literaturbericht," in Radkau and Uekötter, *Naturschutz und Nationalsozialismus*, 447–81.

[3] For a more extensive discussion on the methodology of conservation history, see Uekoetter, "Old Conservation History."

movement. John Alexander Williams published one of the major contributions on conservation ideology in *Central European History* in 1996, which is best read together with Karl Ditt's essay of 2000. In 2005, Franz-Josef Brüggemeier, Mark Cioc, and Thomas Zeller published a collection of nine essays on different aspects of the topic, with a list of themes ranging from the national conservation law and the General Plan East to the Nazis' forest policy and air pollution control.

Compared with the later volume, the book *Naturschutz und Nationalsozialismus*, edited by the present author in cooperation with Joachim Radkau, is narrower in its range of themes, in that it focuses more closely on the nature protection movement. The volume presents the proceedings of the conference that took place under the auspices of the German minister for the environment Jürgen Trittin in Berlin in 2002, and at the risk of self-congratulation, it might be said that it offers the most comprehensive overview of the field that is currently available in print. The Berlin conference coincided with the publication of a number of important books. Thomas Zeller's *Straße, Bahn, Panorama* provides a detailed discussion of the Autobahn project and Alwin Seifert's work in this context. Discussing conservation work in the broader context of the *Heimat* movement in Westphalia, Lippe, and Thuringia, Willi Oberkrome traces the debates and their political implications from the turn of the century to 1960. Michael Hartenstein's dissertation dealt with the Nazis' plans for the annexed part of Poland; a number of further authors, most prominently Jost Hermand, Klaus-Georg Wey, Rolf Peter Sieferle, and Jeffrey Herf, have dealt with conservation in Nazi Germany in monographs with a broader focus. The postwar years have recently come increasingly into focus, with major publications from Jens Ivo Engels, Ute Hasenöhrl, Monika Bergmeier, Andreas Dix, Bärbel Häcker, and the present author. A few years ago, Karsten Runge published an instructive overview on the origins of landscape planning. The history of forests and forestry in Germany still awaits an authoritative monograph; Heinrich Rubner, Wilhelm Bode, and Martin von Hohnhorst provide some valuable information, but they have not exhausted the topic. Another neglected issue is the Nazis' animal rights policy; the essays of Miriam Zerbel and Heinz Meyer have only scratched the surface. On the history of conservation ideas before the Nazis' rise to power, the essential books are Friedemann Schmoll's *Erinnerung an die Natur* and Thomas Rohkrämer's *Eine andere Moderne?* It is advisable to supplement this reading with Andreas Knaut's *Zurück zur Natur* and the essays of Arne Andersen and Edeltraud Klueting.

A number of publications focus on the history of individual conservation associations, and it is gratifying to see that some of these projects were inspired by the leagues themselves. The Deutscher Alpenverein authorized a publication that looked specifically into the league's exceptionally anti-Semitic stance. Dorle Grible published a monograph on the Munich-based Isartalverein, and Susanne Falk dealt with the Sauerländischer Gebirgsverein. The history project of the Naturschutzbund Deutschland (NABU), the former Bird Protection League founded by Lina Hähnle, did not lead to a scholarly publication, but the project's brochure deserves attention for its unusually frank discussion of the association's past. The Heimatschutz movement has long recognized its problematic heritage, as the publications of Edeltraud Klueting and others document. The Bavarian Conservation League has been discussed by Richard Hölzl and Ernst Hoplitschek. Leftist and alternative movements are the subject of books by Jochen Zimmer and Ulrich Linse.

Articles in the field are far too numerous for even a fleeting overview. Michael Wettengel's essay of 1993 is still the most concise introduction into the institutional history of German conservation, especially if read together with the overview articles of Karl Ditt, Kiran Patel, and Burkhardt Riechers. Klaus Fehn wrote a number of important essays on landscape planning in Eastern Europe. Dietmar Klenke published an inspiring article on the Autobahn project, whereas Charlotte Reitsam discussed the ideological implications of Alwin Seifert's work. Helmut Maier's publications discuss the surprising prominence of conservation issues in the context of electric power production. Reinhard Piechocki takes a critical look at Göring's national nature reserves, and Willi Oberkrome describes German conservation in the two world wars.

For those who want to learn about earlier developments in the field, the publications of Gert Gröning and Joachim Wolschke-Bulmahn deserve attention. Gröning and Wolschke-Bulmahn mentioned a number of important facts for the first time, though their pioneering role has sometimes been overestimated; for example, the shameful work of the landscape planning community in World War II was discussed for the first time by Walter Mrass in 1970, more than a decade before Gröning's and Wolschke-Bulmahn's first publications. Gröning's and Wolschke-Bulmahn's interpretations have been criticized from several perspectives, and this publication could not help but correct them on several points, making it advisable to read Gröning's and Wolschke-Bulmahn's publication with a good deal of skepticism. Their recent attacks on fellow researchers (including the present author) have drawn criticism beyond the research community.[4] Even more caution is urged in dealing with the publications of Anna Bramwell, whose biography of Richard Walther Darré created a stir in the 1980s because of its assertion that there was something like a "green party" in Nazi Germany. Scholars as diverse as Raymond Dominick, Gustavo Corni, and Gesine Gerhard have criticized Bramwell's interpretation with the result that Bramwell's description of Darré, as well as her notion of a "Green Party" in Nazi Germany, are clearly discredited at this point.[5]

In spite of lively research, there are still numerous topics and perspectives that are waiting to be explored. Some of the desiderata have already been mentioned: there is a dearth of publications on the history of animal rights and the link between conservation and forestry. The relationship between nature protection and agriculture also awaits a more thorough inquiry than this book could provide: some signs exist that the Nazis' agricultural policy made farmers somewhat more receptive to the demands of conservation. Historians might also look at Nazi Germany more systematically in an international context: with conservation emerging as a political issue in many European countries around 1900 and marked differences in national styles, the topic is ideally suited for comparative work. For example, how does the German discussion over nonnative species appear compared to debates in other countries, where authors could bemoan that "sentiment lauds the exotic"?[6] There is also a need for more research on the history of specific places: quarries, swamps, trees, forests, rivers, landscapes, and so on. Studies of this kind would shed more light on the importance of the Nazi era in both conservation history and landscape history, in addition to the contribution that these studies could make to Germany's collective memory. Research on the Nazi era has always benefited greatly from local historians who wanted to learn more about the history of their hometowns during the Nazi era. Studies on specific localities could also produce a more detailed picture of the ecological effects of the war economy, another field where research is painfully scarce. The project at the top of the author's personal wish

---

[4] See Joachim Wolschke-Bulmahn, "The Search for 'Ecological Goodness' among Garden Historians," in Michel Conan (ed.), *Perspectives on Garden Historie* (Dumbarton Oaks, 1999), 161–80; and Joachim Wolschke-Bulmahn, "Zu Verdrängungs- und Verschleierungstendenzen in der Geschichtsschreibung des Naturschutzes in Deutschland," in Uwe Schneider and Joachim Wolschke-Bulmahn (eds.), *Gegen den Strom. Gert Gröning zum 60. Geburtstag* (Hannover, 2004), 313–34.

[5] See p. 202–3.

[6] Ernest H. Wilson, *Aristocrats of the Trees* (Boston, 1930), xx.

list is a collective biography of the personnel of German conservation: what is it that defined a conservationist as a member of the community, and are there different generations of German conservationists? Finally, the author would generally like to urge researchers to make more use of archival collections. After all, he has found in the preparation of this study that there are an enormous number of files in state and county archives on which historians have never laid their hands.

For anyone planning archival research on the topic, it is important to realize the two-tiered structure of German conservation: whereas the authority to take decisions remained within the administration, officials consulted with conservation advisors on the county, regional, provincial, and state levels. With the conservation advisors standing outside the administrative hierarchy, they often failed to offer their files to state or county archives, and much of their documentation seems to be lost. It is only under special circumstances that files from conservation advisors have been preserved: for example, the advisor's files for the province of Westphalia survived only because the position was affiliated with the natural history museum of Münster. Ironically, the situation is reverse on the national level, where the advisory body, the Reich Conservation Agency, managed to preserve a sizable number of documents, available in the German *Bundesarchiv* as deposit B 245, whereas the surviving files of the German Forest Service (deposit R 3701), the supreme conservation authority in Nazi Germany, do not contain material on conservation issues. When the German Forest Service took charge of conservation in 1935, the Prussian ministry of education delivered its conservation files to Göring's officials, and the material was lost during the war.

Incomplete files are a familiar problem to every historian of the Nazi era because of the bombing of many German cities and intentional destruction of files in the final months of the war. In some cases, it is a good idea to search the files of institutions on the county level because they often provide a rich documentation of events on the regional and provincial level; some conservation advisors have also inherited personal deposits. It is advisable to check at least some of the publications on the legal status quo in preparation for archival work. Contemporary commentaries on the national conservation law include *Das Reichsnaturschutzgesetz vom 26. Juni 1935* of Walther Schoenichen and Werner Weber, Gustav Mitzschke's book of the same title, and the legal dissertation of Karl Cornelius; on legislative changes after 1945, one may consult Albert Lorz or Jürgen Grote. From 1937, decrees of more general relevance were published in the *Reichsministerialblatt der Forstverwaltung*. The leading conservation journal was *Naturschutz*, edited by the Prussian Agency for the Protection of Natural Monuments until 1935 and the Reich Conservation Agency thereafter. Associations often maintained their own journals, and their quality differs widely; they include ambitious publications like the *Blätter für Naturschutz und Naturpflege* produced by the Bavarian Conservation League as well as numerous nonacademic periodicals.

Selected Bibliography

Amstädter, Rainer. *Der Alpinismus. Kultur – Organisation – Politik.* Wien, 1996.
Andersen, Arne. "Heimatschutz. Die bürgerliche Naturschutzbewegung." In Franz-Josef Brüggemeier and Thomas Rommelspacher (eds.), *Besiegte Natur. Geschichte der Umwelt im 19. und 20. Jahrhundert.* 2nd edition. Munich, 1989. 143–57.
Applegate, Celia. *A Nation of Provincials. The German Idea of Heimat.* Berkeley and Los Angeles, 1990.
Bergmeier, Monika. *Umweltgeschichte der Boomjahre 1949–1973. Das Beispiel Bayern.* Münster, 2002.
Bode, Wilhelm, and Martin von Hohnhorst. *Waldwende. Vom Försterwald zum Naturwald,* 4th edition. Munich, 2000.
Bramwell, Anna. *Blood and Soil. Walther Darré and Hitler's Green Party.* Abbotsbrook, 1985.
Bramwell, Anna. *Ecology in the 20th Century. A History.* New Haven and London, 1989.
Brüggemeier, Franz-Josef, Mark Cioc, and Thomas Zeller (eds.). *How Green Were the Nazis? Nature, Environment, and Nation in the Third Reich.* Athens, Ohio, 2005.
Brüggemeier, Franz-Josef, and Jens Ivo Engels (eds.). *Natur- und Umweltschutz nach 1945. Konzepte, Konflikte, Kompetenzen.* Frankfurt and New York, 2005.
Confino, Alon. *The Nation as a Local Metaphor. Württemberg, Imperial Germany, and National Memory, 1871–1918.* Chapel Hill, N.C., 1997.
Confino, Alon. "'This lovely country you will never forget.' Kriegserinnerungen und Heimatkonzepte in der westdeutschen Nachkriegszeit." In Habbo Knoch (ed.), *Das Erbe der Provinz. Heimatkultur und Geschichtspolitik nach 1945.* Göttingen, 2001. 235–51.
Cornelius, Karl. *Das Reichsnaturschutzgesetz.* Bochum-Langendreer, 1936.
Ditt, Karl. *Raum und Volkstum. Die Kulturpolitik des Provinzialverbandes Westfalen 1923–1945.* Münster, 1988.

Ditt, Karl. "Naturschutz zwischen Zivilisationskritik, Tourismusförderung und Umweltschutz. USA, England und Deutschland 1860–1970." In Matthias Frese and Michael Prinz (eds.), *Politische Zäsuren und gesellschaftlicher Wandel im 20. Jahrhundert. Regionale und vergleichende Perspektiven.* Paderborn, 1996. 499–533.

Ditt, Karl. "The Perception and Conservation of Nature in the Third Reich." *Planning Perspectives* 15 (2000): 161–87.

Dix, Andreas. *"Freies Land." Siedlungsplanung im ländlichen Raum der SBZ und frühen DDR 1945–1955.* Cologne, 2002.

Dominick, Raymond H. III. *The Environmental Movement in Germany. Prophets and Pioneers 1871–1971.* Bloomington, Ind., 1992.

Engels, Jens Ivo. *Ideenwelt und politische Verhaltensstile von Naturschutz und Umweltbewegung in der Bundesrepublik 1950–1980.* Habilitationsschrift, Freiburg University, 2004.

Falk, Susanne. *Der Sauerländische Gebirgsverein. "Vielleicht sind wir die Modernen von übermorgen."* Bonn, 1990.

Falk, Susanne. "'Eine Notwendigkeit, uns innerlich umzustellen, liege nicht vor.' Kontinuität und Diskontinuität in der Auseinandersetzung des Sauerländischen Gebirgsvereins mit Heimat und Moderne 1918–1960." In Matthias Frese and Michael Prinz (eds.), *Politische Zäsuren und gesellschaftlicher Wandel im 20. Jahrhundert. Regionale und vergleichende Perspektiven.* Paderborn, 1996. 401–17.

Fehn, Klaus. "Die Auswirkungen der Veränderungen der Ostgrenze des Deutschen Reiches auf das Raumordnungskonzept des NS-Regimes (1938–1942)." *Siedlungsforschung. Archäologie – Geschichte – Geographie* 9 (1991): 199–227.

Fehn, Klaus. "Rückblick auf die 'nationalsozialistische Kulturlandschaft.' Unter besonderer Berücksichtigung des völkisch-rassistischen Mißbrauchs von Kulturlandschaftspflege." *Informationen zur Raumentwicklung* (1999): 279–90.

Fehn, Klaus. "'Artgemäße deutsche Kulturlandschaft.' Das nationalsozialistische Projekt einer Neugestaltung Ostmitteleuropas." In Kunst- und Ausstellungshalle der Bundesrepublik Deutschland (ed.), *Erde.* Bonn, 2002. 559–75.

Gribl, Dorle. *"Für das Isartal." Chronik des Isartalvereins.* Munich, 2002.

Gröning, Gert, and Joachim Wolschke. "Naturschutz und Ökologie im Nationalsozialismus." *Die alte Stadt* 10 (1983): 1–17.

Gröning, Gert, and Joachim Wolschke-Bulmahn. *Die Liebe zur Landschaft. Teil III: Der Drang nach Osten. Zur Entwicklung der Landespflege im Nationalsozialismus und während des Zweiten Weltkrieges in den "eingegliederten Ostgebieten."* Arbeiten zur sozialwissenschaftlich orientierten Freiraumplanung 9. Munich, 1987.

Gröning, Gert, and Joachim Wolschke-Bulmahn. *Die Liebe zur Landschaft. Teil I: Natur in Bewegung. Zur Bedeutung natur- und freiraumorientierter Bewegungen der ersten Hälfte des 20. Jahrhunderts für die Entwicklung der Freiraumplanung.* Arbeiten zur sozialwissenschaftlich orientierten Freiraumplanung 7. Munich, 1986. 2nd edition. Münster, 1995.

Gröning, Gert, and Joachim Wolschke-Bulmahn. "Landschafts- und Naturschutz." In Diethart Kerbs and Jürgen Reulecke (eds.), *Handbuch der deutschen Reformbewegungen 1880–1933.* Wuppertal, 1998. 23–34.

Grote, Jürgen. *Möglichkeiten und Grenzen des Landschaftsschutzes nach dem Reichsnaturschutzgesetz.* Juridical Dissertation, Cologne University, 1971.

Häcker, Bärbel. *50 Jahre Naturschutzgeschichte in Baden-Württemberg. Zeitzeugen berichten.* Stuttgart, 2004.

Hartenstein, Michael A. *"Neue Dorflandschaften."* Nationalsozialistische Siedlungsplanung in den "eingegliederten Ostgebieten" 1939 bis 1944 unter besonderer Berücksichtigung der Dorfplanung. Wissenschaftliche Schriftenreihe Geschichte 6. Berlin, 1998.

Hartung, Werner. *Konservative Zivilisationskritik und regionale Identität. Am Beispiel der niedersächsischen Heimatbewegung 1895 bis 1919.* Hannover, 1991.

Hasenöhrl, Ute. *Zivilgesellschaft und Protest. Zur Geschichte der Umweltbewegung in der Bundesrepublik Deutschland zwischen 1945 und 1980 am Beispiel Bayerns.* WZB Discussion Paper No. SP IV 2003–506. Berlin, 2003.

Herf, Jeffrey. *Reactionary Modernism. Technology, Culture, and Politics in Weimar and the Third Reich.* Cambridge, 1984.

Hermand, Jost. *Grüne Utopien in Deutschland. Zur Geschichte des ökologischen Bewußtseins.* Frankfurt, 1991.

Hölzl, Richard. *Naturschutz in Bayern von 1905–1933 zwischen privater und staatlicher Initiative. Der Landesausschuß für Naturpflege und der Bund Naturschutz.* M.A. thesis, University of Regensburg, 2003.

Hoplitschek, Ernst. *Der Bund Naturschutz in Bayern. Traditioneller Naturschutzverband oder Teil der neuen sozialen Bewegungen?* Berlin, 1984.

Klenke, Dietmar. "Autobahnbau und Naturschutz in Deutschland. Eine Liaison von Nationalpolitik, Landschaftspflege und Motorisierungsvision bis zur ökologischen Wende der siebziger Jahre." In Matthias Frese and Michael Prinz (eds.), *Politische Zäsuren und gesellschaftlicher Wandel im 20. Jahrhundert. Regionale und vergleichende Perspektiven.* Paderborn, 1996. 465–98.

Klueting, Edeltraud. "Heimatschutz." In Diethart Kerbs and Jürgen Reulecke (eds.), *Handbuch der deutschen Reformbewegungen 1880–1933.* Wuppertal, 1998. 47–57.

Knaut, Andreas. *Zurück zur Natur! Die Wurzeln der Ökologiebewegung.* Supplement 1 (1993) of *Jahrbuch für Naturschutz und Landschaftspflege.* Greven, 1993.

Lekan, Thomas. *Imagining the Nation in Nature. Landscape Preservation and German Identity, 1885–1945.* Cambridge, Mass., 2003.

Linse, Ulrich. *Ökopax und Anarchie. Eine Geschichte der ökologischen Bewegungen in Deutschland.* Munich, 1986.

Lorz, Albert. *Naturschutz-, Tierschutz- und Jagdrecht.* 2nd edition. Munich, 1967.

Maier, Helmut. "Kippenlandschaft, 'Wasserkrafttaumel' und Kahlschlag. Anspruch und Wirklichkeit nationalsozialistischer Naturschutz- und Energiepolitik." In Günter Bayerl, Norman Fuchsloch, and Torsten Meyer (eds.), *Umweltgeschichte – Methoden, Themen, Potentiale. Tagung des Hamburger Arbeitskreises für Umweltgeschichte, Hamburg 1994.* Cottbuser Studien zur Geschichte von Technik, Arbeit und Umwelt 1. Münster and New York, 1996. 247–66.

Maier, Helmut. "'Unter Wasser und unter die Erde.' Die süddeutschen und alpinen Wasserkraftprojekte des Rheinisch-Westfälischen Elektrizitätswerks (RWE) und der Natur- und Landschaftsschutz während des 'Dritten Reiches.'" In Günter Bayerl and Torsten Meyer (eds.), *Die Veränderung der Kulturlandschaft. Nutzungen – Sichtweisen – Planungen.* Münster, 2003. 139–75.

May, Helge. *NABU. 100 Jahre NABU – ein historischer Abriß 1899–1999.* Bonn, n.d.

Meyer, Heinz. "19./20. Jahrhundert." In Peter Dinzelbacher (ed.), *Mensch und Tier in der Geschichte Europas.* Stuttgart, 2000. 404–568.

Mitzschke, Gustav. *Das Reichsnaturschutzgesetz vom 26. Juni 1935 nebst Durchführungsverordnung vom 31. Oktober 1935 und Naturschutzverordnung vom 18. März 1936 sowie ergänzenden Bestimmungen.* Berlin, 1936.

Mrass, Walter. *Die Organisation des staatlichen Naturschutzes und der Landschaftspflege im Deutschen Reich und in der Bundesrepublik Deutschland seit 1935, gemessen an der Aufgabenstellung in einer modernen Industriegesellschaft.* Beiheft 1 of *Landschaft + Stadt.* Stuttgart, 1970.

Oberkrome, Willi. "Suffert und Koch. Zum Tätigkeitsprofil deutscher Naturschutzbeauftragter im politischen Systemwechsel der 1920er bis 1950er Jahre." *Westfälische Forschungen* 51 (2001): 443–62.

Oberkrome, Willi. "'Kerntruppen' in 'Kampfzeiten.' Entwicklungstendenzen des deutschen Naturschutzes im Ersten und Zweiten Weltkrieg." *Archiv für Sozialgeschichte* 43 (2003): 225–40.

Oberkrome, Willi. *"Deutsche Heimat." Nationale Konzeption und regionale Praxis von Naturschutz, Landschaftsgestaltung und Kulturpolitik in Westfalen-Lippe und Thüringen (1900–1960).* Paderborn, 2004.

Patel, Kiran Klaus. "Neuerfindung des Westens – Aufbruch nach Osten. Naturschutz und Landschaftsgestaltung in den Vereinigten Staaten von Amerika und in Deutschland, 1900–1945." *Archiv für Sozialgeschichte* 43 (2003): 191–223.

Piechocki, Reinhard. "'Reichsnaturschutzgebiete' – Vorläufer der Nationalparke?" *Nationalpark* 107 (2000): 28–33.

Radkau, Joachim, and Frank Uekötter (eds.). *Naturschutz und Nationalsozialismus.* Frankfurt and New York, 2003.

Reitsam, Charlotte. "Das Konzept der 'bodenständigen Gartenkunst' Alwin Seiferts. Ein völkisch-konservatives Leitbild von Ästhetik in der Landschaftsarchitektur und seine fachliche Rezeption bis heute." *Die Gartenkunst* 13 (2001): 275–303.

Riechers, Burkhardt. "Nature Protection during National Socialism." *Historical Social Research* 29, 3 (1996): 34–56.

Rohkrämer, Thomas. *Eine andere Moderne? Zivilisationskritik, Natur und Technik in Deutschland 1880–1933.* Paderborn, 1999.

Rubner, Heinrich. *Deutsche Forstgeschichte 1933–1945. Forstwirtschaft, Jagd und Umwelt im NS-Staat.* St. Katharinen, 1985.

Runge, Karsten. *Entwicklungstendenzen der Landschaftsplanung. Vom frühen Naturschutz bis zur ökologisch nachhaltigen Flächennutzung.* Berlin, 1998.

Schmoll, Friedemann. *Erinnerung an die Natur. Die Geschichte des Naturschutzes im deutschen Kaiserreich.* Frankfurt and New York, 2004.

Schoenichen, Walther, and Werner Weber. *Das Reichsnaturschutzgesetz vom 26. Juni 1935 und die Verordnung zur Durchführung des Reichsnaturschutzgesetzes vom 31. Oktober 1935 nebst ergänzenden Bestimmungen und ausführlichen Erläuterungen.* Berlin-Lichterfelde, 1936.

Sieferle, Rolf Peter. *Fortschrittsfeinde? Opposition gegen Technik und Industrie von der Romantik bis zur Gegenwart.* Munich, 1984.

Ueköter, Frank. *Naturschutz im Aufbruch. Eine Geschichte des Naturschutzes in Nordrhein-Westfalen 1945–1980.* Frankfurt and New York, 2004a.

Uekoetter, Frank. "The Old Conservation History – and the New. An Argument for Fresh Perspectives on an Established Topic." *Historical Social Research* 29, 3 (2004b): 171–91.

Ueköter, Frank. "Naturschutz und Demokratie. Plädoyer für eine reflexive Naturschutzbewegung." *Natur und Landschaft* 80 (2005): 137–40.

Wettengel, Michael. "Staat und Naturschutz 1906–1945. Zur Geschichte der Staatlichen Stelle für Naturdenkmalpflege in Preußen und der Reichsstelle für Naturschutz." *Historische Zeitschrift* 257 (1993): 355–99.

Wey, Klaus-Georg. *Umweltpolitik in Deutschland. Kurze Geschichte des Umweltschutzes in Deutschland seit 1900.* Opladen, 1982.

Williams, John Alexander. "'The Chords of the German Soul Are Tuned to Nature.' The Movement to Preserve the Natural Heimat from the Kaiserreich to the Third Reich." *Central European History* 29 (1996): 339–84.

Zebhauser, Helmuth. *Alpinismus im Hitlerstaat. Gedanken, Erinnerungen, Dokumente.* Munich, 1998.

Zeller, Thomas. "'The Landscape's Crown.' Landscape, Perceptions, and Modernizing Effects of the German Autobahn System, 1934 to 1941." In David E. Nye (ed.), *Technologies of Landscape. From Reaping to Recycling.* Amherst, Mass., 1999. 218–38.

Zeller, Thomas. *Straße, Bahn, Panorama. Verkehrswege und Landschaftsveränderung in Deutschland von 1930 bis 1990.* Frankfurt and New York, 2002.

Zerbel, Miriam. "Tierschutz und Antivivisektion." In Diethart Kerbs and Jürgen Reulecke (eds.), *Handbuch der deutschen Reformbewegungen 1880–1933.* Wuppertal, 1998. 35–46.

Zimmer, Jochen (ed.). *Mit uns zieht die neue Zeit. Die Naturfreunde. Zur Geschichte eines alternativen Verbandes in der Arbeiterkulturbewegung.* Cologne, 1984.

Index

Printed in the United States
By Bookmasters